Communications in Computer and Information Science   593

Commenced Publication in 2007
Founding and Former Series Editors:
Alfredo Cuzzocrea, Dominik Ślęzak, and Xiaokang Yang

More information about this series at http://www.springer.com/series/7899

Kôiti Hasida · Ayu Purwarianti (Eds.)

Computational Linguistics

14th International Conference of the Pacific Association
for Computaitonal Linguistics, PACLING 2015
Bali, Indonesia, May 19–21, 2015
Revised Selected Papers

Springer

Editors
Kôiti Hasida
Graduate School of Information Science
The University of Tokyo
Bunkyo-ku, Tokyo
Japan

Ayu Purwarianti
School of Electrical Engineering
  and Informatics
Bandung Institute of Technology
Bandung
Indonesia

ISSN 1865-0929   ISSN 1865-0937   (electronic)
Communications in Computer and Information Science
ISBN 978-981-10-0514-5   ISBN 978-981-10-0515-2   (eBook)
DOI 10.1007/978-981-10-0515-2

Library of Congress Control Number: 2015952054

This Springer imprint is published by SpringerNature
The registered company is Springer Science+Business Media Singapore

Preface

We are very pleased to present the proceedings of PACLING 2015: The 2015 Conference of the Pacific Association for Computational Linguistics. The conference was held at The Stones Hotel, Legian, Bali, Indonesia, during May 19–21, 2015. In all, 45 papers were submitted to the conference, of which 18 were accepted as long papers and 16 as short papers. This volume contains the 18 long papers.

The conference provided opportunities for participants to present and discuss their recent achievements and ongoing developments in a wide range of topics such as syntax, semantics, spoken language, dialogue, corpora, message understanding, text mining, information retrieval, language learning, and machine translation. In addition to the submitted contributions, the conference featured two keynote talks. Dr. Dwi Hendratmo Widyantoro gave a talk entitled "Summarization of Multiple Scientific Text: Approaches, Challenges, and Opportunities" and Prof. Chu-Ren Huang's talk was on "Ontology, Language, and Lexicon." These proceedings do not contain the details of these talks, but they were fruitful in introducing recent advances in the respective subfields of computational linguistics.

PACLING 2015 enjoyed 55 international participants, representing Indonesia, Japan, China, Australia, and Italy. The conference is notable in that it included a session for discussing future directions and issues of computational linguistics in Indonesia. The most important result thereof was the agreement to found the Indonesian Association on Computational Linguistics. The conference banquet was held at Ma Joly Restaurant, located on Kuta beach, one of Bali's most renowned tourist destinations.

We would like to thank all the participants and the committee members for their contributions to and support of the conference and these proceedings. Our gratitude also goes to the staff members and students of Bandung Institute of Technology for the local arrangements and hospitality.

PACLING 2015 was the 14th in the series of biannual meetings that started in 1989. The first two of these events were the Japan–Australia Joint Symposium on NLP held in Australia and then in Japan, followed by 12 PACLING conferences held not only in Australia and Japan but also in Canada, Malaysia, and Indonesia. We hope to further extend this tradition, and look forward to the 15th PACLING to be held in Yangon, Myanmar, in 2017.

January 2016   Kôiti Hasida

Organization

Steering Committee

Koiti Hasida   The University of Tokyo, Japan
Hammam Riza   Indonesia Agency for the Assessment and Application
     of Technology, Indonesia

Technical Program Committee

Chair

Masayu Leylia Khodra   Bandung Institute of Technology, Indonesia

Members

Abdul Wahab bin Abdul Rahman	International Islamic University, Malaysia
Anto Satriyo Nugroho	Indonesia Agency for the Assessment and Application of Technology, Indonesia
Kenji Araki	Hokkaido University, Japan
Wirote Aroonmanakun	Chulalongkorn University, Thailand
Arry Akhmad Arman	Bandung Institute of Technology, Indonesia
Ayu Purwarianti	Bandung Institute of Technology, Indonesia
Lawrence Cavedon	RMIT University, Australia
Tetsuro Chino	Toshiba, Japan
Key-Sun Choi	Korea Advanced Institute of Science and Technology, South Korea
Hercules Dalianis	SDSV-Stockholm University, Sweden
Dessi Puji Lestari	Bandung Institute of Technology, Indonesia
Chrysanne Dimarco	University of Waterloo, Canada
Kohji Dohsaka	Akita Prefectural University, Japan
Dwi H. Widyantoro	Bandung Institute of Technology, Indonesia
Tsutomu Endo	Kyushu Institute of Technology, Japan
Hammam Riza	Indonesia Agency for the Assessment and Application of Technology, Indonesia
Koiti Hasida	The University of Tokyo, Japan
Herry Sujaini	University of Tanjungpura, Indonesia
Bowen Hui	University of British Columbia, Canada
Kai Ishikawa	NEC Corp, Japan
Hiroyuki Kameda	Tokyo University of Technology, Japan
Inui Kentaro	Tohoku University, Japan
Alistair Knott	University of Otago, New Zealand
Kiyoshi Kogure	Kanazawa Institute of Technology, Japan

Qin Lu	Hong Kong Polytechnic University, SAR China
Paul McKevitt	Ulster University, UK
Robert Mercer	University of Western Ontario, Canada
Diego Molla	Macquarie University, Australia
Hiromi Nakaiwa	Nagoya University, Japan
Normaziah Abdul Aziz	International Islamic University, Malaysia
Cecile Paris	CSIRO ICT Centre, Australia
Rila Mandala	Bandung Institute of Technology, Indonesia
Ruli Manurung	University of Indonesia, Indonesia
Hiroaki Saito	Keio University, Japan
Saiful Akbar	Bandung Institute of Technology, Indonesia
Kazutaka Shimada	Kyushu Institute of Technology, Japan
Akira Shimazu	Japan Advanced Institute of Science and Technology, Japan
Virach Sornlertlamvanich	Thammasat University, Thailand
Tomek Strzalkowski	University of Albany, USA
Thepchai Supnithi	NECTEC, Thailand
Masami Suzuki	KDDI R&D Laboratories Inc, Japan
Hisami Suzuki	Microsoft, USA
Kumiko Tanaka-Ishii	Kyushu University, Japan
Masato Tokuhisa	Tottori University, Japan
Mutsuko Tomokiyo	École Nationale Supérieure d'Informatique et Mathématiques, France
Chai Wutiwiwatchai	NECTEC, Thailand
Yang Xiang	University of Guelph, Canada
Ingrid Zukerman	Monash University, Australia

Local Organizing Committee

Chair

Ayu Purwarianti	Bandung Institute of Technology, Indonesia

Treasury

Arie Ardiyanti	Telkom University, Indonesia

Secretariat

Ade Romadhony	Telkom University, Indonesia

Sponsorship

Warih Maharani	Telkom University, Indonesia

Publicity and Website

Dody Dharma	Bandung Institute of Technology, Indonesia
Yudi Wibisono	Indonesia University of Education, Indonesia

Contents

Syntax and Syntactic Analysis

Pointwise Prediction and Sequence-Based Reranking for Adaptable Part-of-Speech Tagging

Shinsuke Mori[1], Yosuke Nakata[2], Graham Neubig[3], and Tetsuro Sasada[1(✉)]

[1] Academic Center for Computing and Media Studies, Kyoto University,
Yoshidahonmachi, Sakyo-ku, Kyoto 606-8501, Japan
forest@i.kyoto-u.ac.jp, sasada@ar.media.kyoto-u.ac.jp
[2] NTT Communications, 1-1-6 Uchisachicho, Chiyoda-ku, Tokyo 100-8019, Japan
ruberukuraku@gmail.com
[3] Nara Institute of Science and Technology, 8916-5 Takayamacho,
Ikoma, Nara 630-0192, Japan
neubig@is.naist.jp

Abstract. This paper proposes an accurate method for part-of-speech (POS) tagging that is highly domain-adaptable. The method is based on an assumption that the POS transition tendencies do not depend on domains, and has the following three characteristics: (1) it is trainable from partially annotated data, (2) it uses efficiently trainable pointwise POS taggers to allow for active learning, and (3) is more accurate than the pointwise or sequence-based POS taggers. The proposed method estimates POS tags by stacking pointwise and sequence-based predictors. In the experiments we deal with the joint problem of word segmentation and POS tagging in Japanese. We show that our proposed stacking process improves over pointwise and sequence-based methods (hidden Markov models and conditional random fields) both in the general domain and the target domain. In addition we show the learning curve in a domain adaptation scenario. The result shows that our method outperforms state-of-the-art methods in the same domain as the training data and is better than them in domain adaptation situations as well.

Keywords: Active learning · Reranking · Word segmentation · Part-of-speech tagging · Pointwise prediction

1 Introduction

Part-of-speech (POS) tagging ([2,11] and many others) is a fundamental step of natural language processing (NLP) in many languages, and many NLP applications use POS tagging results. Thus POS tagging accuracy has a great impact on these NLP applications. With large annotated corpora ([10] *inter alia*) and methods based on machine learning techniques, the NLP community achieved a high accuracy around 97 % or more in various languages. However, with the

---

Y. Nakata—This work was done when he was at Kyoto University.

K. Hasida and A. Purwarianti (Eds.): PACLING 2015, CCIS 593, pp. 3–17, 2016.
DOI: 10.1007/978-981-10-0515-2_1

diversification of the domains to which NLP is applied, such as medical texts or texts in user generated contents (blog, twitter, etc.), we sometimes observe a severe degradation in POS tagging accuracy in text domains different from that of the training data.

Therefore we can say that there is still a large demand for improving POS tagging accuracy, especially in domain adaptation situations.

In addition to the machine learning techniques, the NLP community is increasingly aware of importance of language resources, as the easiest way to improve an NLP based on a particular machine learning technique for a certain domain is to just add annotated texts in that domain to the training data. This strategy does require time and money, however, so we are interested in reducing annotation work by allowing annotators to focus on informative points that will provide a good performance/cost trade-off. Thus, there is a large amount of research on training NLP systems from partially annotated data or incomplete data, in which only some points are annotated with labels [18]. In this setting, some points lack the correct labels, and some may have multiple labels.

One of the major tasks to which these methods have been applied is word segmentation (WS) for languages without obvious word boundaries. A method for training conditional random fields (CRFs) from partially annotated data has been proposed and tested in Japanese WS [18]. This CRF extension is used to improve Chinese WS by referring to so-called natural annotations, such as partially segmented sentences converted from Wikipedia assuming that HTML tags are word boundaries [8]. A word segmenter based on a binary classifier [15] is another implementation trainable from partially annotated data. In this method the WS system decides whether there is a word boundary or not at each point between two characters without referring to the estimated labels surrounding the decision point. This is called a pointwise prediction method (or simply a pointwise method). Compared with sequence prediction methods like Markov models or CRFs, pointwise prediction requires less time to estimate model parameters even from partially annotated data, and is thus suitable for active learning, which is performed by alternating rounds of selecting uncertain points for annotation, performing annotation, and retraining the classifier [16].

Given this background, in this paper we propose a POS tagger equipped with following three characteristics:

1. It is trainable from partially annotated data.
2. Training is as fast as pointwise POS taggers to allow active learning.
3. It is more accurate than the pointwise and sequence-based POS taggers.

Our method performs POS estimation by stacking pointwise and sequence-based predictors, using pointwise prediction followed by reranking using sequence-based predictors [1]. The first module, pointwise POS estimation, is trainable from partially annotated sentences. The second module, sequence-based POS reranking, is efficiently trainable only from fully annotated sentences. Thus the training data of the second module is a subset of the first module. However, sequence-based predictors can use POS sequence information, and thus there may be room for improvement by referring to the combination of label candidates. We assume that these POS transition tendencies do not depend on the domain, and thus even if the sequence-based labeler is trained only on general domain data, it might be able to contribute to improve POS tagging accuracy even on texts in the adaptation target domain where only partially annotated data is available.

In the experiment we deal with the joint problem of WS and POS tagging in Japanese, traditionally called morphological analysis (MA).[1] We show that our stacking process improves over pointwise MA [16] and sequence-based MA [6,12,14] both in the general domain and in the target domain. In addition we show the learning curve in a domain adaptation scenario, which finds that the proposed method is as domain adaptable as purely pointwise approaches.

2   Joint Problem Solution Baseline

Our method, which we propose in this paper, uses MA by pointwise classifiers [16] as the first step. MA by pointwise classifiers (PW-MA) solves the problem step-by-step. First, it segments an input sentence into a word sequence. Then, it estimates the POS of each word like an English POS tagger. At each step PW-MA refers only to the input but not to any estimation results (or dynamic information) as features. In [16] linear support vector machines (SVMs) [3] are used because of their classification accuracy and speed. In this section we describe PW-MA in detail.

2.1   Word Segmentation by Pointwise Classification

The two-step approach [16] segments character sequence $x = x_1x_2\cdots x_k$ into the word sequence w. Word segmentation is formulated as a series of binary classification problems, estimating boundary tags b_1, b_2, ..., b_{k-1}. Tag $b_i = 1$ indicates that a word boundary exists between characters x_i and x_{i+1}, while $b_i = 0$ indicates that a word boundary does not exist.

As features it uses information about the surrounding characters (character and character-type n-grams), as well as the presence or absence of words in the dictionary. The details of the features are as follows:

1. Character n-grams: substrings surrounding the decision point i. There are two parameters: the window width m and the length n. Features are all the substrings of the length up to n in the $2m$ long substring $x_{i-m+1}, \cdots ,$ $x_{i-1}, x_i, x_{i+1}, \cdots , x_{i+m}$. Figure 1 shows an example.
2. Character type n-grams: the same as the character n-grams but the characters in the substring are converted into the character type. The character types are Chinese character (K), *katakana* (k), *hiragana* (H), Roman alphabet (R), Arabic number (N), or other (O). Figure 1 shows an example.
3. Dictionary: three flags indicating that the word starting at i, ending at i, or containing i are included in the dictionary, and the length of that word.

---

[1] MA often also performs recovery of word base forms, but we do not handle this element in the present work.

(vaccinate a healthy child with this medicine)

$$x_{i-2} \quad x_{i-1} \quad x_i \quad x_{i+1} \quad x_{i+2} \quad x_{i+3}$$

Text: 健 康 児 に 本 剤 を 接 種 し

↑

t_i: Decision point

Character (type) 1-gram: -3/児 (K), -2/に (H), -1/本 (K),
1/剤 (K), 2/を (K), 3/接 (K)

Character (type) 2-gram: -3/児に (KH), -2/に本 (HK), -1/本剤 (KK),
1/剤を (KH), 2/を接 (HK)

Character (type) 3-gram: -3/児に本 (KHK), -2/に本剤 (HKK),
-1/本剤を (KKH), 1/剤を接 (KHK)

Fig. 1. Features referred to in word segmentation (window width $m = 3$, $n = 1, 2, 3$).

As the above explanation indicates, PW-MA is trained from only the annotated points between two characters and it does not require any modification to estimate its parameters from partially annotated data. Thus it is both simple and fast enough to make active learning realistic.

2.2 POS Tagging by Pointwise Classification

POS tagging by pointwise classification performs one of the following four processes depending on the target word.

1. If the word appears as more than one POS in the training corpus, estimate the POS by a classifier,
2. If the word appears as only one POS in the training corpus, return its POS,
3. If the word does not appear in the training corpus but in the dictionary, return the POS of the first entry,
4. Otherwise, return noun.

In the first case, POS estimation is formulated as a multi-class classification problem, where we choose one tag t_j for each word w_j. The input is a word sequence but the classifier regards it as the target word and the character sequences preceding it ($\boldsymbol{x}_-$) and following it ($\boldsymbol{x}_+$). The POS of w_j is estimated from $\boldsymbol{x}_-$, w_j, and $\boldsymbol{x}_+$. When the window width is m', then the information referred to is $x_{-m'} \cdots x_{-2} x_{-1}, w_j, x_1 x_2 \cdots x_{m'}$. Putting it in another way, it only refers to the fact that there are word boundaries on both sides of w_j and that there is no word boundary inside w_j, and two character sequences $\boldsymbol{x}_-$ and $\boldsymbol{x}_+$.

The features for POS estimation are as follows (see Fig. 2):

1. Word in focus,
2. Character n-grams included in $\boldsymbol{x}_- \boldsymbol{x}_+$,
3. Character type n-grams included in $\boldsymbol{x}_- \boldsymbol{x}_+$.

Similar to PW-MA, POS tagging based on pointwise prediction is trained from only the words annotated with their POS and it does not require any modification to estimate its parameters from partially annotated data and is enough fast to make active learning realistic.

(vaccinate a healthy child with this medicine)

$$x_{-3} \quad x_{i-2} \quad x_{-1} \quad w \quad x_{i+1} \quad x_{i+2} \quad x_{i+3}$$

Text: 健 康 児 に 本剤 を 接 種 し

↑

Word in focus

Character (type) 1-gram: -3/康 (K), -2/児 (K), -1/に (H),
1/を (H), 2/接 (K) 3/種 (K),
Character (type) 2-gram: -3/康児 (KK), -2/児に (KH), -1/にを (HH),
1/を接 (HK), 2/接種 (KK)
Character (type) 3-gram: -3/康児に (KKH), -2/児にを (KHH),
-1/にを接 (HHK), 1/を接種 (HKK)

Fig. 2. Features referred to in POS tagging (window width $m' = 3$, $n = 1, 2, 3$).

2.3 Flexible Language Resource Usage by Pointwise Prediction

WS or POS tagging based on the pointwise prediction allows us to use the following new types of language resources, making it possible to more efficiently adapt the tagger to new domains.

1. Partially annotated corpora: Only some points between two characters in a sentence are annotated with word boundary information or only some words are annotated with POSs. For MA a corpus annotated only with word boundaries is also a partial annotation corpus. Partially segmented or partially POS-annotated corpora also fall in this category.
2. Word dictionary: A list of words without POSs. This type of dictionary is often available in many domains. We can use this for automatic WS.

Of course the pointwise prediction can use a fully annotated corpus in which all the sentences are completely segmented into words and all the words are annotated with their POSs, and a list of words with POSs. These fully annotated corpora and dictionaries are sometimes difficult to prepare in a target domain, but partial annotations are relatively easy to prepare. Thus, MA based on the pointwise prediction makes it easier to adapt to new domains by making it possible to retrieve information even from these various language resources.

3 2-Step POS Estimation

The PW-MA described in the previous section can not use the POS sequence information in the training corpus. This information may be, however, important for POS estimation. In this paper we assume that the domain dependency of POS transition tendencies is low and propose a new method for POS estimation based on this assumption. In this method, we use stacking to combine pointwise and sequence-based predictors, with the domain-specific pointwise predictor capturing domain knowledge, and the domain independent sequence-based predictor reranking the POS estimation result of PW-MA.

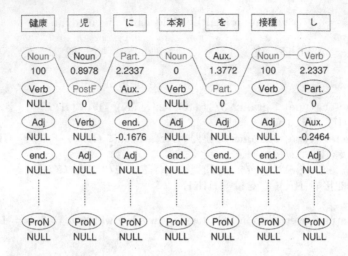

Fig. 3. POS reranking by sequence labeling.

3.1   Overview of the Proposed Method

The proposed method combines the following three processes in a cascade:

1. word boundary estimation by a pointwise prediction,
2. POS-confidence pair estimation by pointwise prediction, and
3. POS reranking by sequence prediction.

Given an input sentence, first we segment it into a word sequence by word boundary estimation based on a pointwise prediction. This process is completely the same as the one described in Sect. 2.1. Then we estimate a POS for each word in the word sequence. This process is similar to the one described in Sect. 2.2, but we enumerate all the possible POSs with confidences. Finally we rerank the POS sequences based on sequence-based prediction referring to the confidences.

3.2   POS Estimation with Confidence by the Pointwise Prediction

The pointwise POS estimation described in Subsect. 2.2 outputs only one POS for each word. In the proposed method, however, we calculate the confidences for all the possible POSs for a word and we use these confidences in the reranking process (see Fig. 3).

The confidence of a POS for a word is defined as follows. First let d_r be the distance (margin) from the separation hyper-plane of the r-th $(r \geq 1)$ POS candidate. And we define the confidence of the r-th POS candidate as $c_r = d_r - d_2$. As a result, the confidence of the first candidate is a positive value (in almost all cases $c_r \ll 100$ because of L2 regularization), that of the second candidate is 0, and those of the other candidates are negative values. If there is no POS candidate (the case 4 in Sect. 2.2), this process returns a noun with confidence 0. And if there is only one POS candidate (the case 2 or 3 in Sect. 2.2), this process returns that POS with confidence 100 (a special value). Figure 3 shows an example of POS candidates and their confidences.

3.3   POS Reranking by a Sequential Prediction

We have a word sequence and all the possible POSs with confidences as the output of the process above. Then we search for the best POS sequence among all the possible POS sequences by referring to the POS-confidence pair estimation result and the POS sequence statistics taken in the training corpus. Note that the word boundaries estimated by the pointwise word segmentation are not changed, because we do not rerank the word boundaries.

As a sequential prediction method we use CRFs [7], a standard method for sequence labeling problems because of their flexible feature design and high classification accuracy. The correct labels in the training data are the POS sequences in the full annotation corpus. The features are divided into two types: context features and confidence features, which we describe in detail in the subsequent section. In the prediction step the CRFs output the most likely POS sequence taking the output of the pointwise prediction results with confidence as the input. In the example shown in Fig. 3, the CRFs output the POS sequence connected by the solid line, where the POS of the word "" (child) has been changed into prefix from noun.

3.4   Features

As we mentioned, the CRFs for POS reranking refer to context features and confidence features. The confidence features are the followings calculated from the POS-confidence pairs output by the pointwise prediction.

Rule 1:
> If the word has multiple POS candidates, the t-th feature ($1 \leq t \leq T$) is the confidence of the t-th POS.

Rule 2:
> If the t-th POS is not a candidate, the $(T+t)$-th feature ($T+1 \leq T+t \leq 2T$) is set be 1.

Rule 3:
> If the t-th POS is the only candidate, the $(2T + t)$-th feature ($2T + 1 \leq 2T + t \leq 3T$) is set be 1.

When the condition of each rule is not satisfied, the feature value is set to be "NULL" (i.e. many features are NULL). The rationale of the rule 2 is to provide information about the POSs not in the candidate list. That of the rule 3 is to indicate POSs with high confidence according to the pointwise prediction, that may not need to be changed.

The other feature set is the context. We list them as follows:

1. word n-grams in the window width m'' including the word in focus at the center.

2. character type set n-grams of the words in the window width m'' including the word in focus at the center.

The character type set is a set of character types included in the spelling of a word. We set 6 character types, which are the same as those used in the word boundary prediction (Subsect. 2.1). Thus the character type set has $2^6 - 1$ combinations. The character type set n-grams are sequences of the character types for a word sequence.

3.5   Training Data Creation

As the training data of the CRFs for POS reranking, we need the correct POS tag sequence and those estimated by the pointwise prediction for a word sequence for feature creation. The estimated POS tag sequence should be similar to that given at the runtime. Thus the confidence estimation target has to be different from the training data of the pointwise prediction for the POS-confidence pair estimation. So we propose the following procedure similar to deleted interpolation [5].

1. Divide the training corpus C into k subsets C_1, C_2, ..., C_k.
2. For each $i \in \{1, 2, ..., k\}$
   (a) Train the i-th pointwise MA from $k - 1$ subsets except for C_i
   (b) Estimate POS-confidence pairs on C_i by the i-th pointwise MA with the model obtained by the step (a)

Figure 4 illustrates the above procedure in the case of $k = 3$. The above procedure produces the subsets annotated with POS candidates and their confidences C'_1, C'_2, ..., C'_k. By adding the correct POS tag sequence in C to them, we have the training data of our CRFs for POS reranking.

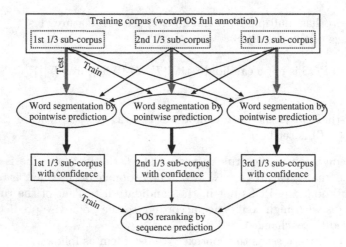

Fig. 4. Procedure for generating the training corpora for POS reranking by sequence labeling ($k = 3$).

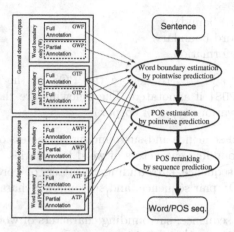

Fig. 5. Relationship between the proposed method and various types of corpora. Theoretically we can use language resources connected by both dotted and solid lines for each process indicated by the ovals. Practically we use language resources connected by solid lines.

General domain (G)		
Word boundary	Full (F): |文-化|交-流|使|事-業|を|	
(W)	Partial (P): ␣文␣化|交-流|使␣事␣業|を␣	
Word boundary	Full (F): |文-化/Noun|交-流/Noun|使/PostF|事-業/Noun|を/PP|	
/POS (T)	Partial (P): ␣文␣化|交-流/Noun|使␣事␣業|を␣	
Target domain (A)		
Word boundary	Full (F): |血|小-板|の|減-少|が|	
(W)	Partial (P): ␣血|小-板|の␣減␣少␣が␣	
Word boundary	Full (F): |血/PreF|小-板/Noun|の/PP|減-少/Noun|が/PP|	
/POS (T)	Partial (P): ␣血|小-板/Noun|の␣減␣少␣が␣	

Fig. 6. Examples of various types of corpora.

3.6 Proposed Method and Language Resource

At the end of this section, we discuss the relationship between the proposed method and the corpus types. In the general domain, many fully annotated corpora (GTF in Fig. 5), in which the sentences are divided into words completely and all the words are annotated with POSs, are available. Almost all annotated corpora produced through corpus annotation research [4,9] fall in this category. The annotation work for the target (adaptation) domain corpus requires, however, domain knowledge in addition to the linguistic knowledge of the annotation standard. Thus the full annotation corpus in the target domain is costly. But a partial annotation corpus, in which some words are identified and some are annotated with POSs, is relatively easy to prepare. Figure 6 shows examples. In Fig. 6, we use a notation called the extended 3-valued notation, which is our extension of the following 3-valued notation [13].

| : There is a word boundary.
- : There is no word boundary.
⊔ : There is no information.

As an extension we add "/" to denote the POS of the word after it like |s-p-e-l-l-i-n-g/POS| if annotated. The following are the information that we can extract from various types of corpora.

- GWF, AWF: Word sequence and surrounding characters of word boundaries
- GWP, AWP: Surrounding characters of word boundaries
- GTF, ATF: Word sequence, surrounding characters of word boundaries, POS sequence, word-POS pair sequence, and surrounding characters of word-POS pairs
- GTP, ATP: Word sequence, surrounding characters of word boundaries, and surrounding characters of word-POS pairs

Theoretically speaking the WS based on a pointwise prediction can use any type of corpora containing one or more word boundaries with the characters surrounding them. So the pointwise WS can be trained from all types of corpora. The POS tagging based on a pointwise prediction can use any type of corpora containing one or more words annotated with their POSs with the characters surrounding them. In the above list, this applies to GWP, GWF, AWP, and AWF. POS tagging based on a sequence prediction can use corpora in which sentences are divided into a word sequence and the words are annotated with their POSs without any missing elements. In the above list, this applies to GTF and ATF.

In practical domain adaptation situations the available training data are a large GTF and AWP or ATP which are relatively easy to build. Full annotation corpora (AWF and ATF) are costly because it requires both linguistic and domain knowledge to build them. Figure 5 summarizes these remarks. In this figure the corpora connected by solid lines are usable by the processes listed on the right hand side: the WS or POS tagging based on pointwise prediction and the POS reranking based on sequence prediction.

4 Evaluation

In order to test the effectiveness of the proposed method, we conducted two experiments. One is a comparison on the general domain among existing methods and the proposed method. The other is a comparison among the major methods in a domain adaptation situation. We set the parameters n in n-gram to 2 and the window width m, m', and m'' to 5 in all cases based on the results of preliminary experiments. We divided the training corpus into 9 parts in the training data creation for the POS reranking (see Sect. 3.5). For the sequence labeling we used CRFsuite [17].

4.1   Corpus

The corpus we used is the core part of Balanced Corpus of Contemporary Written Japanese (BCCWJ) [9] The sentences are divided into words and each word is annotated with a POS. We only used 21 coarse grained POS tags. The sources are white papers, books, newspapers, and Yahoo!QA. As [9] states, Yahoo!QA is different from the others. Thus we regard Yahoo!QA as the target domain and the others as the general domain. Table 1 shows the corpus specifications.

Table 1. Corpus specification.

Name	Source	Usage	#Sent.	#Words	#Char.
BCCWJ	White paper, Book, Newspaper	Training	27,338	782,584	1,131,317
	(General domain as GTF)	Test	3,038	87,458	126,154
	Yahoo!QA	Training	5,800	114,265	158,000
	(Target as ATF or ATP)	Test	645	13,018	17,980

4.2   Evaluation Criterion

As an evaluation criterion we follow [14] and use precision and recall based on word-POS pairs. First the longest common subsequence (LCS) is found between the correct answer and system output. Then let N_{REF} be the number of word-POS pairs in the correct sentence, N_{SYS} be that in the output in a system, and N_{LCS} be that in the LCS of the correct sentence and the output of the system, so the recall R and precision P are defined as follows:

$$R = \frac{N_{LCS}}{N_{REF}}, \quad P = \frac{N_{LCS}}{N_{SYS}}. \tag{1}$$

Finally we calculate F-measure defined as the harmonic mean of the recall and the precision:

$$F = \left\{ \frac{1}{2}(R^{-1} + P^{-1}) \right\}^{-1} = \frac{2N_{LCS}}{N_{REF} + N_{SYS}}. \tag{2}$$

4.3   Evaluation 1: Comparison with Existing Methods

First we compared our method with popular existing methods in the general domain. The methods are based on POS 2-grams model[2] [14], word-POS pair n-grams ($n = 2,3$) [12], CRFs (MeCab) [6], or pointwise prediction (KyTea) [16]. In this experiment, we assumed that only the full annotation corpus (GTF in Figs. 5 and 6) is available to compare our method with existing ones trained from the same language resources.

---

[2] [14] reports POS 3-gram model but POS 3-gram model is less accurate than word-POS pair 3-gram model.

Table 2. Accuracies of WS and the joint problem on the general domain.

Method	Word boundary estimation			Joint		
	Prec. [%]	Rec. [%]	F-measure	Prec. [%]	Rec. [%]	F-measure
POS 2-gram model (HMM)	96.32	96.84	96.58	93.77	94.27	94.02
Pair 2-gram model	97.44	98.52	97.98	96.58	97.65	97.11
Pair 3-gram model	97.49	98.53	98.00	96.70	97.73	97.21
CRFs (MeCab)	97.19	98.30	97.74	96.72	97.84	97.28
Pointwise (KyTea)	98.73	98.71	98.72	98.07	98.06	98.06
Pointwise + Reranking	98.73	98.71	98.72	**98.38**	**98.37**	**98.38**

Table 3. Accuracies of WS and the joint problem on the target domain (Yahoo!QA).

Method	Word boundary estimation			Joint		
	Prec. [%]	Rec. [%]	F-measure	Prec. [%]	Rec. [%]	F-measure
POS 2-gram model (HMM)	93.17	94.44	93.80	86.78	87.96	87.36
Pair 2-gram model	94.52	96.65	95.57	92.01	94.09	93.04
Pair 3-gram model	94.52	96.71	95.60	92.10	94.24	93.16
CRFs (MeCab)	94.89	96.87	95.87	93.69	95.65	94.66
Pointwise (KyTea)	96.93	97.26	97.09	95.19	95.51	95.35
Pointwise + reranking	96.93	97.26	97.09	**95.86**	**96.18**	**96.02**

To train the CRFs for reranking in the proposed method, we used the corpus generated from the general domain corpus produced by the procedure described in Subsect. 3.5. We tested the methods on the corpora in general domain and in the target domain. First we performed MA using pointwise prediction and then reranked the resulted POSs using sequence-based prediction.

Tables 2 and 3 show the accuracies in the general domain and the target domain respectively. In these tables, "pointwise" means the results of "pointwise prediction," the second oval from the top in Fig. 5. "pointwise + reranking" means the results of the POS reranking by the proposed method, that is the third oval in Fig. 5. Since we do not rerank the WS results, word boundary estimation accuracies of these two methods are the same. From the tables we can say that the proposed method improves the joint problem accuracy both in the general domain and the target domain. The improvement is larger in the target domain. From these results, our assumption that the POS transition tendencies does not depend on the domain (see Sect. 3) is plausible and we can improve PW-MA based on this assumption without losing the flexibility in choosing language resources. From the above observations, we can say that the proposed method is effective.

4.4 Evaluation 2: Adaptation Case

Second, we evaluate our method in a domain adaptation scenario. The existing method that is the most flexible in this scenario is pointwise MA, as it is trainable from partial annotations. In the experiment, we emulated active learning by adding partially annotated sentences. Along with the proposed method we tested pointwise MA and sequence-based MA. We started with the training corpus in the general domain and added partially annotated sentences gradually.

The concrete procedure is as follows (see Fig. 7).

1. Train the pointwise MA from the training corpus in the general domain (GTF in Figs. 5 and 6),
2. Estimate confidences of the training corpus in the target domain by the above obtained model without referring to the correct tags.
3. Annotate 100 points of low confidence in the corpus in the target domain with word boundary or POS producing a partial annotation corpus in the target domain (ATP in Figs. 5 and 6), and
4. Add the above partial annotation corpus to training corpus and train the model again and go to 2).

We repeated this procedure for 200 iterations. Each time we measured the accuracies on the target domain. The baselines are the pointwise MA (pointwise:part) trained from the same corpus as the proposed method (pointwise+CRFsuite:part) and the CRFs with new words appearing in the partially annotation corpus added to the dictionary (CRF:part).

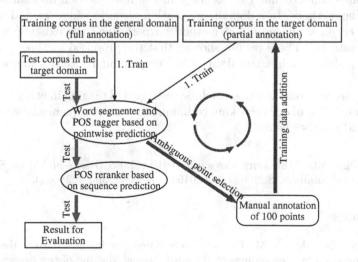

Fig. 7. Domain adaptation scheme based on active learning using partial annotation.

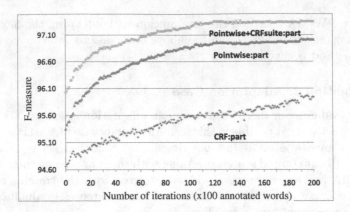

Fig. 8. Learning curve in the case of domain adaptation.

The result is shown in Fig. 8. From this graph we see that the proposed method outperforms the pointwise MA consistently. In addition the proposed method improves the accuracy in the domain adaptation case. Putting it in other words, the proposed method successfully increased the accuracy without losing the domain adaptability of pointwise MA. Therefore we can say that the proposed method is superior to existing ones in this case as well.

5 Conclusion

In this paper we have proposed a POS tagging method allowing flexible usage of language resources. The method is based on pointwise prediction and reranking by sequence-based prediction combined in the cascaded manner. The experimental results showed that the accuracy in the resource-rich domain is higher than existing methods. In a domain adaptation scenario where we add partially annotated corpora, the proposed method outperformed the existing pointwise method constantly. These results showed that the proposed method is capable of providing high domain adaptability while keeping high accuracy in the general domain.

Interesting research directions include testing POS tagging in other languages and the application of our reranking technique in various sequence labeling problems in NLP or other fields.

Acknowledgments. This work was supported by JSPS Grants-in-Aid for Scientific Research Grant Numbers 26280084, 26540190, 24240030, and 26280039.

References

1. Charniak, E., Johnson, M.: Coarse-to-fine n-best parsing and maxent discriminative reranking. In: Proceedings of the 43rd Annual Meeting of the Association for Computational Linguistics, pp. 173–180 (2005)

2. DeRose, S.J.: Grammatical category disambiguation by statistical optimization. Comput. Linguist. **14**(1), 31–39 (1988)
3. Fan, R.E., Chang, K.W., Hsieh, C.J., Wang, X.R., Lin, C.J.: LIBLINEAR: a library for large linear classification. J. Mach. Learn. Res. **9**, 1871–1874 (2008)
4. Japan Electronic Dictionary Research Institute Ltd.: EDR Electronic Dictionary Technical Guide (1993)
5. Jelinek, F.: Self-organized language modeling for speech recognition. Technical report, IBM T. J. Watson Research Center (1985)
6. Kudo, T., Yamamoto, K., Matsumoto, Y.: Applying conditional random fields to japanese morphological analysis. In: Proceedings of the Conference on Empirical Methods in Natural Language Processing, pp. 230–237 (2004)
7. Lafferty, J., McCallum, A., Pereira, F.: Conditional random fields: probabilistic models for segmenting and labeling sequence data. In: Proceedings of the Eighteenth ICML (2001)
8. Liu, Y., Zhang, Y., Che, W., Liu, T., Wu, F.: Domain adaptation for crf-based chinese word segmentation using free annotations. In: Proceedings of the 2014 Conference on Empirical Methods in Natural Language Processing, pp. 864–874 (2014)
9. Maekawa, K., Yamazaki, M., Maruyama, T., Yamaguchi, M., Ogura, H., Kashino, W., Ogiso, T., Koiso, H., Den, Y.: Design, compilation, and preliminary analyses of balanced corpus of contemporary written japanese. In: Proceedings of the Seventh International Conference on Language Resources and Evaluation (2010)
10. Marcus, M.P., Santorini, B.: Building a large annotated corpus of english: the penn treebank. Comput. Linguist. **19**(2), 313–330 (1993)
11. Merialdo, B.: Tagging english text with a probabilistic model. Comput. Linguist. **20**(2), 155–171 (1994)
12. Mori, S., Kurata, G.: Class-based variable memory length markov model. In: Proceedings of the InterSpeech2005, pp. 13–16 (2005)
13. Mori, S., Oda, H.: Automatic word segmentation using three types of dictionaries. In: Proceedings of the Eighth International Conference Pacific Association for Computational Linguistics (2009)
14. Nagata, M.: A stochastic japanese morphological analyzer using a forward-dp backward-a* n-best search algorithm. In: Proceedings of the 15th International Conference on Computational Linguistics, pp. 201–207 (1994)
15. Neubig, G., Mori, S.: Word-based partial annotation for efficient corpus construction. In: Proceedings of the Seventh International Conference on Language Resources and Evaluation (2010)
16. Neubig, G., Nakata, Y., Mori, S.: Pointwise prediction for robust, adaptable japanese morphological analysis. In: Proceedings of the 49th Annual Meeting of the Association for Computational Linguistics, pp. 529–533 (2011)
17. Okazaki, N.: Crfsuite: a fast implementation of conditional random fields (2007). http://www.chokkan.org/software/crfsuite/
18. Tsuboi, Y., Kashima, H., Mori, S., Oda, H., Matsumoto, Y.: Training conditional random fields using incomplete annotations. In: Proceedings of the 22nd International Conference on Computational Linguistics (2008)

Semantics and Semantic Analysis

Japanese Semantic Role Labeling with Hierarchical Tag Context Trees

Yasuhiro Ishihara[✉] and Koichi Takeuchi

Graduate School of Natural Science and Technology,
Okayama University, Okayama, Japan
{ishihara,koichi}@cl.cs.okayama-u.ac.jp

Abstract. In this paper we describe that the hierarchical tag context tree (HTCT) approach improves the accuracy of semantic role labeling on Japanese text. In Japanese language there are functional multiword expressions such as *no-tame-ni* and *yotte* that have potential to designate semantic relations between a predicate and its arguments. Since these expressions come to the end part of each argument, the performance of the CRF-based semantic role labeler can be improved by taking into account the last morphemes of each argument as features. We apply our proposed system to the annotated corpus of semantic role labels on a balanced Japanese corpus. The experimental results show that the CRF-based labeler with features extracted by HTCT approach outperforms the normal CRF-based labeler.

Keywords: Hierarchical Tag Context Trees · Semantic role labeling · CRFs

1 Background Issues

Analyzing semantic roles of arguments for a predicate must be a fundamental technology to capture deeper semantic relations between sentences. Since annotated corpora of semantic role labels (i.e., SRLs) and their frames are well developed in English, e.g., FrameNet [1] and PropBank [2], a lot of SRL detection systems have been developed mainly on English language [3–5]. In contrast to this, the most of the recent annotated corpora of predicate-argument structure in Japanese [6–8] are not on the level of semantic roles but on the level of surface case marker level.

In this situation, recently several language resources such as Japanese FrameNet [9] and Predicate Thesaurus (PT) [10] containing annotated semantic role information are constructed on Balanced Corpus of Contemporary Written Japanese (BCCWJ) [11]. Since the balanced corpus contains various text genres, the annotated data of SRLs on BCCWJ must be a profitable language resource for constructing a robust SRLer for Japanese. Currently the annotated corpus

© Springer Science+Business Media Singapore 2016
K. Hasida and A. Purwarianti (Eds.): PACLING 2015, CCIS 593, pp. 21–32, 2016.
DOI: 10.1007/978-981-10-0515-2_2

[**Reason** 悪天候 の-ため-に] [**Theme** フライト-は] 中止-さ-れ-た
akutenkou   no-tame-ni   furaito-ha   chuushi-sa-re-ta
bad weather because of   flight-TOP   was cancelled
The flight was cancelled because of the bad weather.

Fig. 1. An example of multiword expression *no-tame-ni*.

based on PT is available[1] thus we use PT-based annotated corpus as a gold standard of SRLs that contains 72 types of SRLs[2].

The previous work on constructing English semantic role labeling system [3,4] reveals that syntactic information is indispensable feature for recognizing SRLs, however, Japanese case markers, which are main clues of syntactic structure, do not have enough variety compared with prepositions in English; for example, English prepositions *in, at, with, by* can be mapped to a Japanese case marker *de*. Thus it must not be possible to apply the approaches of English SRL systems to a Japanese SRL system.

Besides case markers, functional multiword expressions (e.g., *no-tame-ni* (because of), *to-shi-te* (as), and so on) can be clues to estimate semantic relation types between a predicate and its arguments. The example of *no-tame-ni* (because of) is shown in Fig. 1.

In Fig. 1 the brackets indicates arguments for the predicate *chuushi-sa-re-ta*, and *Reason* and *Theme* are SRLs in Fig. 1. Functional multiword *no-tame-ni* (because of) indicates that the SRL of the first argument must be *Reason*. Functional multiwords are manually collected and distributed as a dictionary Tsutsuji[3], however,

(1) Japanese dependency parser (e.g., cabocha+mecab) does not detect the functional multiwords; and then the functional multiwords are separated into morphemes and are sometimes wrongly POS-annotated depending on the context, and

(2) even though the functional multiword dictionary is available, there is still possibility to exist unrecognized functional multiwords.

Therefore we propose an approach to improve performance of SRL system by capturing the functional multiword expressions in each argument. In this paper, we apply hierarchical tag context tree model (HTCT) [13] that can extract automatically effective sequences of morphemes and/or POSes. The extracted sequences of morphemes and/or POSes are applied to a CRF-based SRL system as features. In the experimental results we show that the CRF with HTCT system outperformed a simple CRF-based SRL system.

---

[1] http://pth.cl.cs.okayama-u.ac.jp.

[2] The EDR corpus [12] also contains SRLs on Japanese texts, however, the texts are not balanced, thus we select PT corpus.

[3] http://kotoba.nuee.nagoya-u.ac.jp/tsutsuji/.

2 Hierarchical Tag Context Tree Approach for Extracting Effective Sequences

The basic idea of the HTCT-based proposed approach is almost the same as an approach to construct a context tree from input sequences. The context tree is a framework to capture frequent sequences, and the characteristics of HTCT is that a context tree is constructed not only for input words but also for tags (e.g., POSes) taking into account a hierarchy of tags [13]. In the rest of the section, we describe the information-theoretical framework of how we find effective sequences from input sequences with hierarchical tags, and then describe how we adapt the HTCT framework for finding effective feature sequences of SRLs.

The key issue of constructing a context tree from input sequences is to define a criteria where a new context should be added to a tree or not. Assuming the situation to add a new tag b to a context sequence s at a leaves of a context tree, we define $\delta(sb)$ as an evaluation measure that indicates the gain of expanding the context s to a new context sb on the basis of Kullback-Leibler divergence between the probability distributions given the context sequences sb and s. The equation is shown in Eq. (1).

$$\delta(sb) = n(sb) \sum_{a \in A} \frac{n(a|sb)}{n(sb)} log \frac{P(a|sb)}{P(a|s)}$$

$$= n(sb) \sum_{a \in A} P(a|sb) log \frac{P(u|sb)}{P(a|s)}$$

$$= n(sb) D_{KL}(P(\cdot|sb), P(\cdot|s)) \tag{1}$$

Where $n(sb)$, $P(\cdot|sb)$ denote the number of occurrence of sb and the conditional probability of a target given by sb, respectively. The idea of the evaluation measure is that the new tag b should be added to the tree node s when the new context sb gives enough information gain compared with the base context s. Then a new tag will be added when the measure $\delta(sb)$ is larger than the threshold we define in Sect. 3.

The algorithm of construction of a context tree for input sequences is processed by a greedy algorithm, i.e., the possibility of adding new tags are evaluated only on the leaves of the context tree that have already been fixed. This situation is shown in Fig. 2, where each node indicates a context tag sequence and each arrow indicates a tag added to a leaf of the context tree; the first node ϵ denotes an empty context; the dashed nodes and arrows denote not generated nodes and arrows, respectively.

In Fig. 2 once a new arrow r is rejected to add the context s by the above evaluation using Eq. (1), our approach will not take the context sr into account any more. This indicates that even if the longer context src was an effective context sequence, our approach would not take the context src because the context sr was not registered in the base context tree.

In the above description, tags are flat, and now we incorporate tags that have a hierarchical structure. Since the unit of the tags are morphemes in Japanese,

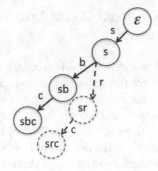

Fig. 2. Making a context tree with a greedy algorithm.

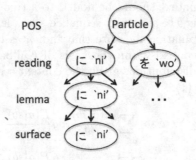

Fig. 3. Hierarchical structure of tags.

we assume that four-layer is-a hierarchy, i.e., part-of-speech, reading, lemma and surface are annotated to all the morphemes in the corpus (see Sect. 3).

Figure 3 shows an example of a hierarchy of Japanese case marker 'ni' whose POS is Particle, reading is 'ni', lemma is 'ni' and surface is 'ni'. Since the hierarchical structure expresses abstraction levels of a morpheme, our approach takes only one element from the four hierarchical levels for a morpheme on the basis of Eq. 1. This indicates that the elements (i.e., tags) in a context sequence contain surface expressions, lemmas, readings and POSes of morphemes, and then our approach takes the best tag from all of the possible morphemes with hierarchical tags in extending a context tag sequence.

In the above explanation, we describe the theoretical framework of HTCT approach, and now we describe how we adapt the HTCT framework for finding effective tag sequences for SRLs.

As described in Sect. 1, case markers and multiwords i.e., functional morpheme sequences at the end of arguments can be effective for disambiguation of SRLs. Thus we apply the HTCT approach to extraction of effective tag sequences of ending morphemes in each argument of sentences.

To realize this adaptation, we prepare an annotated corpus of SRLs such as Fig. 1 and apply the HTCT approach to the annotated corpus by the following modification steps.

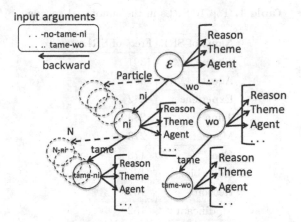

Fig. 4. Construction of an HTCT for finding effective tag sequence of SRLs.

(1) An HTCT is constructed not for morphemes but for SRLs, and
(2) An HTCT is constructed backward from the last morpheme of each argument.

In the modification step **(1)**, we define the target $a \in A$ in Eq. 1 as SRLs. Thus we need to evaluate the conditional probability of SRLs given by various context tags such as $P(Theme|\cdot)$ and $P(Reason|\cdot)$ using the annotated corpus.

To describe the details of the modification **(2)**, Fig. 4 shows the situation of constructing an HTCT for *no-tame-ni* and *tame-wo*. The left bracket denotes the target SRLs and each node has a conditional probability of SRLs given the context tag sequence. For example, at the top node ϵ, the conditional probabilities are defined as $P(Theme)$ and $P(Agent)$ which indicate no context tags, while at the second node, e.g., *ni*, the conditional probability is defined as $P(Theme|ni)$. Since these conditional probabilities of SRLs are used in the evaluation measure of Eq. (1), the extracted context tag tree can be effective for predicting SRLs.

Figure 4 shows that the context tree is constructed backward, i.e., the first level of the context tags are evaluated on the morphemes *ni* and *wo*, and then the second level of the context is evaluated on *tame*. Since a leaf node of the context tree will be extended if the information gain of the new node is enough large, the context tag tree is expected to capture characteristic tag sequences as long as possible.

In every step of adding a new tag to a leaf of context tree, the proposed approach takes into account hierarchical tags for the target morphemes. Figure 4 shows the case that the surface level, i.e., *ni* and *wo* are selected at the second nodes of the context tree. Since hierarchical consistency will be kept in the context tree, if the POS level, i.e., *PARTICLE* were selected at the second nodes, the surface level nodes *ni* and *wo* might be merged into *PARTICLE* node; and then the third node *tame* would be evaluated in the context of *PARTICLE-tame*.

Table 1. Top 10 SRLs in the annotated corpus

Name of SRL	Freq. of SRLs
Theme	1391
Agent	567
Experiencer	242
Time	233
Manner	223
Goal	178
Adverbial	165
Reason	161
Modificant	152
Method	140
Total	4844

3 Experiments of Semantic Role Labeling and Discussions

3.1 Experimental Set Up

The PT corpus contains 2662 annotated sentences and head verbs and their arguments (4844) are annotated with the 62 types of SRLs in the sentences of BCCWJ. In the corpus all of the sentences are broken down to morphemes, and then SRLs are annotated to the morphemes with IOB2 tag format for arguments. The statistics of the top 10 SRLs are shown in Table 1[4]. The top two frequent SRLs are *Theme* and *Agent* that are the same as an English SRL annotated corpus PropBank [5].

Since each chunk, i.e., argument is annotated, the proposed CRF-based SRL system recognize (1) boundary of each argument and (2) SRL for each argument. The performance of the system is evaluated by precision, recall and f-measure. Let an output of the system be correct if the system correctly detect both a boundary and its SRL.

To evaluate the SRL system, we divide the TP corpus in half, i.e., training corpus and test corpus. In the both corpora all of the morphemes are correctly annotated with surface, lemma, reading, and POS on the basis of UniDic [11].

3.2 CRF Model and CRF with HTCT Model

We execute three types of experiments. The first is applying normal CRFs[5] with taking into account a fixed number of morphemes at the end of each argument (Table 7); the second is CRFs with variable length features from the HTCT

---

[4] See more details of the annotated corpus at http://pth.cl.cs.okayama-u.ac.jp.

[5] We use CRF++ http://crfpp.googlecode.com/svn/trunk/doc/index.html?source= navbar.

Table 2. Base features of CRF

No.	Description of feature
1	Surface of the target morpheme
2	Lemma of the target morpheme
3	Reading of the target morpheme
4	POS of the target morpheme
5	Surface of the final Noun morpheme in the argument
6	Lemma of the final Noun morpheme in the argument
7	Case marker of the argument
8	Lemma of the head verb

Table 3. Contextual features of CRF

No.	Description of feature
t1	Surface of the next morpheme
t2	Surface of the previous morpheme
t3	Reading of the next morpheme
t4	Reading of the previous morpheme
t5	POS of the next morpheme
t6	POS of the previous morpheme

model[6]; and the third is CRFs with the first experiments' settings and the features extracted from the HTCT model. In the rest of the section, we describe how we utilize the HTCT to a CRF model as well as the details of the features in each CRF model.

We prepare three types of CRF-based models with different features; they are (1) normal CRF (denoted as CRF), (2) CRF taking into account the features of the last a few morphemes in arguments (denoted as CRF+2suf and CRF+3suf, respectively), and (3) CRF that extends the second model by adding the combinations of features of the last two morphemes of arguments (denoted as CRF+3suf+c).

Table 2 shows the base features of the CRF model. The features No. **7** and **8** must be key information to decide SRLs. The features of the normal CRF model has also the contextual information as seen in Table 3 and the combinatorial features in Table 4. The features defined in Tables 2, 3 and 4 are used in the all of CRF models.

Table 5 shows the features of the last three morphemes used in the CRF+3suf model, while the CRF+2suf model uses the features of the last two morphemes in arguments, i.e., the features from No. **15** to **112** in Table 5. These features consist of four attributes, that are, surface, lemma, reading, and POS, and thus

---

[6] We set the threshold to 0 in these experiments.

Table 4. Combination of base features in CRF

No.	Description of feature
c1	Combination of 1 and t1
c2	Combination of 1 and t2
c3	Combination of 4 and t5
c4	Combination of 4 and t6
c5	Combination of 5 and 8
c6	Combination of 6 and 8
c7	Combination of 7 and 8
c8	Combination of 5, 7 and 8
c9	Combination of 6, 7 and 8

Table 5. Features of enhancing the last three morphemes in arguments for CRF+3suf

No.	Description of feature
l1	Surface of the third last morpheme in the argument
l2	Lemma of the third last morpheme in the argument
l3	Reading of the third last morpheme in the argument
l4	POS of the third last morpheme in the argument
l5	Surface of the second last morpheme in the argument
l6	Lemma of the second last morpheme in the argument
l7	Reading of the second last morpheme in the argument
l8	POS of the second last morpheme in the argument
l9	Surface of the last morpheme in the argument
l10	Lemma of the last morpheme in the argument
l11	Reading of the last morpheme in the argument
l12	POS of the last morpheme in the argument

the CRF models can learn various kinds of abstracted levels of the characteristics of ending multiwords of arguments.

The features of the CRF+3suf+c model consist of combinations of the features in Table 6 and the features used in the CRF+3suf. Table 6 shows all of the binary combinations between the second last morpheme and the last morpheme; the base features are surface, lemma, reading, and POS, and then the combinations are 16 features in total. Thus the CRF+3suf+c can capture effective combined features for SRLs.

Next, we describe the CRF with HTCT models. The first model is the CRF model with the features using the output of the HTCT model for characterizing the ending multiwords of arguments instead of using fixed length features of the last a few morphemes, i.e., the features of the CRF with HTCT model are the

Table 6. Combination of features at the last two morphemes in CRF+3suf+c

No.	Description of feature
f1	Combination of l5 and l9
f2	Combination of l5 and l10
f3	Combination of l5 and l11
f4	Combination of l5 and l12
f5	Combination of l6 and l9
f6	Combination of l6 and l10
f7	Combination of l6 and l11
f8	Combination of l6 and l12
f9	Combination of l7 and l9
f10	Combination of l7 and l10
f11	Combination of l7 and l11
f12	Combination of l7 and l12
f13	Combination of l8 and l9
f14	Combination of l8 and l10
f15	Combination of l8 and l11
f16	Combination of l8 and l12

base features of CRF in Tables 2, 3 and 4 with a feature of the best context tag sequence outputted by the HTCT. Several HTCT models are constructed with varying different maximum depth of context tag trees from two to five, and then they are denoted as HTCT-2 to HTCT-5 learned from the training corpus. The second models of the CRF with HTCT take all the features of the CRF model and the HTCT model that shows the best performance among HTCT models in the experiments of Sect. 3.3.

3.3 Experimental Results and Discussions

In this section we will show the preliminary experimental results of detecting SRLs for the test data; that is, all of learning CRF models and construction of HTCT models are done on the training corpus, and the following scores are evaluated on the test corpus described in Sect. 3.1.

Table 7 shows the experimental results of detecting SRLs by the CRF models. In the table, the normal CRF without the features of the ending morphemes of arguments does not work well compared with the cases taking care of the ending morphemes of arguments. Note that the normal CRF also takes into account all of the morphemes in arguments, that is, multiwords at the end of arguments are contained in the features; however, the functional multiwords are separated to individual morphemes then it must be hard for the CRF model to associate the morphemes with the SRLs. In consract, the CRF+2suf model

Table 7. Experimental results of CRF + fixed length of the last a few morphemes in arguments

Model	Precision (%)	Recall (%)	F-measure
CRF	46.74	19.61	27.63
CRF+2suf	47.74	33.96	39.69
CRF+3suf	48.77	37.26	42.25
CRF+3suf+c	47.90	37.22	41.89

Table 8. Experimental Results of CRF + HTCT

Model	Precision (%)	Recall (%)	F-measure
HTCT-2	48.85	35.51	41.12
HTCT-3	51.05	34.53	41.20
HTCT-4	51.09	31.55	39.01
HTCT-5	50.35	29.27	37.02

Table 9. Experimental Results of CRF + fixed + HTCT

Model	Precision (%)	Recall (%)	F-measure
CRF+3suf+HTCT-3	49.71	37.87	42.99
CRF+3suf+c+HTCT-3	49.42	39.79	44.08

and the CRF+3suf model take two or three morpheme sequences as one new features, then the performance of recognizing SRLs is significantly improved.

Comparing the results between the CRF+2suf and the CRF+3suf models, we found that the length of the effective morpheme sequences would be three. Besides, comparing the CRF+3suf with the CRF+3suf+c, the simple application of the combinatorial features of the last two morphemes in arguments does not work well in SRL detection.

The experimental results of the CRF with HTCT model are shown in Table 8. Comparing the different length models of HTCT in F-measure, the HTCT-3 model shows the best performance. This indicates that the HTCT model estimates the effective morpheme length for SRLs must be three on the training corpus, which is the same results in Table 7. Comparing the HTCT models with the CRF+3suf in F-measure, however, the CRF+3suf outperforms all of the HTCT models. If we focus on the precision rates, the HTCT-3 model performs 51.05 % in precision rate whose score is better than the CRF+3suf. This indicates that the arguments annotated correctly by the HTCT model might be different from those by the CRF+3suf, and thus there might be room for improvement of the performance of detecting SRLs by using both features.

The experimental results of the CRF+3suf model or the CRF+3suf+c model combined with HTCT-3 are shown in Table 9. The table shows that the both combined models outperforms the original models, i.e., CRF+3suf, CRF+3suf+c and HTCT-3 in F-measure. Especially comparing the results in Table 9 with those in Table 7, both the precision and recall rates are improved. These are preliminary results, however, these improvements must indicate that the context tag sequences extracted by HTCT would be different characteristics from manually defined features, and those must be effective for annotating SRLs.

4 Conclusion

We proposed a hierarchical tag context tree approach for capturing the multi-word expressions in arguments of Japanese sentences and show the effectiveness of extracting SRLs by applying the extracted hierarchical context tag sequences to the feature of CRFs. In the future work we will do more detailed analysis of these results.

Acknowledgments. This research received support from JSPS KAKENHI Grant Number 26370485.

References

1. Baker, C.F., Fillmore, C.J., Lowe, J.B.: The Berkeley FrameNet project. In: Proceedings of the 36th Annual Meeting of the Association for Computational Linguistics, pp. 86–90 (1998)
2. Palmer, M., Gildea, D., Kingsbury, P.: The proposition bank: an annotated corpus of semantic roles. Computat. Linguist. **31**(1), 71–105 (2005)
3. Gildea, D., Jurafsky, D.: Automatic labeling of semantic roles. Comput. Linguist. **28**(3), 1–45 (2002)
4. Surdeanu, M., Johansson, R., Meyers, A., Marquez, L., Nivre, J.: The CoNLL-2008 shared task on joint parsing of syntactic and semantic dependencies. In: Proceedings of the 12th Conference on Computational Natural Language Learning, pp. 159–177 (2008)
5. Palmer, M., Gildea, D., Xue, N.: Semantic Role Labeling. Morgan & Claypool Publishers, San Rafael (2009)
6. Kawahara, D., Kurohashi, S., Hashida, K.: Construction of a Japanese relevance-tagged corpus. In: Proceedings of the 8th Annual Meeting of the Association for Natural Language Processing, pp. 495–498 (2007) (in Japanese)
7. Iida, R., Komachi, M., Inui, K., Matsumoto, Y.: Annotating a Japanese text corpus with a predicate-argument and coreference relations. In: Proceedings of the 1st Linguistic Annotation Workshop, pp. 132–139 (2007)
8. Komachi, M., Iida, R.: Annotating a Japanese balanced corpus (BCCWJ) with a predicate-argument and coreference relations. In: Workshop for Japanese Corpus, pp. 352–330 (2011) (in Japanese)
9. Ohara, K., Kato, J., Saito, H.: Annotation of Japanese framenet to BCCWJ. In: Proceedings of the Workshop of Japanese Corupus in Grant-in-Aid For Scientific Research on Priority Areas, pp. 513–518 (2011) (in Japanese)
10. Takeuchi, K., Ueno, M., Takeuchi, N.: Annotating semantic role information to Japanese balanced corpus. In: Proceedings of MAPLEX 2015 (2015)

11. Maekawa, K.: Balanced corpus of contemporary written Japanese. In: Proceedings of the 6th Workshop on Asian Language Resources (ALR), pp. 101–102 (2008)
12. EDR, EDR: Electric Dictionary the Second Edition, Japan Electronic Dictionary Research Institute, Ltd. (1995)
13. Haruno, M., Matsumoto, Y.: Mistake-driven mixture of hierarchical tag context trees. In: Proceedings of the 35th Annual Meeting of the Association for Computational Linguistics, pp. 230–237 (1997)

Spoken Language and Dialogue

Arabic Dialect Identification Using a Parallel Multidialectal Corpus

Shervin Malmasi[1]([⊠]), Eshrag Refaee[2], and Mark Dras[1]

[1] Centre for Language Technology, Macquarie University, Sydney, NSW, Australia
{shervin.malmasi,mark.dras}@mq.edu.au
[2] Interaction Lab, Heriot-Watt University, Edinburgh EH144AS, UK
eaar1@hw.ac.uk

Abstract. We present a study on sentence-level Arabic Dialect Identification using the newly developed Multidialectal Parallel Corpus of Arabic (MPCA) – the first experiments on such data. Using a set of surface features based on characters and words, we conduct three experiments with a linear Support Vector Machine classifier and a meta-classifier using stacked generalization – a method not previously applied for this task. We first conduct a 6-way multi-dialect classification task in the first experiment, achieving 74 % accuracy against a random baseline of 16.7 % and demonstrating that meta-classifiers can large performance increases over single classifiers. The second experiment investigates pairwise binary dialect classification within the corpus, yielding results as high as 94 %, but also highlighting poorer results between closely related dialects such as Palestinian and Jordanian (76 %). Our final experiment conducts cross-corpus evaluation on the widely used Arabic Online Commentary (AOC) dataset and demonstrates that despite differing greatly in size and content, models trained with the MPCA generalize to the AOC, and vice versa. Using only 2,000 sentences from the MPCA, we classify over 26 k sentences from the radically different AOC dataset with 74 % accuracy. We also use this data to classify a new dataset of MSA and Egyptian Arabic tweets with 97 % accuracy. We find that character n-g are a very informative feature for this task, in both within- and cross-corpus settings. Contrary to previous results, they outperform word n-grams in several experiments here. Several directions for future work are outlined.

1 Introduction

The Arabic language, the official language of more than 20 countries, is comprised of many regional dialects with the Modern Standard Arabic (MSA) variety having the role of a common dialect across the Arabic-speaking population.

Arabic is a morphologically sophisticated language with many morphemes that can appear as prefixes, suffixes or even circumfixes. These mark grammatical information including case, number, gender, and definiteness, amongst others. This leads to a sophisticated morphotactic system. Its orthography is very different to English with right-to-left text that uses connective letters. Moreover,

© Springer Science+Business Media Singapore 2016
K. Hasida and A. Purwarianti (Eds.): PACLING 2015, CCIS 593, pp. 35–53, 2016.
DOI: 10.1007/978-981-10-0515-2_3

this is further complicated due to the presence of word elongation, common ligatures, zero-width diacritics and allographic variants – resulting in a degree of orthographic ambiguity. All of these properties pose a challenge for NLP [1].

These varieties of Dialectal Arabic (DA) and MSA vary among each other across the major linguistic subsystems, including phonology, morphology, orthography and to a lesser degree, syntax. For written Arabic – the focus of the present work – the greatest differences exist in lexicon, morphology and orthography.[1]

The availability of robust and accurate dialect identification models can be of great benefit to Arabic NLP tasks and this has fuelled the recent drive in investigating Arabic Dialect Identification (ADI). Potential applications of ADI are:

- As a useful preprocessing step for other tasks, such as statistical machine translation. Here they could be used to determine the most suitable dialect-specific models to be used for the input data.
- For building dialect-to-dialect or dialect-to-MSA lexicons, such as the work presented in [3] which uses information mined from the web to induce such lexicons. Another example is [4], which presents an electronic three-way lexicon, Tharwa, comprising Dialectal Arabic, Modern Standard Arabic and English correspondents. This can be helpful in linguistic research and can also aid learners who are studying a specific dialect.
- The generated dialectal mappings can be used in Natural Language Generation (NLG) for selecting the appropriate lexeme or morphological inflection using dialect-based word choice criteria [5]. This is useful for tailoring the output for a particular dialect or region.
- As a tool for Authorship profiling and attribution in the forensic linguistics domain.
- In an Information Retrieval context this method can be used to filter documents according to their dialect. Practical applications include, *inter alia*, filtering of news articles or search engine results according to user preferences.

These potential applications have generated recent interest in the task of automatically identifying the Arabic dialect of given texts.

The rise of microblogs and social media have also spurred researchers to investigate NLP tasks at smaller scales.[2] In this spirit, our work also focuses on dialect identification at the sentence level. This is a more challenging task due to sparsity and the amount of information available per item.

There have been concerns that the word unigram models used in previous research are affected by topic bias, as discussed in Sect. 2. We attempt to investigate this by running the first ADI experiments using a parallel corpus that is inherently balanced by topic. We further investigate this issue by using cross-corpus evaluation on previous datasets.

Another limitation with previous work is that almost all studies have distinguished between only two classes. There are likely to be many more classes in

---

[1] See [2, §2] for a more detailed discussion.
[2] e.g. on short texts such as Tweets, SMS messages and status updates.

practical application and we perform a 6-way dialect identification experiment to evaluate our system.

In sum, the broad aim of the present study is to assess the utility of surface features for multi-class Arabic dialect identification on a parallel corpus that is balanced by topic and size across classes. In addition to the standard single-classifier setup, we also experiment with a meta-classifier approach which to the best of our knowledge, has not hitherto been applied to dialect identification. Finally, we also aim to evaluate the generalizability of models trained on specific datasets through cross-corpus evaluation.

2 Background

A number of recent works have attempted to perform automatic dialect identification of Arabic texts.[3] In this section we briefly review some of this previous work.

The Arabic Online Commentary (AOC) Dataset, a 52 m word monolingual dataset rich in dialectal content was developed in [7]. A total of 108 k sentences were labelled for dialect and used for automatic dialect identification. The authors take a Language Model approach and report an accuracy of 69.4 % on a 4-way classification task (MSA and three dialects). On a binary classification between Egyptian Arabic and MSA, an accuracy of 80.9 % was reported.

Similarly, [8] also take a supervised learning approach to sentence-level binary classification of Egyptian Arabic and MSA data from the AOC dataset. They utilize a Naive Bayes classifier along with word n-grams combined with core (token- and perplexity-based features) and meta features. Their system achieves as accuracy of 85.5 %, an improvement over the 80.9 % reported in [7] for the same task.

In [9] the authors extend their previous work on the AOC dataset to include letter and word features. They report that word unigrams are the best performing feature. They report an accuracy of 81.0 % on a 4-way classification task (MSA vs. three dialects). For Egyptian Arabic *vs.* MSA, an accuracy of 87.9 % is reported.

Also focusing on the Egyptian-MSA binary classification task, [10] use a range of lexical and morphological features to classify 700 tweets with 95 % accuracy against a 50 % baseline. This set of 700 tweets was constructed specifically for evaluation and is different to the training data. A total of 880 k Arabic tweets were crawled from Twitter in March 2014 and this manually selected subset of 350 Egyptian and MSA tweets were selected to create the test set. We also use this test set in our cross-corpus evaluation.

Much of the previous work in Arabic Dialect Identification has used the Arabic Online Commentary (AOC) dataset. This dataset is not controlled for topic and the number of sentences across the different dialects are not balanced. The authors of [10] state that since the data are sourced from singular sources,

---

[3] Spoken Arabic dialect identification is a another area of research, as discussed in [6].

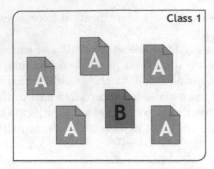
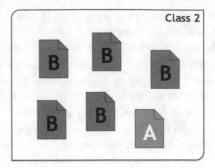

Fig. 1. An example of a dataset that is not balanced by topic: class 1 contains mostly documents from topic A while class 2 is dominated by texts from topic B. Here, a learning algorithm may distinguish the classes through other confounding variables related to topic.

these models may not generalize to other data as they implicitly capture topical cues and are thus susceptible to *topic bias*. This is a claim that we aim to assess in this work.

Topic bias can occur as a result of the themes or topics of the texts to be classified not being evenly distributed across the classes, leading to correlations between classes and topics [11,12]. For example, if in our training data all the texts written by Egyptian Arabic speakers are on topic A, while all the MSA texts refer to topic B, then we have implicitly trained our classifier on the topics as well. In this case the classifier learns to distinguish our target variable through another confounding variable. This concept is illustrated in Fig. 1.

3   Data

For our experiments we use the Multidialectal Parallel Corpus of Arabic (MPCA) which was recently released by [2]. They present the first parallel multidialectal Arabic dataset, comprised of 2,000 sentences in Modern Standard Arabic, five regional dialects, as well as English. This data was transcribed native-speaker translators who translated the source sentences into their dialect. This corpus is a valuable resource as such parallel cross-dialect translations do not occur naturally and are useful for studying dialectal differences while controlling for topic bias. Moreover, as this data has been transcribed, it is not prone to the issues found in noisy social media or web crawled data.

The corpus covers seven dialects/languages: Modern Standard Arabic (MSA), English (EN), Egyptian (EG), Tunisian (TN), Syrian (SY), Jordanian (JO) and Palestinian (PA). An example sentence is shown in Fig. 2, which highlights the wide ranging differences among the dialects. We use 1,000 sentences[4] from the Arabic data for our experiments, excluding the English translations.

---

[4] Given that this is a parallel corpus, this is 1,000 sentences per dialect, 6,000 sentences in total.

Dialect/Language	Example
English	*Because you are a personality that I can not describe.*
Modern Standard Arabic	لأنك شخصية لا أستطيع وصفها. *lÂnk šxSyħ lA ÂstTyς wSfhA.*
Egyptian Arabic	لأنك شخصية وبجد مش هعرف أوصفها. *lÂnk šxSyħ wbjd mš hςrf ÂwSfhA.*
Syrian Arabic	لأنك شخصية وعنجد ما رح أعرف أوصفها. *lÂnk šxSyħ wςnjd mA rH Âςrf ÂwSfhA.*
Jordanian Arabic	انت جد شخصية مستحيل اقدر اوصفه *Ant jd šxSyħ mstHyl Aqdr AwSfhA.*
Palestinian Arabic	عن جد ماشاء الله عليك شخصيتك ما بتنوصف. *ςn jd mA šA' Allh ςlyk šxSytk mA btnwSf.*
Tunisian Arabic	على خاطرك شخصية بلحق منجمش نوصفها. *ςlý xATrk šxSyħ blHq mnjmš nwSfhA.*

Fig. 2. A comparison of the translations for one sentence in the Multidialectal Parallel Arabic Corpus. We use the six Arabic dialects in our experiments.

In this work we also explore cross-corpus evaluation and use AOC and Egyptian-MSA tweet datasets, both described in the previous section, to test our system.

4 Methodology

We take a supervised classification approach for this task, similar to previous research. Our features, classifier and evaluation method are described in this section.

4.1 Features

We employ two lexical surface feature types for this task, as described below. We do not perform any preprocessing steps (e.g. tokenization or orthography normalization) prior to feature extraction.

Character n-grams. This is a sub-word feature that uses the constituent characters that make up the whole text. When used as *n*-grams, the features are *n*-character slices of the text. From a linguistic point of view, the substrings captured by this feature, depending on the order, can implicitly capture various sub-lexical features including single letters, phonemes, syllables, morphemes and suffixes.

Word n-grams. The surface forms of words can be used as a feature for classification. Each unique word may be used as a feature (i.e. unigrams), but the use of bigram distributions is also common. In this scenario, the *n*-grams are extracted along with their distributions.

The features frequencies are weighted using the *tf-idf* weighting scheme. This choice is based on our preliminary experiments showing that they outperformed a binary feature representation.

4.2   Classifier

We use a linear Support Vector Machine to perform multi-class classification in our experiments. In particular, we use the LIBLINEAR[5] SVM package [13] which has been shown to be efficient for text classification problems with large numbers of features and documents. We use cross-validation to optimize the SVM's C hyperparameter.

Ensemble classifiers have been found to be useful in other multi-class text classification tasks including language identification [14] and Native Language Identification [15,16]. In this work we also experiment with a stacked generalization model [17]. This is done through creating an ensemble of classifiers by training a single linear SVM classifier for each feature type and using the class probability outputs from each of these classifiers to train a higher level classifier. This meta-classifier, also a linear SVM, may be able to map the outputs from the lower level classifiers to their true labels by learning patterns such as certain classifiers being more likely to misclassify some classes [18, §3.6].

4.3   Evaluation

We report our results as classification accuracy under cross-validation. We experiment with two types of cross-validation.

Consistent with most previous studies, we use *k*-fold cross-validation, with $k = 10$. For creating our folds, we employ stratified cross-validation which aims to ensure that the proportion of classes within each partition is equal [19].

The accuracy estimated by *k*-fold cross-validation is a variable value that depends on the randomly chosen splits of the data. To reduce the variability introduced by this random splitting we also experiment with Leave-one-out (LOO) cross-validation where each data point is predicted by a learner trained on every other data point.[6]

No previous baselines are available here as this is the first application of dialect identification to this data. We use a *random baseline* for comparison purposes. This is commonly employed in classification tasks where it is calculated by randomly assigning labels to documents. It is a good measure of overall performance in instances where the training data is evenly distributed across

---

[5] http://www.csie.ntu.edu.tw/%7Ecjlin/liblinear/.

[6] For a dataset with *n* items, this is equivalent to *n*-fold cross-validation.

Table 1. Arabic Dialect Identification classification accuracy for all six dialects, using our feature set. The best results for each column are in bold.

Feature	Accuracy (%)	
	10-fold CV	LOO CV
Random Baseline	16.67	16.67
Oracle Baseline	81.21	81.74
(1) Character unigrams	46.12	46.27
(2) Character bigrams	62.16	62.40
(3) Character trigrams	65.26	65.60
(4) Character 4-g	59.62	60.12
(5) Word unigrams	57.53	57.76
(6) Word bigrams	24.10	24.27
All Character n-grams (1–4)	65.60	66.10
Character 1/2/3-g (1–3)	66.48	66.63
All Word n-g (5–6)	54.40	54.44
All features combined (1–6)	65.25	66.07
Meta-classifier (all features)	**74.32**	**74.35**

the classes, as is the case here. For example, an 11-class dataset has a random baseline of $\frac{1}{11} = 9.1\,\%$.

Additionally, we also compare against the oracle baseline used by [20]. Here the oracle correctly classifies a text if any single feature type alone correctly predicts its label. It is useful in defining an upper-bound for classification accuracy.

5 Experiments and Results

5.1 Multi-dialect Classification

Our first experiment evaluates our feature set for distinguishing all of the dialects from each other. This is a 6-way classification task with a random baseline of 16.67 %. The oracle baseline – the estimated maximum accuracy possible on this data – is 81 %, meaning that not any of our feature types can correctly classify around 19 % of this data. The results for all of our features under both cross-validation methods are shown in Table 1.

These results show that character n-grams are the best feature type, with trigrams yielding the highest accuracy and performance dropping sharply with 4-g. Word unigrams are also an informative feature, although not as accurate as the other features.

We also experiment with combining different feature types into a single feature vector, with results shown in the third section of Table 1. Here we observe that a combination of character 1/2/3-g provides the best result for this type of simple combination.

Finally, we also test our stacked generalization model for this task with all 6 feature types, achieving an accuracy of 74 %. This is an 8 % increase over the best single-classifier model and is only 7 % lower than the oracle upper-bound.

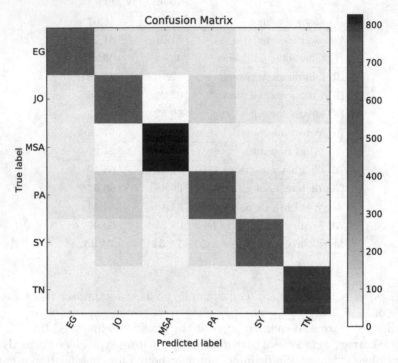

Fig. 3. The confusion matrix of our multi-class classification using stacked generalization with all features, visualized as a heatmap.

We can also assess the degree of confusion between classes; a confusion matrix of the results obtained using the stacked generalization model is presented in Fig. 3. Egyptian Arabic has the highest degree of confusion, mostly with MSA and Palestinian Arabic. We also see a significant amount of confusion between Jordanian Arabic and the Syrian and Palestinian varieties. This is not surprising and likely a result of geographical proximity as all three classes are Levantine dialects. MSA and Tunisian are the dialects that are most accurately identified.

Finally, we can also assess the learning curve for our best feature, a combination of character 1/2/3-g. This is shown in Fig. 4. It can be seen that there is rapid increase with the first 1,000 training instances and steady increases until the curve begins to stabilize at around 4,000 training examples. The accuracy does continue to increase after this, albeit at a slower pace. This suggests that the addition of more training data could help increase performance.

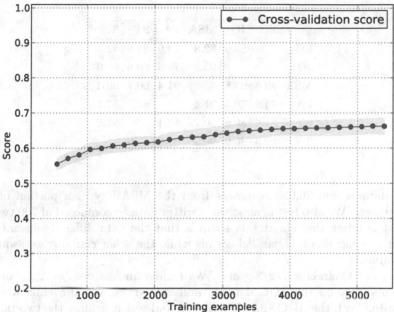

Fig. 4. The learning curve for Character 1/2/3-g. The curve begins to stabilize after around 4 k training sentences.

5.2 Pairwise Classification

Given that much of the previous dialect identification work has focused on binary classification of two dialects, we perform pairwise classification between all six varieties in the MPCA dataset. The results are shown in Table 2.

MSA and Jordanian Arabic are the most distinguishable pair with an accuracy of 93.8 %. Conversely, Palestinian and Egyptian Arabic are the most challenging to discriminate, resulting in the lowest accuracy of 74.9 %. Most other pairs are discriminated well. The accuracy for the widely-investigated MSA-Egyptian pair is similar to the previous results reported in Sect. 2.

5.3 Cross-Corpus Evaluation

Our final experiment aims to assess the generalizability of the features learned by our system. We do this through a cross-corpus evaluation using the MPCA and the AOC dataset described in Sect. 2. Additionally, we also test our system on the set of tweets constructed by [10].

As the datasets cover different dialects, we use the overlapping MSA and Egyptian dialects for binary classification. We take 2,000 sentences from the

Table 2. Pairwise Arabic Dialect Identification classification accuracy using Character 1/2/3-g.

	EG	JO	MSA	PA	SY	TN
EG		83.0	82.8	74.9	81.6	82.3
JO	83.0		93.8	76.3	80.8	86.0
MSA	82.8	93.8		91.4	90.7	90.2
PA	74.9	76.3	91.4		83.1	87.3
SY	81.6	80.8	90.7	83.1		87.9
TN	82.3	86.0	90.2	87.3	87.9	

MPCA dataset and 26,039 sentences from the MSA-Egyptian portion of the AOC dataset.[7] We also test against the Twitter dataset composed of 700 tweets.

What is interesting about this setup is that the data differ significantly in size and content; one is a parallel corpus while the other contains web-sourced user comments.

Using our Character 1/2/3-g and Word unigram features, we train on the MPCA and test on the AOC dataset, and vice versa. We also train a single model using both the AOC and MPCA data and test it against the tweets. The results for all of these evaluations are listed in Table 3.

These results again show that the character features perform very well in both cross-corpus scenarios. The accuracy for training on the MPCA is over 20 % higher than the AOC baseline. This is particularly impressive considering that we are using only 2 k sentences from one corpus to classify over 26 k sentences from a radically different corpus with 73.6 % accuracy. Word unigrams are also useful and only a few percentage points behind the character n-grams.

This pattern is mirrored for training and the larger AOC and testing on the MPCA, but with higher accuracies. This is not surprising given that the training data is 13 times larger. Character n-grams provide the best cross-corpus accuracy of 83.85 % compared to 80.20 % for the word unigrams, both of which are against a 50 % random baseline.

A key finding here is that the models trained here do generalize across datasets with a high degree of accuracy, despite their striking differences in size and content. Although this result does not evidence the absence of topic bias, it may indicate that its negative effects are tolerable.

These results also suggest that, at least for small dataset like the MPCA, character n-grams generalize the most. However, it may be the case that word unigrams may perform better with a large enough dataset; character n-grams may be performing better here as there may not be much lexical overlap between the unrelated datasets.

---

[7] This contains 13,512 MSA sentences, resulting in a majority class baseline of 51.89 %.

Table 3. MSA vs. Egyptian Arabic cross-corpus classification results for training on one dataset and testing on the other, and vice versa. Bold indicates best result in column.

	Cross-corpus accuracy (%)		
Train	MPCA[a]	AOC	AOC+MPCA
Test	AOC[b]	MPCA	Tweets[c]
Baseline	51.89	50.00	50.00
Character 1/2/3-g	**73.60**	**83.35**	94.00
Word unigrams	68.82	80.20	**96.71**
All Features	73.16	83.00	95.14

[a] Includes 2,000 sentences, distributed evenly across the two classes.
[b] Has 26,039 sentences, majority baseline used as not evenly distributed
[c] Includes 700 Tweets distributed equally across both classes.

6 Error Analysis

In this section we isolate and analyze the misclassified sentences in the MPCA data to gain a better understanding of the challenges for sentence-level dialect identification.

6.1 Sentence Length Analysis

Sentence length, measured by the number of tokens, is an important factor to consider in sentence-level classification tasks [21,22]. There may not be enough distinguishing features if a sentence is too short. Conversely, very long sentences will likely have more features that facilitate correct classification. Here we investigate the length of misclassified items.

The MPCA data has a mean sentence length of 8.9 tokens (SD=5.3) while the misclassified subset has a substantially smaller average length of 6.8 tokens per sentence (SD=4.07). Histograms for this data are shown in Fig. 5. We also observe that very few of the longer sentences are misclassified.

An analysis of the cumulative frequency shown that 65 % of the misclassified sentences have 7 tokens or less. In sum, evidence from this analysis points to the challenges of distinguishing smaller sentences.

6.2 Human Evaluation of Misclassified Sentences

We also perform a human evaluation on the misclassified sentences. Such analyses of misclassified items can help better understand the difficulty of a task [20] and provide further insights about the task.

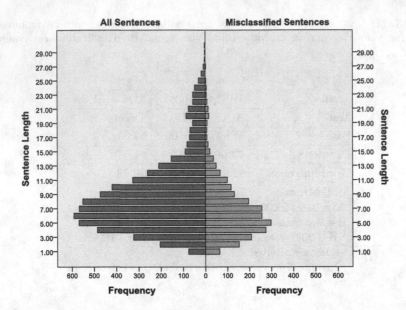

Fig. 5. Histograms of the sentence lengths (tokens) in our data for the entire corpus (left) and only for misclassified sentences (right).

For this analysis 20 misclassified sentences from each dialect were randomly selected to create a set of 120 sentences. The second author, a native speaker with experience in dialectal Arabic research, was then required to label each sentence with the most probable dialect.

Only 23 sentences (19.17 %) were correctly classified, only slightly above the random baseline of 16.67 %. Analysis and evaluator feedback from the task provided some relevant insights:

- A large proportion of the sentences are very short and therefore lack contextual and dialect-specific cues that can be effective in determining the dialect class accurately.
- The above issue results in many texts being acceptable into any of dialect classes.
- A number of other instances can be confidently ruled out as being MSA, but it is not clear which non-MSA dialect they belong to.
- A narrower subset of sentences can fit within any of the Levantine dialects.
- Most of the correctly labelled sentences (65 %) were MSA or Egyptian Arabic.

These results and highlighted issues comport with our confusion matrix and sentence length analyses. All of these findings could also explain why the MPCA data has an oracle baseline of 81 %.

Future work can use an oracle classifier [20] to isolate the subset of sentences that no feature type can predict correctly.

7   Feature Analysis

In this section we perform an analysis of the most discriminative features associated with each class in the MPCA data. We do this using the method proposed by [23] to extract lists of features associated with each dialect.

7.1   Egyptian Arabic

A large portion of discriminative features here are dialect specific function words and highly dialectal content words. Some discriminative features are shown in Fig. 6.

Egyptian Arabic	English
ده, دی, دي	Egyptian specific references
كد, كدا, كده	Like that
ايه, بجد	Denoting questions
اوي, اوى	Egyptian specific intensifiers
حصل	Verb meaning 'happened'
بقى, بق	Word denotes inferring/reasoning
واد	Noun meaning "boy"
ريس	Noun meaning "president"
فيش, دش, حدش, مش	Negators
بتا	Token denoting possession

Fig. 6. Discriminative features for Egyptian Arabic.

7.2   Jordanian Arabic

The discriminative features of Jordanian Arabic tend to be more content words rather than function words. We also note that some of the content words are conversational (*i.e.* بحكي ، حكي ، حكتلو ،). This might reflect a genuine trend in this dialect or it could merely be an artefact due to the size of the dataset. Example features are listed in Fig. 7.

Jordanian Arabic	English
عال	Common token meaning "good/fine"
اشي	Common token meaning "something"
حدا	Common token meaning "someone"
زلم	Common token meaning "men"
هاي	A reference, "this"
لسا, مش	Negators
رح	Denoting future actions, "will"
ليش, شو	Denoting questions

Fig. 7. Discriminative features for Jordanian Arabic.

Palestinian Arabic	English
هسه	"Now"
في, عن, على, حقي	Prepositions overused by this dialect
مره	A woman
مش	Negator
شو	Denoting questions
هدا, هد	Denoting references
بد	A common prefix in Levantine dialects that denotes a desire to do something. "I'd like to".

Fig. 8. Discriminative features for Palestinian Arabic.

7.3 Palestinian Arabic

This dialect is also distinguished by more unique content words rather than function words. Some examples from this dialect are listed in Fig. 8.

7.4 Syrian Arabic

This dialect has some features that overlap with the other Levantine dialects. Examples are shown in Fig. 9.

7.5 Tunisian Arabic

As shown by the features in Fig. 10, this dialect has a set of highly specific negators, prefixes, intensifiers, interrogative prefixes and verbs.

7.6 Modern Standard Arabic

Function words are the most discriminative features for MSA, some of which are listed in Fig. 11.

8 Discussion and Conclusion

We presented a number of Arabic dialect identification experiments using the newly released MPCA dataset. These results inform current research in several ways.

We demonstrated the utility of a parallel corpus for ADI, achieving 74 % accuracy on a 6-dialect classification task with a random baseline of 16.7 %. Pairwise binary dialect classification within this corpus also yielded results as high as 94 %, but also highlighted poorer results between closely related dialects such as Palestinian and Jordanian (76 %). This was also evident in our feature analysis where we observed that the Levantine dialects share a lot of common features, making it harder to distinguish them. The results also show that leave-one-out cross-validation leads to very similar results as 10-fold cross-validation.

We demonstrated that a meta-classifier can provide significant increases for multi-class dialect identification. This is a direction that requires further investigation as this is the first application of such a method for this task.

Syrian Arabic	English
عم	Denote actions currently happening
رح	Denotes future actions, "will"
متل	Syrian spelling variation "like/similar to"
هلئ	Word shared among Levantine dialects meaning "now"
تعي	Syrian specific verb "come"
مو, ليش	Negators
هاد, هنن, حنا, عنا	References

Fig. 9. Discriminative features for Syrian Arabic.

Tunisian Arabic	English
نيش, فما, موش, بلا	Negators
باش	Function word meaning "In order to"
شن, شنو, شكو	Interrogative prefixes
ش, وش	Usually appear as affixes of an integrative word
نحب	Verb meaning "to like"
برشة	A Tunisian-specific intensifier
لحق	Adverb means "Truly"
هكا	"Like that"

Fig. 10. Discriminative features for Tunisian Arabic.

MSA	English
سوف, قد	Denoting future actions, "will"
ليس, لم	Negators
ماذا	"What"
له	Denoting possession (masculine)
هذه	A reference (feminine)
أن	That (connects parts of a sentence)
قوم	People
ندم	A verb or noun meaning "regret"
وجد, تجد	Present and past verbs meaning "find"

Fig. 11. Discriminative features for Modern Standard Arabic (MSA).

Our cross-corpus experiment demonstrated that models trained with the MPCA generalize to other data. This was also the case for the AOC dataset when tested against the MPCA. Data from both corpora was also used to classify 700 Egyptian Arabic and MSA tweets with 97% accuracy.

Similar to the results of [10], we find that character n-grams are in most scenarios the best single feature for this task, in both within- and cross-corpus settings. This is in contrast to the results of [7–9] that establish word unigrams as being the best feature type. This discrepancy merits further scrutiny and we plan to investigate it in future research.

One possibility is that previous experiments report higher accuracies due to topic bias *within* their corpora, which is most strongly present in words. This may also be due to the smaller size of our dataset; there may not be a sufficient amount of data and unique tokens to train a learner on words.

The use of the two feature types is not mutually exclusive. In a system that operates on both the token and sentence levels, such as that of [8], the character n-grams could be used to classify out of vocabulary (OOV) tokens which are previously unseen.

The key shortcoming of this study, albeit beyond our control, is the limited amount of data available for the experiments. In this regard, we are surprised by relatively high classification accuracy of our system, given the restricted amount of training data available. Future work includes the application of our methods to additional data as it becomes available. Only 1 k parallel sentences from the MPCA dataset were available to us at the time of our study, but this is to be expanded in the future.

Another limitation is the absence of data preprocessing. The integration of additional task-specific preprocessing steps, namely tokenization and orthography normalization, could lead to improved performance according to the results reported by [8, p.459].

There are also a number of other potential directions for future work. The overall accuracy can be increased by focusing on improving the most commonly confused classes (as shown in the confusion matrix in Sect. 5.1) and the worst performing dialect pairs from the pairwise classification analysis.

We also note that conducting an even more comprehensive error analysis could also provide to be a fruitful line of future inquiry. This analysis could provide valuable insights about the most common errors being committed by the current system – such as those related to the above-mentioned class confusion – thus helping guide future efforts in this area.

Another possibility is to experiment with a wider range of features and to assess the diversity of these features, for example, using the method proposed by [24].

Further to increasing the dataset sizes, the number of dialects can also be increased. More datasets could also be used to perform additional cross-corpus experiments. This data can be sourced from everyday natural language productions found in social media and Twitter.

Acknowledgments. We would like to thank Houda Bouamor for making the MPCA data available. We also thank the three anonymous reviewers for their helpful comments.

References

1. Habash, N.Y.: Introduction to arabic natural language processing. Synth. Lect. Hum. Lang. Technol. **3**(1), 1–187 (2010)
2. Bouamor, H., Habash, N., Oflazer, K.: A multidialectal parallel corpus of arabic. In: Proceedings of the Ninth International Conference on Language Resources and Evaluation (LREC 2014). European Language Resources Association (ELRA), Reykjavik, Iceland, May 2014
3. Al-Sabbagh, R., Girju, R.: Mining the web for the induction of a dialectical arabic lexicon. In: Proceedings of the Seventh International Conference on Language Resources and Evaluation (LREC 2010). European Language Resources Association (ELRA), Valletta, Malta, May 2010
4. Diab, M., Albadrashiny, M., Aminian, M., Attia, M., Elfardy, H., Habash, N., Hawwari, A., Salloum, W., Dasigi, P., Eskander, R.: Tharwa: A Large Scale Dialectal Arabic - Standard Arabic - English Lexicon, May 2014
5. Stede, M.: Lexical choice criteria in language generation. In: Proceedings of the sixth conference on European chapter of the Association for Computational Linguistics, pp. 454–459. Association for Computational Linguistics (1993)
6. Biadsy, F., Hirschberg, J., Habash, N.: Spoken arabic dialect identification using phonotactic modeling. In: Proceedings of the EACL 2009 Workshop on Computational Approaches to Semitic Languages, pp. 53–61, Association for Computational Linguistics (2009)
7. Zaidan, O.F., Callison-Burch, C.: The Arabic online commentary dataset: an annotated dataset of informal Arabic with high dialectal content. In: Proceedings of the 49th Annual Meeting of the Association for Computational Linguistics: Human Language Technologies, pp. 37–41. Association for Computational Linguistics (2011)
8. Elfardy, H., Diab, M.T.: Sentence level dialect identification in arabic. In: Proceedings of the 51st Annual Meeting of the Association for Computational Linguistics (ACL), pp. 456–461 (2013)
9. Zaidan, O.F., Callison-Burch, C.: Arabic dialect identification. Comput. Linguist. **40**(1), 171–202 (2014)
10. Darwish, K., Sajjad, H., Mubarak, H.: Verifiably effective arabic dialect identification. In: Proceedings of the 2014 Conference on Empirical Methods in Natural Language Processing (EMNLP). Association for Computational Linguistics, Doha, Qatar, October 2014
11. Brooke, J., Hirst, G.: Measuring interlanguage: native language identification with L1-influence metrics. In: Proceedings of the Eight International Conference on Language Resources and Evaluation (LREC 2012), Istanbul, Turkey, pp. 779–784, May 2012
12. Malmasi, S., Dras, M.: Arabic native language identification. In: Proceedings of the Arabic Natural Language Processing Workshop (EMNLP 2014). Association for Computational Linguistics, Doha, Qatar, pp. 180–186, October 2014. http://aclweb.org/anthology/W14-3625
13. Fan, R.E., Chang, K.W., Hsieh, C.J., Wang, X.R., Lin, C.J.: LIBLINEAR: a library for large linear classification. J. Mach. Learn. Res. **9**, 1871–1874 (2008)
14. Malmasi, S., Dras, M.: Language Identification using Classifier Ensembles. In: Proceedings of the Joint Workshop on Language Technology for Closely Related Languages, Varieties and Dialects (LT4VarDial 2015). Association for Computational Linguistics, Hissar, Bulgaria, september 2015

15. Malmasi, S., Wong, S.M.J., Dras, M.: NLI shared task 2013: MQ submission. In: Proceedings of the Eighth Workshop on Innovative Use of NLP for Building Educational Applications. Association for Computational Linguistics, Atlanta, Georgia, pp. 124–133, June 2013. http://www.aclweb.org/anthology/W13-1716
16. Malmasi, S., Dras, M.: Large-scale native language identification with cross-corpus evaluation. In: Proceedings of NAACL-HLT 2015. Association for Computational Linguistics, Denver, Colorado, pp. 1403–1409, June 2015. http://aclweb.org/anthology/N15-1160
17. Wolpert, D.H.: Stacked generalization. Neural Netw. **5**(2), 241–259 (1992)
18. Polikar, R.: Ensemble based systems in decision making. IEEE Circuits Syst. Mag. **6**(3), 21–45 (2006)
19. Kohavi, R.: A study of cross-validation and bootstrap for accuracy estimation and model selection. IJCAI **14**, 1137–1145 (1995)
20. Malmasi, S., Tetreault, J., Dras, M.: Oracle and human baselines for native language identification. In: Proceedings of the Tenth Workshop on Innovative Use of NLP for Building Educational Applications. Association for Computational Linguistics, Denver, Colorado, June 2015
21. Malmasi, S., Dras, M.: Automatic language identification for persian and dari texts. In: Proceedings of the 14th Conference of the Pacific Association for Computational Linguistics (PACLING 2015). Bali, Indonesia, May 2015
22. Gottron, T., Lipka, N.: A comparison of language identification approaches on short, query-style texts. In: Gurrin, C., He, Y., Kazai, G., Kruschwitz, U., Little, S., Roelleke, T., Rüger, S., van Rijsbergen, K. (eds.) ECIR 2010. LNCS, vol. 5993, pp. 611–614. Springer, Heidelberg (2010)
23. Malmasi, S., Dras, M.: Language transfer hypotheses with linear SVM weights. In: Proceedings of the Conference on Empirical Methods in Natural Language Processing (EMNLP). Association for Computational Linguistics, Doha, Qatar, pp. 1385–1390 (10 2014). http://aclweb.org/anthology/D14-1144
24. Malmasi, S., Cahill, A.: Measuring feature diversity in native language identification. In: Proceedings of the Tenth Workshop on Innovative Use of NLP for Building Educational Applications. Association for Computational Linguistics, Denver, Colorado, pp. 49–55, June 2015. http://aclweb.org/anthology/W15-0606

Filled Pause Detection in Indonesian Spontaneous Speech

Auliya Sani[✉], Dessi Puji Lestari, and Ayu Purwarianti

Institut Teknologi Bandung, Bandung, Indonesia
13509067@std.stei.itb.ac.id, dessipuji@stei.itb.ac.id,
ayu@informatika.org

Abstract. Detecting filled pause in spontaneous speech recognition is very important since most of the speech is spontaneous and the most frequent phenomenon in Indonesian spontaneous speech is filled pause. This paper discusses the detection of filled pauses in spontaneous speech of Indonesian by utilizing acoustic features of the speech signal. The detection was conducted by employing statistical method using Naïve Bayes, Classification Tree, and Multilayer Perceptron algorithm. To build the model, speech data were collected from an entertainment program. Word parts in the data were labeled and its features were extracted. These include the formant and pitch stability, energy-drop, and duration. Half an hour of sentences contains 295 filled pause and 2082 non-filled pause words were employed as training data. Using 25 sentences as testing data, Naïve Bayes gave best detection correctness, 74.35 % on a closed data set and 71.43 % on an open data set.

Keywords: Spontaneous speech · Filled pause · Acoustic

1   Introduction

Speaking is one way of conveying information. Despite many kinds of speaking styles, it can be divided into three categories based on the preparation: prepared speech; semi-spontaneous; and spontaneous. A prepared speech is produced when the speaker read a text that has been prepared in advance. Semi-spontaneous speech means the speaker already has a topic prepared but delivers it freely. Spontaneous speech does not have any preparation or guidance that must be followed.

Speech in everyday life expressed spontaneously and becomes a common way to communicate with others [12]. Generally people speak while thinking what they would say later. This makes spontaneous speech has some phenomena [10]. These phenomena are not appeared in the prepared speech whose speech transcription will be exactly same as the prepared text. These phenomena can cause problems in processing the speech. Some of these phenomena are [5, 17].

1. Filled pause is a sound created by the speaker which has no related meaning to the rest of the sentence, for example /ah/, /uh/, /um/, etc.
2. Repetition means a phrase correction which is the same with previously uttered word. Generally, the edit region structure consists of a reparandum, an interruption point (IP), an optional interregnum, and a repair region.

© Springer Science+Business Media Singapore 2016
K. Hasida and A. Purwarianti (Eds.): PACLING 2015, CCIS 593, pp. 54–64, 2016.
DOI: 10.1007/978-981-10-0515-2_4

3. Revision is a case where the repair phrase corrects the reparandum.
4. Restart (also called as a false start) happens when an utterance is aborted and then restarted with a new thought.
5. Interjection is extraneous phrases, usually for showing the speaker's feeling about what he just said or stating it's just his opinion.
6. Ellipsis is a style of speaking where the speaker only delivers necessary information, like label specification or amount, without a proper sentence's forms.
7. Wrong grammatical sentence.

Phenomenon 1 to 4 is generally classified as disfluencies in spontaneous speech. These phenomena also occur in semi-spontaneous speech. They will affect the result transcription of spontaneous and semi-spontaneous speech processing. Because the similarity of speech phenomena on both speaking style, henceforth in this paper we will call both as spontaneous speech for short.

One technology that processes information from the sound signal as input is speech recognition technology. Speech recognition technology transforms a computerized voice signal into words in the written form. Recognized words can be a final output as well as an input into other systems, including NLP (Natural Language Processing).

Speech generated by reading the text is able to be recognized with accuracy above 95 % by utilizing state-of-the-art sound processing technology. However, the accuracy of such systems decreases dramatically when recognizing spontaneous speech. This is because the acoustic models and language models are generally made of a set of proper grammar sentences, instead made of spontaneous speech. Since spontaneous speech and prepared speech has some different both in terms of acoustics and grammar, the characteristics of spontaneous speech have not been handled well here.

Research on spontaneous speech and the development of spontaneous speech recognition has been widely applied to several languages such as English [1, 8], Japanese [7], and Dutch [15, 16]. For Indonesian, speech recognition is now able to process prepared or read speech with good accuracy. However research for Indonesian spontaneous speech is still on the preliminary stage. The paper presents our experiment as a preliminary study in developing speech recognition for Indonesian spontaneous speech.

Table 1. Disfluencies in indonesian spontaneous speech

Respondent	Frequencies of phenomena			
	Filled pause	Revision	Repetition	Restart
1	28	9	13	3
2	28	7	13	–
3	36	10	6	6
4	24	7	2	4
total	116	33	34	13

In order to study phenomena that usually be appeared in Indonesian spontaneous speech, a preliminary experiment about speech disfluencies in Indonesian was conducted by involving 4 respondents. They were asked to answer some questions for about 10 min. Speech disfluencies in their spontaneous answers are recorded in Table 1.

The experiment result shows filled pause as the most occurred speech disfluency in Indonesian spontaneous speech. Therefore, filled pause was chosen as the main focus in this study. Filled pause is one of speech disfluency which can show speaker hesitance, asking time for thinking or as a signal of revision or repetition. It can take form as a word or phrase but has no meaning in the uttered speech [3, 16]. Based on the conducted preliminary experiment, filled pauses in Indonesian spontaneous speech can be classified into two categories:

1. Filled pause which has no meaning as a standalone word. Example: /aah/, /əəh/, / um/, /ng-/, etc.
2. Filled pause which has a meaning as a standalone word. This filled pause group consists of words listed in the dictionary, but sometimes used as filled pause. They can be a word or a phrase, and can be vary depending on the speaker characteristic and speaking habits. Some example of this filled pause group are *jadi*, *terus*, *ya*, *itu*, and *apa ya*. English word for those examples respectively: so, then, yeah, that's, like what.

In this work, we built an automatic system to detect filled pause in Indonesian spontaneous speech. In order to build such system, we built a filled pause and non-filled pause model from Indonesian spontaneous speech. Indonesian spontaneous speech that is used in the experiments is explained in Sect. 2. Section 3 explains filled pause detection methods while Sect. 4 explains the selected method to be conducted in this experiment. The experiment itself is explained in Sect. 5, and the conclusion of the experiment is shown in Sect. 6.

2 Corpus

Currently, there is no Indonesian spontaneous speech corpus. To build such corpus, we used Indonesian TED[1] presentation videos which are semi-spontaneous speech. There were 9 presentations (7 male speakers and 2 female speakers) of half an hour long selected and cut into 225 sentences. Most of the speech sentences contain at least one filled pause.

Next, we labeled the sentences manually by employing the Transcriber [2]. There are 4 kinds of labels:

1. Filled Pause (FP) for filled pause, revision word, and not fully-form word,
2. Non-Filled pause (NFP) for meaningful word,
3. Short Pause (SP) for short pause, and
4. Short Pause Noise (SP-noise) for labels pause contains noises like sound of breath captured by microphone, claps, and other technical problem.

---

[1] http://www.youtube.com/user/TEDxTalks.

The statistical information about label distribution is shown in Table 2.

Table 2. Total labels

Label	Count
FP	330
NFP	2,318
SP	2,130
SP-noise	919
total	5,697

3   Filled Pause Detection Method

Various methods for detecting filled pause can be divided into 4 major lines:

1. Detection using voice features, the voice feature is subdivided into using prosodic features, spectral, and acoustics [1, 7, 8, 11, 15];
2. Detection using acoustic models [18];
3. Detection using language models [13];
4. The merger of two or more of the methods above [9, 14].

A combination of several studies of filled pause voice features characteristics such as duration, pitch, spectral, and formant outlined in a filled pause detection method proposed in [8]. First of all, energy of the speech signal is analyzed to detect silent, low energy areas. Since the duration of vowels in a filled pause is longer than the duration of fluent vowels, only voiced parts with duration greater than 0.5 times the average voiced duration are extracted. In this step, the words that are often confused as a filled pause such as 'a', 'the', 'me', and 'you' can be excluded. The next step is calculating four formant frequencies (F1, F2, F3, F4) from parts with stable F0. Having knowledge that the energy of the filler dropped dramatically at the end of the speech, Edrop (energy

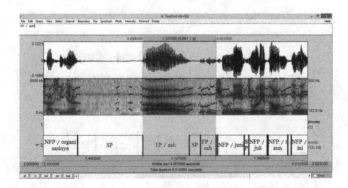

Fig. 1. Formants of filled pause /aah/and /eeh/in a sentence

drop) of the extracted parts is also calculated from energy of the latter part of voiced region. These six categories are named as the stable F0 transition (F0sd), minimum standard deviation of formant (F1sd, F2sd, F3sd, and F4sd), and the maximum end-utterance spectral Edrop and combined in to a single decision factor which was calculated as follows:

$$\text{Decision factor} = \text{F0sd} * \text{F1sd} * \text{F2sd} * \text{F3sd} * \text{F4sd} * (1/\text{Edrop}) \qquad (1)$$

Giving the formula means a filled pause is detected when the decision factor is smallest for a given utterance. The testing of filled pause detection using 60 sentences as data test from 3 different speakers with only one filled pause was present in each segment achieves detection accuracy of 80 %.

Up until now, filled pause detection is not possible to be made independently of languages. Some language has different characteristics of filled pause. Take Indonesian as an example. In Indonesian, we face a condition that there exist two categories of filled pause (see Sect. 1, categorization of filled pause in Indonesian). The second category rarely happens in spontaneous speech from other languages. Therefore, a research for spontaneous speech should be conducted for each language.

4   Method Selection

Research on the filled pause in Indonesian has never been conducted before. This resulted in the absence of references to the filled pause in Indonesian, including variants of filled pauses that are often used in everyday life. This experiment is a preliminary study to detect filled pause. Due to the lack of information regarding the filled pause in Indonesian, detection using acoustic models and language models are difficult to be conducted. By taking the hypothesis that the voice feature of filled pause is different from the non-filled pause, detection using voice features was chosen.

The method outlined in Sect. 3 above brings the formant stability in the filled pause words. It turns out that this is true in most filled pause in Indonesian. Formant illustration of the word in a sentence can be seen in Figs. 1 and 2. Both figures show that the filled pause in Indonesian has a fairly stable formant. Formant depicted by dots in the center

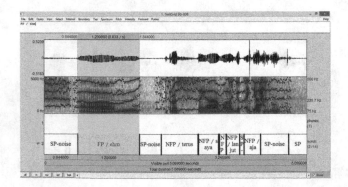

Fig. 2. Formants of filled pause /ehm/in a sentence

of the image, respectively from the bottom is the F1, F2, F3, F4, and a bit of F5. This experiment utilized only the first four formant frequencies while F5 is ignored.

5 Experiment

The experiment utilized extracted voice features from 10 ms segments of each label such as formant frequencies, pitch, and edrop. Training and testing data were used in the form of labels features. Testing was conducted by calculating the decision factors and by using models built from training data with machine learning algorithms. The correctness of the classification using decision factor was calculated by sorting the value of decision factor. The correctness of classification using the model was obtained by calculating the percentage of correctly recognized labels.

Experiments conducted in [8] utilizing VAD (Voice Activity Detector) to extract non-pause sections. Then these sections are processed. However, because the owned data is spontaneous utterances contain unnecessary pauses and noises, it is difficult to completely extract the meaningful non-pause parts using VAD. The purpose of processing data with VAD is to take words of the sentence, which in fact, has been done through manual labeling. For subsequent experiments, the data, that is processed, is only the FP and NFP labeled data.

Required features of 10 ms samplings from FP and NFP labeled data were extracted. The required features are F0, F1, F2, F3, F4, and intensity. Duration feature was also collected at the level of words. Features extraction was conducted using Praat [4].

Words whose duration less than 0.1 s were eliminated. Elimination aimed to reduce the non-filled pause words consisting of only one syllable and also have stable features for example *ke* 'to', *di* 'in', and *yang* 'the'. Words such as these can be considered as filled pause because of their similar features. The average durations of this kind of non-filled pause words are distributed around 0.1 s. The value of formant and pitch stability of each word were taken from SD (Standard Deviation) values throughout the 10 ms sampling.

In experiment [8], they calculated edrop in the spectral envelope of the last 20 samples of each voiced segment. That criterion couldn't be conducted in this experiment. In our data, the shortest duration is 0.1 s which is only contains 10 samples. Based on this, we calculated edrop only of the last 7 samples of each segment. If the energy of a segment is really dropped toward the end of the word, last 7 samples are indeed affected regardless the duration. Thus, features of each label are the SD of the four formants F1SD, F2SD, F3SD, F4SD; SD values of pitch F0SD; Edrop; and word duration.

Testing whether a label is a filled pause or not was conducted in two ways. The first way is by calculating Decision factor of all features using formula (1). The second way is by building a model with Naïve Bayes algorithm, Tree J48, and Multilayer Perceptron with Weka [6].

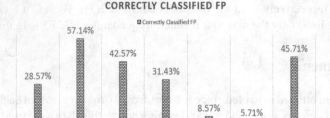

CORRECTLY CLASSIFIED FP

Fig. 3. FP detection graph result from experiment I

5.1 Experiment I

Filled pause detection was conducted by calculating the decision factor with the formula (1) in Sect. 3. Starting with the assumption that filled pause has stable both pitch and formant and has energy that dropped dramatically at the end of the word, then the filled pause has a small value of decision factor. The difference in this experiment with the experiment in [8] lies in the selection of label which considered as filled pause. Experiment in [8] used artificial data where there is only one filled pause in each sentence, while the data used for this experiment has some sentences that contain more than one filled pause. Therefore, the ranking method based on the smallest decision factor and duration limits was used. FP and NFP labels of 25 sentences as the testing data were processed and decision factor was calculated. Testing data contains 35 FP and 236 NFP segments.

The graph in Fig. 3 shows the results of filled pause detection by ranking values of each feature ascendingly and values of all features incorporated in the calculation of the smallest decision factor. Of the top 35 ranking which has the smallest decision factor, 16 filled pause words are correctly detected. Thus, the classification correctness is 45.7 %. Classification by ranking the feature values ascendingly is also can be used against each feature group. By simply using F2SD, 20 filled pauses are found from top 35 rank of the smallest F2SD with 57.1 % classification correctness.

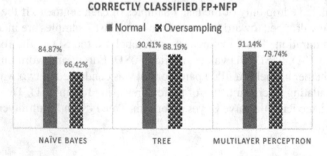

CORRECTLY CLASSIFIED FP+NFP

Fig. 4. FP and NFP classification (detection) correctness

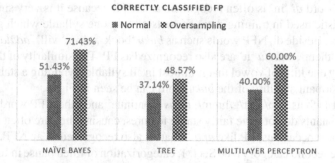

Fig. 5. FP classification (detection) correctness

5.2 Experiment II

The model was built from F1SD, F2SD, F3SD, F4SD, F0SD, and Edrop data of each word. Two hundred sentences containing 295 FP and 2082 NFP words were used as training data while the rests, 25 sentences, were used as data test. Because of the unbalanced distribution of the data, balancing the amount of data through oversampling was also conducted. Oversampling was performed by multiplying FP labeled data until reach the same amount as NFP labeled data using weka. From this more balanced data, a model was also been built. The overall comparison of classification correctness from all models can be seen in Fig. 4 while the correctness of FP classification can be seen in Fig. 5.

From Fig. 4 we can see that the highest correctness was achieved by the model built from the normal amount of data using multilayer perceptron algorithm. Unfortunately, that same model did not provide good correctness in classifying FP. Because the purpose of the experiment is for detecting FP, we focused on FP classification correctness in Fig. 5 instead of overall classification correctness in Fig. 4. Figure 5 shows that models built from a balanced amount of training data provided better FP detection result than the ones with unbalanced amount of data. Of the three algorithms used, Naïve Bayes gave the best results in the FP detection.

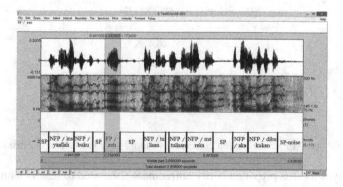

Fig. 6. The word *buku* 'book' (third from left) has fairly stable formants

The NFP word *di* 'in' is often recognized as the FP because it is very similar to the FP characteristic used in training data: consists of only one syllable which generates a stable formant. Beside di, NFP words such as *buku* 'book', *akan* 'will', *adalah* 'is', *atau* 'or', *mereka* 'them', and *itu* 'it' are also recognized as FP. The similarity of these words is having only one kind of vowel that is almost in all syllables, yielding a stable formant frequency. Formant stability of the *buku* word can be seen in Fig. 6.

FP words such as /um/, /er/, /hmm/, *terus* 'continue' and others FP words that have striking consonants do not have fairly stable features, causing they are often recognized as NFP. In some occasions, FP like *apa* 'what' is also recognized as an NFP. This word belongs to the second category (see Sect. 1, categorization of filled pause in Indonesian). FPs that are almost always recognized correctly are /aah/and /eeh/which have fairly stable features and in accordance with the filled pause characteristics described in [8]. FP from the second category like *ya* 'yeah' is also recognized correctly sometimes, although not as much as /aah/and /eeh/do. Three of them have same feature: consists of only one syllable and does not have striking consonants. From this result, it can be concluded that the proposed method in [8] can be used to recognize filled pause that consists of only one syllable and not have a striking consonants, such as /aah/, /eeh/, and *ya*.

5.3   Testing Method Comparison

Testing methods in experiment I and II were compared. Naïve Bayes models using training data with oversampling was selected to detect filled pauses on the closed set (using training data) and open testing data set. Classification by using decision factor was also conducted on the closed and open data set.

The graph in Fig. 7 below shows a comparison of the overall classification correctness throughout the FP and NFP of four experiments. NB(c) means classification using Naïve Bayes model on closed set while NB(o) means classification using Naïve Bayes model on open set. On the other hand, DF(c) and DF(o) means classification using Decision factor in closed and open testing data consecutively. The graph shows

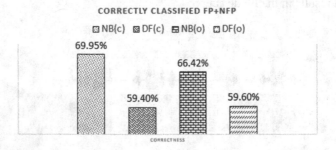

Fig. 7. FP and NFP classification correctness using Naïve Bayes and decision factor

Naïve Bayes models provided better correctness compared to results using decision factor method though the numbers do not differ much.

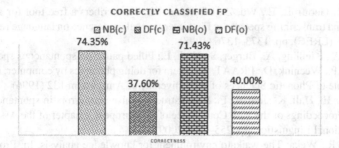

Fig. 8. FP classification (detection) correctness for FP using Naïve Bayes and decision factor

The graph in Fig. 8 shows a comparison of the FP classification correctness of those four experiments. The classification correctness using Naïve Bayes models with over-sampled data gives the best results when detecting FP alone. This applies to both the closed and open data set.

6 Conclusion

We have presented our study in detecting filled pause in Indonesian spontaneous speech. Given the FP classification correctness 74.35 % on closed data set and 71.43 % on open data set, it can be considered that filled pause in Indonesian spontaneous speech can be detected by collaborating the method proposed in [8] and supervised learning algorithms. The results reveal that detecting filled pause containing many same vowels and does not have striking consonants such as /aah/, /eeh/, and ya by using acoustic features such as the stability of the first four formant frequencies, pitch stability, and large energy drop at the end of the word gives good results because the filled pause has values of formant frequencies and pitch that tends to be more stable. Unfortunately, filled pause containing a short vowel and striking consonant sound like /um/have less stable formant frequencies and pitch, so it is difficult to detect them using these methods. Most filled pause words belong to the second category also have striking consonants so they are also difficult to be detected.

There are also some suggestions for future related research. The Indonesian speech recognition that is developed by employing large corpus can be utilized to handle the incorrectly recognized non-filled pause as a filled pause. To cut down the process, a VAD (voice activity detection) can be employed so that the input can be a complete sentence without having to define all words manually.

References

1. Audhkhasi, K., Kandhway, K., Deshmukh, O., Verma, A.: Formant-based technique for automatic filled-pause detection in spontaneous spoken English. In: IEEE International Conference on Acoustics, Speech and Signal Processing, ICASSP 2009, pp. 4857–4860 (2009)

2. Barras, C., Geoffrois, E., Wu, Z., Liberman, M.: Transcriber: a free tool for segmenting, labeling and transcribing speech. In: First international conference on language resources and evaluation (LREC), pp. 1373–1376 (1998)
3. Batliner, A., Kießling, A., Burger, S., Nöth, E.: Filled pauses in spontaneous speech (2011)
4. Boersma, P., Weenink, D.: PRAAT: A system for doing phonetics by computer, in Report of the Institute of Phonetic Sciences of the University of Amsterdam 132 (1996)
5. Fitzgerald, E., Hall, K., Jelinek, F.: Reconstructing false start errors in spontaneous speech text. In: Proceedings of the 12th Conference of the European Chapter of the Association for Computational Linguistics, pp. 255–263 (2009)
6. Garner, S.R.: Weka: The waikato environment for knowledge analysis. In: Proceedings of the New Zealand computer science research students conference, pp. 57–64 (1995)
7. Goto, M., Itou, K., Hayamizu, S.: A real-time filled pause detection system for spontaneous speech recognition. In: Proceedings of the 6th European Conference on Speech Communication and Technology (Eurospeech 1999), pp. 227–230 (1999)
8. Kaushik, M., Trinkle, M., Hashemi-Sakhtsari, A.: Automatic detection and removal of disfluencies from spontaneous speech. In: Australasian International Conference on Speech Science and Technology, Melbourne Victoria (2010)
9. Liu, Y., Shriberg, E., Stolcke, A.: Automatic disfluency identification in conversational speech using multiple knowledge sources. In: Proceedings of Eurospeech, vol. 1, pp. 957–960 (2003)
10. O'Shaughnessy, D.: Recognition of hesitations in spontaneous speech. In: IEEE International Conference on Acoustics, Speech, and Signal Processing, ICASSP 1992, vol. 1, pp. 521–524 (1992)
11. Shriberg, E., Bates, R., Stolcke, A.: A prosody-only decision-tree model for disfluency detection. In: Proceedings of Eurospeech, vol. 5, pp. 2383–2386 (1997)
12. Shriberg, E.: Spontaneous speech: How people really talk and why engineers should care. In: Proceedings of. European Conference on Speech Communication and Technology (Eurospeech) (2005)
13. Stolcke, A., Shriberg, E.: Automatic linguistic segmentation of conversational speech. In: Proceedings Fourth International Conference on Spoken Language, ICSLP 1996, IEEE, vol. 2, pp. 1005–1008 (1996)
14. Stolcke, A., Shriberg, E., Bates, R.A., Ostendorf, M., Hakkani, D., Plauche, M., Lu, Y.: Automatic detection of sentence boundaries and disfluencies based on recognized words. In: ICSLP (1998)
15. Stouten, F., Martens, J.P.: A feature-based filled pause detection system for Dutch. In: IEEE Workshop on Automatic Speech Recognition and Understanding, ASRU 2003, pp. 309–314 (2003)
16. Swerts, M., Wichmann, A., Beun, R.J.: Filled pauses as Markers of Discourse Structure (1996)
17. Ward, W.: Understanding spontaneous speech. In: Proceedings of the workshop on Speech and Natural Language of Association for Computational Linguistics, pp. 137–141 (1989)
18. Žgank, A., Rotovnik, T., Sepesy Maučec, M.: Slovenian spontaneous speech recognition and acoustic modeling of filled pauses and onomatopoeas. In: WSEAS Transactions on Signal Processing (2008)

Automatic Extraction Phonetically Rich and Balanced Verses for Speaker-Dependent Quranic Speech Recognition System

Rahmi Yuwan[✉] and Dessi Puji Lestari

School of Electrical Engineering and Informatics,
Institut Teknologi Bandung, Bandung, Indonesia
13510031@std.stei.itb.ac.id,
dessipuji@stei.itb.ac.id

Abstract. This paper discussed how to collect phonetically rich and balanced verses as speech corpus for quranic recognition system. The Quranic phonology was analyzed based on the qira'a of 'Asim in the riwaya of Hafs to transform arabic text of Holy Quran into alphabetical symbols that represent all possible sounds (QScript) when Holy Quran is read. The entire verses of Holy Quran were checked to select verses-set which met the criteria of a phonetically rich and balanced corpus. The selected verses contained 180 verses of 6236 whole verses in Quran. Statistical phonemes distribution similarity of selected verses was 0.9998 compared to phonemes distiribution in whole Quran. To determine the effect of using this corpus, early development speaker-dependent Quranic recognition system based on CMU Sphinx was developed. MFCC was used as feature extraction. The system used HMM with 3-emitting-states based on tri-phone. For language model, the system used N-gram with word as a basis. The system was trained using recitation from 3 speakers and obtained a recognition accuracy of 97.47 %.

Keywords: Phonetically rich and balanced quranic corpus · Quranic automatic speech recognition · Quran phonology · Acoustic model · Statistical language model

1 Introduction

Automatic speech recognition for many languages has been developed. One of them is automatic speech recognition for Arabic Language [1, 5, 8]. Arabic, as main language, is used only by a large community in the Middle East and Africa. But there is the Holy Book written in Arabic and also known by almost all people of the world, namely Al-Quran. Al-Quran must be recited correctly as elaborated in tajweed. Reciting the Quran has a variety styles and rhythms (qira'a) leaning from one of the seven priests qurra (qira'a Nafi', qira'a Ibn Kathir, qira'a 'Ashim, etc.) according to the guidance of the Prophet Muhammad [3]. In the development of Quranic speech recognition system, tajweed and qira'a contributes to the determination of Quranic phonology such as the duration of long vowel and *imalah* (occurance of phoneme 'e') in Quran. The correct method to learn Quran is *talaqqi*. During *talaqqi*, teachers dictate how to recite Holy

© Springer Science+Business Media Singapore 2016
K. Hasida and A. Purwarianti (Eds.): PACLING 2015, CCIS 593, pp. 65–75, 2016.
DOI: 10.1007/978-981-10-0515-2_5

Quran correctly to a student [2]. However, teacher's availability and time requirement for doing *talaqqi* became obstacles of this method. By acknowledging this, many researchers began to develop an automatic speech recognition of Quranic recitation to assist learners in learning Quran independently [4, 7, 9].

H. Tabbal et al. (2006) establish a system "Automatic Delimiter Quranic Verse" based on HMM. The system is trained using about 1 h recitation of surah Al-Ikhlas recited by 20 different speakers. System obtained correct recognition in range of 85 %–92 %. There is also a system namely E-Hafiz. This system uses vector quantization as a data compression technique. E-Hafiz uses training data from first 5 chapters recited by 30 speakers. Recognition accuracy rate of the system are 92 %, 90 %, and 86 % for 10 speakers men, 10 women, and 10 children respectively [4].

As mentioned above, the existing Automatic Speech Recognition (ASR) system for the Quran only modeled first 5 chapters and short chapters in 30th section of the Quran. Whereas, the ASR system for the Quran requires an acoustic model that covers all phonetic aspects when the Quran is recited. Basically, modelling the entire Quranic verse is necessary due to the limitation of sound variations in Quran recitation. It means, a new sound is not possible to be found except if it occurs because of qira'a differences or error recitation. However, modelling the entire Quranic verse takes a long time and requires large space in the database. Therefore, providing minumum amount of Quranic verses but covering all phonetic aspects when the Quran recited is required. This concept is also known as phonetically rich and balanced corpus.

In this research, the corpus was collected by implementing an algorithm to process the entire Quranic verse until phonetically rich and balanced corpus was obtained. However, extracting the entire Quranic speech corpus directly is not possible to be done. Hence, the extraction process was done by using the Quranic transliteration written by alphabetical symbols to represent Quranic sounds. Here, it is called *QScript*. QScript was developed independently by analyzing Quranic phonology based on the qira'a of 'Ashim in the riwaya of Hafs and tajweed rules. A phonetically rich and balanced corpus is then used in speaker-dependent ASR system for the Quran.

This paper is organized as follows. Section 2, describes analysis to build QScript. Then, an explanation about algorithm to select phonetically rich and balanced verses and statistic of the verses is given in Sect. 3. Section 4 explains the experiment using the corpus in speaker-dependent quranic recognition system. The last Sect. 5 gives conclusion of the work.

2 Constructing *QScript*

Many references provide Quranic verse transliteration using particular symbols. The right transliteration for Qur'anic verse was not easy to obtain. This is due to several things, such transliteration verses of the Quran is not freely accessible, has elusive pattern, and has invalid source. Therefore, in this paper the standardized Buck-walter Arabic transliteration was used to build Quranic transliteration. The mapping of Arabic symbols to Buck-walter notation given in Table 1 [6]. To get Buckwalter transliteration of the entire Quran, quran-uthmani.xml developed by Dukes (2009), is converted into Buckwalter transliteration.

Table 1. The mapping of Arabic symbols to Buckwalter notation

UNICODE			BUCKWALTER	
Decimal	Hex	Glyph	ASCII	Orthography
1569	U+0621	ء	'	Hamza
1571	U+0623	أ	>	Alif + HamzaAbove
1572	U+0624	ؤ	&	Waw + HamzaAbove
1573	U+0625	إ	<	Alif + HamzaBelow
1574	U+0626	ئ	}	Ya + HamzaAbove
1575	U+0627	ا	A	Alif
1576	U+0628	ب	b	Ba
1577	U+0629	ة	p	TaMarbuta
1578	U+062A	ت	t	Ta
1579	U+062B	ث	v	Tha
1580	U+062C	ج	j	Jeem
1581	U+062D	ح	H	Hha
1582	U+062E	خ	x	Kha
1583	U+062F	د	d	Dal
1584	U+0630	ذ	*	Thal
1585	U+0631	ر	r	Ra
1586	U+0632	ز	z	Zain
1587	U+0633	س	s	Seen
1588	U+0634	ش	$	Sheen
1589	U+0635	ص	S	Sad
1590	U+0636	ض	D	Ddad
1591	U+0637	ط	T	Tta
1592	U+0638	ظ	Z	Dtha
1594	U+063A	غ	g	Ghain
1600	U+0640	-		Tatweel
1601	U+0641	ف	f	Fa
1602	U+0642	ق	q	Qaf
1603	U+0643	ك	k	Kaf
1604	U+0644	ل	l	Lam
1605	U+0645	م	m	Meem
1606	U+0646	ن	n	Noon
1607	U+0647	ه	h	Ha
1608	U+0648	و	w	Waw
1609	U+0649	ى	Y	AlifMaksura
1610	U+064A	ي	y	Ya
1611	U+064B	ً	F	Fathatan
1612	U+064C	ٌ	N	Dammatan

(Continued)

Table 1. (*Continued*)

1613	U+064D	.	K	Kasratan
1614	U+064E	ٙ	a	Fatha
1615	U+064F	ٙ	u	Damma
1616	U+0650	ٟ	i	Kasra
1617	U+0651	ّ	~	Shadda
1618	U+0652	ْ	o	Sukun
1619	U+0653	~	^	Maddah
1620	U+0654	ٔ	#	HamzaAbove
1648	U+0670	ٰ	`	AlifKhanjareeya
1649	U+0671	ٱ	{	Alif + HamzatWasl
1756	U+06DC	ۜ	:	SmallHighSeen
1759	U+06DF	۟	@	SmallHigh RoundedZero
1760	U+06E0	۠	"	SmallHighUpright RectangularZero
1762	U+06E2	ۢ	[	SmallHighMeem IsolatedForm
1763	U+06E3	ۣ	;	SmallLowSeen
1765	U+06E5	ۥ	,	SmallWaw
1766	U+06E6	ۦ	.	SmallYa
1768	U+06E8	ۨ	!	SmallHighNoon
1770	U+06EA	۪	=	EmptyCentreLowStop
1771	U+06EB	۫	+	EmptyCentreHighStop
1772	U+06EC	۬	%	RoundedHighStop WithFilledCente
1773	U+06ED	ۭ	]	SmallLowMeem

Although, Quran is written in Arabic, the correct pronunciation of some letters on Quranic verses may totally change from its original sound [10]. Tajweed explains the rules how to pronounce Al-Quran correctly. Thus, these rules give an effect to the Quranic phonology. According to Hamid (2005), the phonological aspects of the Quran can be summarized in 5 conditions, which are pronunciation of emphatic letter Raa "ر", pronunciation of letter Noon "ن", pronunciation of letter Meem "م", extra lengthening of vowel and semivowel, and agitation qalqala "القلقلة". Not only tajweed, the differences qira'a used while reciting the Quran also produces different sound. Here, Buckwalter notation was analyzed and modified, according to the Quranic phonology based on tajweed rules [7, 8] and the qira'a of 'Ashim in the riwaya of Hafs, to build QScript. QScript is representative text of the Quranic sound using alphabetical symbols. It will be used to get phonetically rich and balanced corpus. A total 44 phonemes, with 34 basic phonemes in Arabic, 28 consonants, 3 short vowels and 3 long vowels [7], and additional 10 phonemes, was used in the constructing QScript. Given in

Table 2. List of used phonemes in *QScript* and its frequencies

Phonemes	Frequency	Frequency percentage (%)	Phonemes	Frequency	Frequency percentage (%)
a	78181	15.6059	d	6615	1.3204
i	36810	7.3477	N	5316	1.0611
l	35888	7.1637	c	5269	1.0518
m	33956	6.7780	H	4150	0.8284
A	31328	6.2534	O	4146	0.8276
u	27891	5.5674	j	3435	0.6857
n	27610	5.5113	Y	2759	0.5507
e	19420	3.8765	x	2543	0.5076
w	15528	3.0996	S	2431	0.4853
h	15010	2.9962	X	2388	0.4767
t	13553	2.7053	L	1936	0.3864
r	13476	2.6900	W	1804	0.3601
b	12768	2.5486	z	1777	0.3547
y	11855	2.3664	D	1766	0.3525
U	11733	2.3420	v	1451	0.2896
I	11465	2.2886	T	1417	0.2829
k	10707	2.1372	g	1221	0.2437
E	9414	1.8791	Z	1008	0.2012
f	8915	1.7795	Q	633	0.1264
o	8773	1.7512	V	570	0.1138
q	7365	1.4701	F	1	0.0002
s	6689	1.3352	G	1	0.0002

Table 2 is the statistical frequency of all used phonemes in QScript. The analysis of additional 10 phonemes are:

1. Representative phoneme for the empathic of short vowel denoted by "o". For example, fatha qaf (قَ) written as "qo",
2. Representative phoneme for the empathic of long vowel denoted "O". For example, قا written as "qO"
3. Representative phonemes for diphthong sounds, "ai", "au", "oi", and "ou" denoted by "Y", "W", "V", and "Q" respectively. For example بين written as "bYna", سوف written as "sWfa", خير written as "xVr", and قول written as "qQl"
4. Representative phoneme for lam jalalah in word الله denoted by "L"
5. Representative phoneme for ghunnah in ikhfa rule denoted by "N"
6. Representative phoneme for *imala* sound denoted by "F". This sound occurs only once in 41th verse of 11th chapter, based on the qira'a of 'Ashim in the riwaya of Hafs.
7. Representative phoneme for *tasheel* sound denoted by "G". This sound occurs only once in 44th verse of 41th chapter, based on the qira'a of 'Ashim in the riwaya of Hafs.

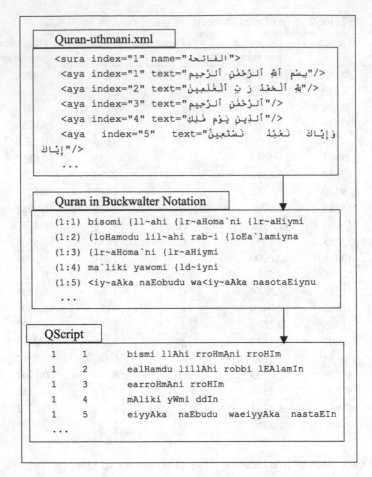

Fig. 1. Summary of QScript construction

Overall, the process of QScript construction is equipped with the modified sample script, can be seen in Fig. 1. QScript has some limitations. These are:

1. Stop sign
   When reciting the Quran, the ways to stop reading are quite flexible. There are stop signs such as compulsory stop, prohibited stop, good stop, etc. Also, reciter may stop their reciting depend on the length of their breath and then continue reading in the right way. In quran-utsmani.xml file, there is no symbol to represent *waqafl* stops. It makes *QScript* also has no stop symbol.

2. Rules of optional recitation
   Tajweed rule, especially for *mad*/extra lengthening vowel and semi-vowel has an optional rule to recite it. For example *mad jaiz munfasheel* may be read for 2 or 5 harakah. To symbolize this sound in *QScript*, one of several rules was selected.

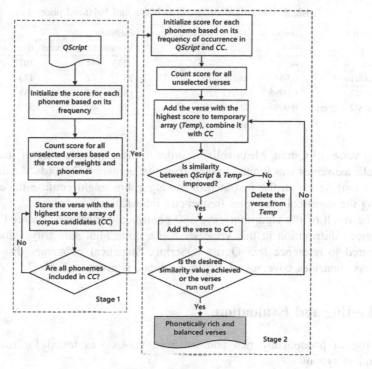

Fig. 2. Flow chart of the algorithm selection corpus

Because the script in QScript will be used as transcription of corpus, using the corpus in ASR system makes the recognition process of the recognized speech strict to the transcription.

3 Corpus Selection

An algorithm was implemented to select phonetically rich and balanced corpus from *QScript*, by adapting the algorithm of *Two-stage Sentence Selection Algorithm* proposed by Wang (1998) [12] with some modifications. The main ideas of the algorithm are:

1. To cover all Quranic phonemes in corpus
2. All phonemes in the corpus should resemble frequencies distribution as close as possible to the original corpus/references text (*QScript*)
3. A corpus contains a minimum verses.

The algorithm consisted of two stages. Figure 2 shows the flow chart of algorithm to select phonetically rich and balanced corpus. The first stage tried to cover all phonemes with minimum verses. In the second stage, verses selection was done to achieve balance distribution phonemes of the corpus candidates corresponding to QScript. In this algorithm, the inspection of phonemes collection was done only for 42 phonenems, excluding phonems "F" and "G". Both of them appear only once, for each phoneme, in

Table 3. Statistic distribution richness and balanced phonemes

Dokumen	cos(α) sim	(α)	Balance (phones)	Richness			
				Verses	Mono-phone	Bi Phone	Tri-phone
QScript	–	–	–	6236	44	1077	8845
CorpusSt1	0.962	0.276	3	13	42	175	232
CorpusSt2	0.9998	0.017	29	180	42	548	1955
CorpusSt2 + 2verses	0.9998	0.019	30	182	44	557	2000

a long verses of Quran. Meanwhile, in order to meet the balancing of statistical data, the selected verses was limited to the verses that contain 4–7 words. Adding too short or too long verses in the first step of the algorithm might confuse the algorithm in getting the statistical phonemes frequencies information.

The result of the algorithm gave 180 phonetically rich and balanced verses. The phonemes distribution in this verse set had a quite high similarity value of 0.9998 compared to reference text Quran (QScript). Statistical phonemes distribution and richness phonemes coverage of corpus candidate is given in Table 3.

4   Testing and Evaluation

The use of phonetically rich and balanced verses was tested for small speaker-dependent system.

4.1   Collecting Speech Corpus

Subjectively, sound recording of three reciter (Ibrahim Al-Akhdar, Emad Zuhair, and Muhammad Ayyub) was chosen based on the following characteristics:

1. The recitation tend to be constant and monotonous
2. The speed not too fast or too slow
3. Low noises and echos

Speech corpus collection was done manually. The usage of the existing developed corpus is not possible to do because the existing corpus is constructed only by several part of the Quran. Whereas, the verses for building phonetically rich and balanced corpus was selected "randomly" from the entire Quran by the algorithm.

4.2   Acoustic Model

The system used *3-emitting-states* of *Hidden Markov Model* (HMM) based on tri-phone. The transition probabilities of Context-Independent (CI) HMMs are estimated using Baum-Welch algorithm [11]. For Context- Dependent (CD), 45 phonemes (including silence) were refined into tri-phones. For each tri-phone HMM state was build. There are 31441 number of tri-phones obtained during modelling process.

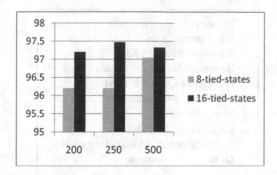

Fig. 3. Accuracy rate corresponding to combination tied-state and senone

To get the best accuracy, the experiment to choose optimal modelling parameter was done. Combination of 2 tied-state values (8, 16) and 3 senone numbers (200, 250, 500) was compared. The optimal parameter was combination of 16 tied-state and 250 senones. Figure 3 show the visualization of accuracy rate corresponding to the combinations of tied-state and senone.

4.3 Language Model and Lexicon

Language model for the system was based on statistical approach, n-gram model. The CMU Sphinx toolkit, CMUCLTK, for building language model is used [11]. The checking of uni-gram, bi-gram and tri-gram words sequences was assumed to be adequate to get the context of verses during the modeling process. Furthermore, the development of lexicon was done by checking all unique words contained in *QScript*. Identified 20599 unique words appear in *QScript*.

4.4 Testing and Evaluation

The testing of the system used similar verses and speaker between training data and test data. Data description is given in Fig. 4. After the testing phase, the system obtained 97.47 % accuracy rate and word error rate (WER) 2.53 %. This rate is good enough for speaker-dependent automatic speech recognition system. The errors identification was found mostly in long duration phonemes recitation. Long duration recitation is one of the challenging aspects in Quranic phonology that affected accuracy rate of automatic speech recognition system. Every speakers can recite mad (tajweed rules of long duration sound) with different duration but keep recitation consistently. The different style of long duration recitation cannot be recognized as wrong recitation. In order to correct this error, the manual checking to match between transcription and audio recitation for every speaker can be done. Another error was found in wrong recognition of similar phonemes characteristic. For example, the word "YUQSIRUN" recognized wrongly as "YUB-SIRUN" by the system. The phonemes Q and B in Arabic, represent qaf (ق) and ba (ب) respectively. Both of Q and B are included in voiced and plosives sound.

Speaker: 3
File Format: .wav
Sampling Rate: 16 KHz
Sampling Accuracy: 16 bits
Number of Channel: 1 (Mono)
Total File: 546 audio files
Size: 109 MB
Dictionary: 20599 words
Total Phoneme: 45 including silence
Duration: 55 minutes

Fig. 4. Data description for training and testing

5 Conclusion

In this research, phonetically rich and balanced Quranic corpus was built. This work created the entire Quran transcription, named *Qscript,* and implemented proposed algorithm to achieve phonetically rich and balanced corpus. The usage of this corpus in Quranic speaker-dependent recognition system should help system to recogize Quran recitation with fairly high recognition accuracy rate.

For future research, the development of Quranic speaker independent recognition system using phonetically rich and balanced corpus is recommended. To achieve this goal, it is necessary to collect corpus from various speakers, about 30 speakers or more. In this work lexicon was contructed by mapping one pronunciation for each word. Lexicon development to provide some alternative pronunciation for each word shall be done.

References

1. Abushariah, M., et al.: Phonetically rich and balanced speech corpus for arabic speaker-independent countinous automatic speech recognition systems. In: ISSPA International Conference on Information Science, Signal Processing and their Applications, p. 65 (2010)
2. Annuri, H.A.: Panduan Tahsin Tilawah Al-Quran dan Ilmu Tajwid. Al-Kautsar, Jakarta (2010)
3. Gus, A., Faqih, S.A.: Al-Quran Sang Mahkota Cahaya. PT. Elex Media Komputindo, Jakarta (2010)
4. Aslam, M., et al.: E-Hafiz: intelligent system to help muslims in recitation and memorization of quran. Life Sci. J. **9**, 534 (2012)
5. Chenfour, N., et al.: Introduction to Arabic Speech Recognition Using CMUSphinx System (2005)
6. Dukes, K.: The Quranic Arabic Corpus (2009). http://corpus.quran.com/. Accessed January 2014

7. Hamid, S.E.: Computer Aided Pronounciation Learning System Using Statistical Based Automatic Speech Recognition Techniques. Ph.D. Thesis Faculty of Engineering Cairo University, Giza (2005)
8. Harrag, A., Mohamadi, T.: QSDAS: new quranic speech database for arabic speaker recognition. Arab. J. Sci. Eng. **35**(2C), 7–19 (2010)
9. Hassan, T., et al.: Analysis and implementation of an automated delimiter of "Quranic" verse in audio files using speech recognition techniques (2007)
10. Razak, Z., et al.: Quranic verse recitation recognition module for support in j-QAF learning: a review. IJCSNS Int. J. Comput. Sci. Netw. Secur. **8**(8), 207–216 (2008)
11. CMU Sphinx Website. Overview of CMUSphinx Toolkit. CMUSphinx: http://cmusphinx. sourceforge.net. Accessed December 2014
12. Wang, H.M.: Statistical analysis of mandarin acoustic units and automatic extraction of phonetically rich sentences based upon a very large chinese text corpus. Comput. Linguist. Chin. Lang. Process. **2**(3), 93–114 (1998)

Corpora and Corpus-Based Language Processing

3-Step Parallel Corpus Cleaning
Using Monolingual Crowd Workers

Toshiaki Nakazawa[1]([✉]), Sadao Kurohashi[1], Hayato Kobayashi[2],
Hiroki Ishikawa[2], and Manabu Sassano[2]

[1] Graduate School of Informatics, Kyoto University, Yoshida-honmachi, Sakyo-ku,
Kyoto 606-8501, Japan
nakazawa@nlp.ist.i.kyoto-u.ac.jp, kuro@i.kyoto-u.ac.jp
[2] Yahoo Japan Corporation, Midtown Tower, 9-7-1 Akasaka, Minato-ku,
Tokyo 107-6211, Japan
{hakobaya,hishikaw,msassano}@yahoo-corp.jp

Abstract. A high-quality parallel corpus needs to be manually created to achieve good machine translation for the domains which do
not have enough existing resources. Although the quality of the corpus to some extent can be improved by asking the professional translators to translate, it is impossible to completely avoid making any mistakes. In this paper, we propose a framework for cleaning the existing
professionally-translated parallel corpus in a quick and cheap way. The
proposed method uses a 3-step crowdsourcing procedure to efficiently
detect and edit the translation flaws, and also guarantees the reliability
of the edits. The experiments using the fashion-domain e-commerce-site
(EC-site) parallel corpus show the effectiveness of the proposed method
for the parallel corpus cleaning.

Keywords: Parallel corpus cleaning · Crowdsourcing · Machine
translation

1 Introduction

Bilingual sentence-aligned parallel corpora are essential language resources
for corpus-based machine translation systems. The translation quality highly
depends on the quality and quantity of the parallel corpora. Parallel sentences
can be extracted from the Web [14] for general domain translations. For some
domains such as patent documents [15] or parliamentary proceedings [8], parallel sentences can be extracted from the existing resources. Some methods of
extracting parallel sentences [6,13] or fragments [5] from comparable corpora
have also been proposed. However, for the domains without existing language
resources, researchers have to create parallel corpora manually.

Constructing a parallel corpus by hand is both time-consuming and expensive. A number of studies have been done recently in the direction of reducing
the translation costs by post-editing the output of machine translation systems

© Springer Science+Business Media Singapore 2016
K. Hasida and A. Purwarianti (Eds.): PACLING 2015, CCIS 593, pp. 79–93, 2016.
DOI: 10.1007/978-981-10-0515-2_6

[3, 12], but this kind of framework may not work well when constructing a parallel corpora for a new domain. Another solution to reduce the translation cost is using crowdsourcing [1, 2]. Crowdsourcing workers basically are not professional translators, and some of them "cheat" on completing the task by using online translation services, which is why it is difficult to guarantee the translation quality. Some researchers have tried to predict the hidden reliability of translators and translations to choose the more appropriate translations [16], but still it is difficult to achieve the quality level of professional translators.

Another important issue, which is the main target of our study, is detecting and editing translation flaws in human-translated parallel corpora. Although we ask professionals to perform translation, the outcome occasionally contains translation flaws for various reasons. If the target text size is small, we can reduce the number of mistakes by making several reviewers check the translation. However, high-quality machine translation requires tens of thousands of parallel sentences to hundreds of thousands of parallel sentences; thus it is almost impossible to check the whole corpus. In this paper, we propose a framework to detect and edit the translation flaws contained in the existing manually-translated parallel corpus. The framework uses crowdsourcing in 3 steps: Step 1 detects the translation flaws, Step 2 edits the flaws and Step 3 validates the edits. By using crowdsourcing, corpus cleaning process can be done quicker and cheaper compared to professional cleaning. In addition, by dividing the cleaning into 3 steps, the quality of cleaning can be guaranteed.

The organization of the present paper is as follows: In Sect. 2, we briefly describe the fashion-domain e-commerce-site (EC-site) parallel corpus which we use in our experiments. We explain the way of constructing this corpus, and the translation flaws it contains. Section 3 explains the proposed framework for the parallel corpus cleaning. Sections 4 and 5 show the experimental results of parallel corpus cleaning and translation, and Sect. 6 summarizes this paper.

2   Fashion-Domain EC-site Parallel Corpus

Yahoo! JAPAN was running an e-commerce site named "Yahoo! China Mall"[1] where customers could purchase Chinese items using Japanese interface. Originally, the descriptions of items were automatically translated into Japanese using a rule-based machine translation system. However the quality of translation was quite poor. We launched a joint project to improve the translation quality by changing the translation paradigm from rule-based to corpus-based. The Chinese-Japanese Fashion-Domain EC-site parallel corpus (we call it FDEC corpus) containing 1.2 M sentences (6.3 M Chinese words, 8.7 M Japanese words) was created during the project.

The FDEC corpus was created by manual translation of the Chinese sentences from the fashion item pages. The pages are basically composed of 3 sections, *Title*, *Feature* and *Description*. Although longer sentences can be extracted from the Description section, the sentences in the Title and Feature sections are

---

[1] Unfortunately, this service has been closed now.

shorter or sometimes containing only one word. The parallel corpus construction of EC-site is different from that of novels [4] and newspapers [17]. In this section, we present some of the issues we have discovered so far and describe the know-how which we acquired during the corpus construction.

2.1 Translation Company Selection

The translation company should be carefully chosen because the quality of the machine translation highly relies on the quality of the parallel corpus. We first prepared trial sentences to check the translation quality of each company, and asked 3 different companies to translate the trial sentences. After considering the translation quality and price per unit, we have chosen two translation companies as contractors. Choosing multiple companies provides some flexibility in case of unexpected matters such as decrease of the translation quality or increase of the unit price. Moreover, we can acquire various translation choices because each company has its own characteristics in the translations, and also two companies can uses their own translation technology, which can balance the drawbacks of each company's translation.

2.2 Notes for Chinese-Japanese EC-site Translation

It is important to pay attention to the technical terms, ambiguities of words, and the difference of cultures to create a high quality parallel corpus in a specific domain. Below we describe some examples which we took care of during the corpus creation.

Domain-Specific Expressions. Some of the basic words have different meanings in a specific domain. For example, the Chinese word "不规则 (*disorder*)" is also used in Japanese "不規則 (*disorder*)". However, in fashion domain, it is used like "不规则的下摆 (*wavy skirt*)". In this case, it is meaningless to translate it as "不規則 (*disorder*)", but it should be translated as "波打った (*wavy*)" or "フレアの (*flare*)".

Similarly, "木耳" originally means "wood ear" in both Chinese and Japanese. However it should be translated as "フリル (*frill*)" in Japanese.

EC-Specific Expressions. Some expressions appear in all EC-sites (not only those belonging to the fashion domain): for example, "秒殺 (*sold out in no time*)" or "淘金币 (*bargain sale*)". Many EC-sites have a seller-ranking system. In our case, there are ranking names "钻 (*diamond*)", "皇冠 (*silver crown*)", "金冠, 金 皇冠 (*gold crown*)", and so on. It is important to take this fact into consideration in order to provide correct translation.

We also need to identify items which should not be translated (user IDs in the review posts, for example). These are proper nouns, which is why it is better not to translate them.

Cultural Difference. Blatant expressions are more commonly used in Chinese, while euphemistic expressions are favorable in Japanese. This holds true for EC-sites. For example, "大きめサイズのレディース (*larger size ladies' wear*)" in Japanese is expressed as "胖女人 (*fat ladies*)". If Japanese female customers see the direct translation of the Chinese, they will displeased. Chinese descriptions often contain words like "我们 (*we*)" and "您 (*you*)". However the corresponding Japanese expressions are "当店 (*our shop*)" and "お客様 (*customers*)".

Some slang words are also used in the EC-site. For example, "MM" and "GG" in Chinese mean "girls" and "boys", respectively. These come from the Chinese pronunciation of "妹妹 (MeiMei/*girls*)" and "哥哥 (GeGe/*boys*)". These words had better to be translated properly to convey the intent correctly.

Unnatural or Unsuitable Compound Nouns in Japanese. Chinese and Japanese share Chinese characters, and some of the Chinese compound nouns make sense in Japanese as they are. In the Chinese-to-Japanese translation, translators tend to preserve Chinese compound nouns as they are without consideration. However, in some cases, they are unnatural or unsuitable in Japanese. For example, the Chinese compound noun "特別 (*special*) 強調 (*emphasis*)" is understandable in Japanese but "注意事項 (*caution*)" is more natural. Another example is "着用 (*wear*) 効果 (*effect*) 图 (*figure*)": it means not "figure of effect to wear", but "picture of wearing".

Technical Terms, Proper Nouns. Technical terms and proper nouns are often difficult to translate, which also holds for the case of EC-site translation. General item names such as "磨毛 (*fleece*)" and "风衣 (*windbreaker*)" have their corresponding Japanese translations, but some items such as "开裆裤[2]" do not have corresponding translations in languages, other than Chinese. In addition, company names are often not translated into other languages. The rules for handling these kinds of words should be defined beforehand. In our project, only proper nouns that have corresponding Japanese expressions were translated into Japanese.

Extremely Long Chinese Sentences. Chinese sentences tend to be long because Chinese sub-sentences are often joined by commas. When performing Chinese-Japanese translation, it is better to divide translations of sub-sentences, if there is no strict relation between the sub-sentences. For example, the sentence in Fig. 1 is easy to understand if it is translated after being divided into three sub-sentences at the || marks.

Repetitions. There are many fixed expressions repeatedly used in the EC-site such as sales copies, material names and so on. If we translate whole item page every time, we cannot increase the coverage of the parallel corpus because of

---

[2] Pants for children without the inside of a thigh being sewn up.

Zh: 上面的刺绣和亮片均为原厂工人原厂设备精心缝制，‖ 挑剔的姐妹们在看到货品之后会发现绝对可以和专柜货品比肩，而且绣工精细清晰，‖ 精棉质地，密度高，手感好，穿着舒适，质量超好。

Ja: 上の刺繍とスパンコールは、全てオリジナル工場の作業員とオリジナル工場の設備で心を込めて作成したものです、‖ あら捜しをするお客様も、この商品を見れば、専門店の商品に匹敵するほど、作りが精細で、はっきりしたものだと思われるはずです、‖ 精綿生地で、密度が高く、手触りも良く、着用すると快適で、品質もとても良いです。

En: *The embroidery and spangles above are all made with care by original factory workers with our original factory equipment, ‖ even the most demanding customers should rank this product with one from a specialist shop and consider it finely and exactly made, ‖ it is made of fine cotton, is dense, has a good feel, is comfortable to wear and the quality is very high.*

Fig. 1. Very long Chinese sentence joined by commas, and its Japanese translation provided by the translation company (it is natural to divide the sentence at ‖ marks).

the repetitions. It is necessary to carefully choose the sentences to be translated so as not to repeat the translation process for the sentences which have already been translated before.

2.3 Translation Specification for Parallel Corpus Construction

Parallel corpus construction for MT has certain specific requirements, which are different from those for usual publishing translation:

- Avoid liberal translations
  Liberal translations are hard to be correctly handled by the majority of the current MT systems. We requested the translators to translate obediently rather than finically.
- Prohibit omissions and additions
  Omissions and additions (adding explanations of some technical terms using parentheses, like this) decreases the machine translation quality.
- Stick to one-to-one sentence translation
  Most of the current MT systems assume that the sentences in the parallel corpus have one-to-one correspondences.
- Respect the sections
  We requested to the translators to pay attention to the characteristics of each section: the Title section should be translated as a noun phrase, and the Feature section should be translated as a sequence of nouns or numerals. For example, Chinese expression "到货" should be translated as "入荷 (*Arrival!*)" in the Title section, and "入荷しました (*is arrived!*)" in the Description section.
- Divide the long sentences into appropriate units
  The background of this request is as follows:
  - The original Chinese sentences are automatically extracted from Web pages; thus they contain errors of sentence boundary detection.

- Chinese sentences tend to be joined by commas, which results in gener-ating very long sentences (see Sect. 2.2). However it is natural to divide them into smaller parts in other languages.

We documented the translation guidelines to correctly convey these requests along with the notes for Chinese-Japanese translation (Sect. 2.2) to the transla-tion companies. However, some mistakes are still present, even after using the guidelines' recommendations. Table 1 shows examples of translation flaws found in the sampling survey. In addition, there are some sentences forcibly translated as one sentence by joining with commas as in Fig. 1. Translation companies have many translation workers and it is difficult to ask all the workers to thoroughly obey the guidelines; thus translation flaws are unavoidable.

To reduce the number of translation mistakes to the minimum and keep the quality of the parallel corpus high, we conducted sampling survey of the translations by Japanese-native observers who can understand Chinese. The low-quality translations and translation flaws were sent to the translation companies as feedback to improve translation in future. The translation companies have also sent feedback to us which points out the unclear or ambiguous parts of the guidelines. We can improve the guidelines by modifying the imperfections and augmenting it to handle new phenomena.

However, this kind of solution cannot modify the sentences which have been already translated. Taking into consideration the high costs, it would have been unwise to send the completed translation to the companies back for additional post-editing. Therefore, we propose using crowdsourcing to clean the existing parallel corpus in a comparatively quick and cheap way.

3 Parallel Corpus Cleaning Using Crowdsourcing

Although the percentage of the sentences which include translation mistakes is small, it is difficult to automatically detect them. We need to check the whole corpus in order to correct all the translation flaws, which is quite expensive.

To solve this problem, we propose a framework of cleaning an existing corpus efficiently and cheaply using crowdsourcing. The framework is composed of 3 steps:

1. Fluency Judgement
2. Edit of Unnatural Sentences
3. Verification of Edits

In the crowdsourcing, any number of workers paticipate the task, and each worker completes the very small part of it. Each step is basically conducted by the monolingual workers of the target language (in our case, Japanese workers). The number of monolingual workers is much greater than that of bilingual workers; thus the tasks can be done efficiently. This framework mainly aims at correcting the unnatural sentences as in Table 1. In the following sections, each step is explained in detail.

Table 1. Examples of translation flaws.

Omission	
Input	看看有没有其他合适的商品
Translation	**看看有没有**その他合適的商品
Reference	他に良いものがないかご覧ください

Mistranslation	
Input	加湿器功能:
Translation	除湿器の機能：(*functions of dehumidifier:*)
Reference	加湿器の機能: (*functions of humidifier:*)
Input	买家秀身上穿的是两件，一口价是一件的价格!
Translation	お客様ショーの体に着ているのは２点、ワンプライスは一枚の値段です！
Reference	モデルが着ているものは２着で、価格は１着の値段です！

Insertion	
Input	不要随便拍下一种
Translation	随意にに１種類だけ注文するのではなく
Reference	随意に１種類だけ注文するのではなく

Chinese Character	
Input	精神焕发之效果
Translation	元気あふれるという効果があります
Reference	元気があふれるという効果があります

Unnatural	
Input	在清洁保养时应切断电源，拔下插头防止意外事故发生。
Translation	お手入れの時、電源を切れ、プラグを抜いてください。
Reference	お手入れの時は、電源を切り、プラグを抜いてください。

3.1 Step 1: Fluency Judgement

The first step detects the translation flaws by asking the crowd workers to judge if the sentences are natural and grammatically correct. This task is done by only showing the translated sentences. Some technical words and proper nouns remain in the translated sentences as they are in the source sentences, and the workers may judge them as unnatural. The workers are instructed to ignore such special words.

This is a choice-based task. If we ask two or more workers to answer the same task, we can increase the reliability of the judgement by putting all decisions together.

3.2 Step 2: Edit of Unnatural Sentences

In the second step, the workers are asked to edit the translated sentences. This task is also done by only showing the translated sentences. However it is possible to show the source sentence as well for the reference[3]. The bilingual workers, if they are available, would edit the translations more precisely with the reference source sentence, and monolingual workers just ignore them.

This is a free writing task. If we ask two or more workers to answer the same task, we can acquire a variety of edits. Different from the studies to create a parallel corpus using crowdsourcing (see Sect. 1), this task is just editing, not translating.

3.3 Step 3: Verification of Edits

In the last step, each edit made by each worker is validated by asking the workers to judge if the edited translation is better than the original one. This step is important to further improve the quality of the outcome because the edits are not necessarily correct.

This is a choice-based task; thus we can increase the reliability of the judgement by asking two or more workers to answer the same task.

4 Corpus Cleaning Experiments

To evaluate the effectiveness of the proposed framework, we conducted corpus cleaning experiments using the FDEC corpus introduced in Sect. 2. We used Yahoo! Crowdsourcing[4] as the crowdsourcing service. We can carry out several styles of crowdsourcing tasks such as Yes/No questions and free writings with this service. In the following sections, we explain the experimental settings and discuss the results. The service is run in Japan; therefore most of the workers are Japanese. In addition we cannot select the workers by their abilities, and the workers who participated in our experiments do not necessarily understand Chinese (perhaps almost all of them does not).

4.1 Step 1

We used 358,085 sentences from the FDEC corpus with length between 10 and 130 characters excluding numerals, Roman characters, symbols and white spaces. We asked 5 different workers to answer the same question. Table 2 shows the results. 108,340 sentences (30.2 %) are flawed translations if we set the threshold of the flawed translation at 3 or more, and 48,104 sentences (13.4 %) are flawed if we set the threshold at 4 or more. Below are examples of the results.

- 5 workers judged as unnatural
  お支払終了後、値切ことは承りません。
- 4 workers judged as unnatural
  もし同僚やガードマンが代印されるなら、事前に確認作業をされて下さい。

---

[3] In our experiments, we showed both source and translated sentences.
[4] http://crowdsourcing.yahoo.co.jp.

- 3 workers judged as unnatural
  商品を受け取ったら、すぐ評価をご確認ください！！
- 2 workers judged as unnatural
  2010 年 3 月、春はぽかぽかと花が満開になる季節。
- 1 worker judged as unnatural
  当店ではすべての商品の実物写真をご用意しております。
- 0 worker judged as unnatural
  最後には、具体的な状態で検討すべきです。

We asked Japanese native speakers to check the results and confirmed that the results are reasonable. It is surprising that the parallel corpus is constructed manually and yet contains 30 % incorrect translations. One reason for this is that most of the sentences are translated by native Chinese speakers, not Japanese speakers. It is often said that translations should be done by native speakers of the target language. However, native speakers of the source language are very knowledgeable about the source sentences including culture and background, and this is an advantage for correctly translating the input sentences.

Table 2. Experimental result of fluency judgement.

# unnatural judegement	# sentences	percentage
5	13,056	(3.6 %)
4	35,048	(9.8 %)
3	60,200	(16.8 %)
2	83,150	(23.2 %)
1	93,187	(26.0 %)
0	73,444	(20.5 %)

4.2   Step 2

From the results of Step 1, we used 47,420 sentences which were judged as unnatural by 4 or more workers[5] in Step 2. We asked 3 different workers to edit the translations. The workers can skip the task if they think that the sentences do not need to be edited. The original Chinese sentences are also shown to the workers. However the workers do not necessarily understand the Chinese.

The results are shown in Table 3. 34,542 sentences (72.8 %) are edited and a total number of 54,550 edits are acquired. The following are examples of edits.

- edited by 3 workers
  Original: 100%適するとは言えないので最終的な決めるのはご自身になります。
    Edit1: 100%適するとは断言できませんので最終的に決めるのはご自身になります。
    Edit2: 100%適するとは言えないので最終的に決めるのはご自身となります。
    Edit3: 100%適してるとは言えないので最終的に決めるのはご自身になります。

---

[5] We excluded some sentences which are garbled.

– edited by 2 workers
  Original: 100%実物写真、実際の物品は絶対にいっそうきらめいて、更に心や目を楽
  しませます。
    Edit1: 100%実物写真です、実際の物品はよりいっそうきらめいて、更に心や目を
  楽しませます。
    Edit2: 100%実物写真です、実際の物品は絶対にいっそうきらめいて、更に心や目
  を楽しませます。
– edited by 1 worker
  Original: お支払終了後、値切ことは承りません。
    Edit1: お支払終了後、値切ることは承りません。

We asked Japanese native speakers to check the edits and confirmed that the
edits are reasonable and correct.

Table 3. Statistics of the edits of unnatural sentences.

# workers edited	# sentences	percentage
3	3,755	(7.9 %)
2	12,498	(26.4 %)
1	18,289	(38.6 %)
0	12,878	(27.2 %)

4.3   Step 3

The quality of a total number of 54,550 edits were verified. The workers were
asked to judge which of the original and edited translations is more natural. The
original Chinese sentences were also shown along with the two translations. We
asked 5 different workers to answer the same question.

Table 4 shows the results of the validation looking at each edit independently.
49,237 edits (90.3 %) were judged to be better than the original translations by
the majority of the workers, which is much greater number than the other. This
result clearly shows that the proposed parallel corpus cleaning framework works
well. Looking at the result by the original sentence, 32,244 sentences (93.3 %)
among 34,542 edited sentences have one or more better edits. The following are
examples of the validations.

– 5 workers judged the edit is more natural
  Original: お支払終了後、値切ことは承りません。
  Edited: お支払終了後、値切ることは承りません。
– 4 workers judged the edit is more natural
  Original: 定期な得意先への連絡と潜在な忠実な取引先の掘り起こし
  Edited: 定期的な得意先への連絡と潜在的に忠実な取引先の掘り起こし
– 3 workers judged the edit is more natural
  Original: 10 元追加すると、ノートブックの放熱台座を差し上げます。
  Edited: 10 元追加すると、ノートブックの放熱パッドを差し上げます。

- 2 workers judged the edit is more natural
  Original: 100％のゼロリスク、頑張ってくださいね
  Edited: 100、リスクなし。頑張ってくださいね。
- 1 worker judged the edit is more natural
  Original: 24K ゴールドの新鮮なバラで、永遠にしおれないバラ
  Edited: 24K ゴールドは新鮮なバラで、永遠にしおれないバラ
- 0 worker judged the edit is more natural
  Original: 写真の説明通りでした（少し異臭がしますが、理解できます）
  Edited: 写真の説明通りでした（少しがしますが、理解できます）

Although the edited sentences are natural as Japanese sentences, they might be incorrect as translations. We reviewed the 100 edits randomly sampled from the ones which are judged to be more natural than the original sentence by 5 workers. We found three types of inequalities: (1) deletion of symbols, (2) omission and (3) mistranslation, and the number of each inequality was 8, 13 and 5 respectively. The following are examples of the inequalities.

1. deletion of symbols
   Chinese: 亲们拍下后联系客服修改价格就好呢 ～～～
   Original: お客様にはご購入後にカスタマーサービスオペレーターに連絡し価格を訂正してください ～～～
   Edited: お客様はご購入後、カスタマーサービスオペレーターへ連絡し価格を訂正してください
2. omission
   Chinese: 但是实际颜色稍微深点，衣服素雅大方
   Original: 実際の色はちょっと深くて、衣裳もさっぱりとしていて大方です。
   Edited: 実際の色はちょっと深くて、衣裳もすっきりとしています。
3. mistranslation
   Chinese: 引用一位资深黄钻买家买这款衣服时对我说的话：
   Original: あるかなり経歴のあるイエローダイヤモンドのお客様がその商品を買った話によると：
   Edited: 歴史あるイエローダイアモンドを買ったお客様の話によると：

In the first example, the symbols at the end of the sentence are removed. This effect can be avoided by correctly instructing the workers to keep the symbols. In the second example, the Chinese word "大方" is omitted. Actually this is a very complicated problem. The Chinese word "大方" has several meanings such as *generous*, *liberal* and *stylish*. There is the same word in Japanese, but it means *almost* or *nearly* which is completely different from the Chinese meanings. The professional translators left the word in the Japanese sentence. However it is completely unnatural, and the crowd workers removed it.

In the third example, "黄钻 (*yellow diamond*)" is the name of a rank in the rating system of the EC-site. However, the crowd workers thought it as the real diamond, and edited the sentence incorrectly. The second and third effects are difficult to prevent, and this is left as future work.

Table 4. Validation results of each edit.

# judged better	# sentences	percentage
5	25,053	(45.9 %)
4	16,478	(30.2 %)
3	7,706	(14.1 %)
2	3,338	(6.1 %)
1	1,462	(2.7 %)
0	513	(0.9 %)

4.4 Crowdsourcing Cost

In our experiments, Step 1 costs 2 million Japanese Yen (JPY), Step 2 costs 310 thousand JPY and Step 3 costs 280 thousand JPY, in total 2.6 million JPY. Of course the fee varies depending on the number of workers for each question (this time 5, 3 and 5 workers respectively). We cannot directly compare with professional editing, but one editing company costs at least 6 JPY per English word[6]. If we apply this rate to our Chinese-to-Jpanaese translation editing, all the sentences containing 6.8 M words costs about 40 million JPY, which is 15 times larger than using crowdsourcing.

As for the editing time, Step 1 took 115 h, Step 2 took 35 h and Step 3 took 36 h, in total 186 h. Note that this is not the sum of the active working time of all the workers, but the time from when we submit the task until we get the results. The professional edits 4000 words per day; thus it takes 1700 days to edit all the sentences. Using crowdsourcing, we can greatly reduce both the time and cost.

5 Translation Experiment

To evaluate the crowdsourcing cleaning extrinsically, we also conducted a translation experiment. We used the original FDEC corpus as the baseline and divided it into training, development and test sets. Then, part of the Japanese sentences were replaced by the edits which were judged to be reasonable by the majority of the workers in Step 3. For the sentences which have more than one edits, we duplicated the sentences to use all the edits (cleaned 1) or randomly chose one (cleaned 2) for only development and test sets. We did not use cleaned 2 for the training data because bigger training data basically makes the translation quality better. Table 5 shows the statistics of the corpus.

We used a dependency tree based alignment model [9] for word alignment and KyotoEBMT system [11] for decoding with the default settings and evaluated the translation quality by BLEU [10] score. The results are shown in Table 6. The baseline (setting 1) score was 21.39 and it was improved by 0.3 points BLEU score in setting 2 where only the training data is cleaned. The p-value calculated

---

[6] http://www.editage.com.

by the bootstrap resampling [7] was 0.052. From this result we conclude that the proposed framework actually cleans the parallel corpus, and it contributes to improve the translation quality.

In other settings where one or both of the development and test data sets were cleaned, the BLEU scores slightly decreased. We think this is due to the inequalities between the original Chinese and the edited Japanese (See Sect. 4.3). The effect of the inequalities in the training data can be moderated during word alignment by handling them as NULL aligned words. However those in the development and test data are not negligible because all the automatic evaluation scores suppose the content of the input and output are strictly equal.

Table 5. The number of sentences for the translation experiments.

	original (OR)	cleaned 1 (CL1)	cleaned 2 (CL2)
train	1,220,597	1,256,908	-
dev	11,186	11,489	11,186
test	11,200	11,495	11,200

Table 6. Experimental Results.

setting	1(base)	2	3	4	5	6
train	OR	CL1	CL1	CL1	CL1	CL1
dev	OR	OR	CL1	CL1	CL2	CL2
test	OR	OR	OR	CL1	OR	CL2
BLEU	21.39	**21.69**	21.34	21.12	21.37	21.09

6 Conclusion

This paper proposed a framework of cleaning existing corpora efficiently and cheaply using crowdsourcing. The framework is composed of 3 steps and is able to clean existing parallel corpora containing noise reliably. The experimental results show the effectiveness of the proposed method.

As stated in Sect. 4.3, there still remain translation flaws which are not easy to prevent and correct, and solving this problem is future work. One possible solution is to ask the workers to give confidence scores of their edits. By only passing the edits with low confidence to the professional checkers, we might clean the corpus more reliably while keeping the cost low.

Another remained issue is that this framework can improve the translation fluency, but not able to improve the translation accuracy. We need to come up with a new idea to effectively improve the translation accuracy of the existing parallel corpora.

Acknowledgments. This work is supported by the Yahoo Japan Corporation. We want to thank the anonymous reviewers for many very useful comments.

References

1. Ambati, V., Vogel, S.: Can crowds build parallel corpora for machine translation systems? In: Proceedings of the NAACL HLT 2010 Workshop on Creating Speech and Language Data with Amazon's Mechanical Turk, pp. 62–65 (2010)
2. Ambati, V., Vogel, S., Carbonell, J.: Active learning and crowd-sourcing for machine translation. In: Proceedings of the Seventh International Conference on Language Resources and Evaluation (LREC 2010) (2010)
3. Aranberri, N., Labaka, G., de Ilarraza, A.D., Sarasola, K.: Comparison of post-editing productivity between professional translators and lay users. In: Proceedings of the Third Workshop on Post-Editing Technology and Practice, pp. 20–33 (2014)
4. Cao, D., Nakano, H., Xu, Y., Kumai, H.: Development of "Chinese-Japanese bilingual corpus" and its remaining tasks. IPSJ SIG Notes **99**(95), 1–8 (1999)
5. Chu, C., Nakazawa, T., Kurohashi, S.: Accurate parallel fragment extraction from quasi-comparable corpora using alignment model and translation lexicon. In: Proceedings of the 6th International Joint Conference on Natural Language Processing (IJCNLP 2013), pp. 1144–1150 (2013)
6. Chu, C., Nakazawa, T., Kurohashi, S.: Chinese-Japanese parallel sentence extraction from quasi-comparable corpora. In: Proceedings of the 6th Workshop on Building and Using Comparable Corpora (BUCC 2013), pp. 34–42 (2013)
7. Koehn, P.: Statistical significance tests for machine translation evaluation. In: Lin, D., Wu, D. (eds.) Proceedings of EMNLP 2004, pp. 388–395. Association for Computational Linguistics, Barcelona, July 2004
8. Koehn, P.: Europarl: A parallel corpus for statistical machine translation. In: Proceedings of the Tenth Machine Translation Summit (MT Summit X), pp. 79–86 (2005)
9. Nakazawa, T., Kurohashi, S.: Alignment by bilingual generation and monolingual derivation. In: Proceedings of COLING 2012, pp. 1963–1978. The COLING 2012 Organizing Committee, Mumbai, December 2012. http://www.aclweb.org/anthology/C12-1120
10. Papineni, K., Roukos, S., Ward, T., Zhu, W.J.: BLEU: a method for automatic evaluation of machine translation. In: ACL, pp. 311–318 (2002)
11. Richardson, J., Cromières, F., Nakazawa, T., Kurohashi, S.: KyotoEBMT: an example-based dependency-to-dependency translation framework. In: Proceedings of 52nd Annual Meeting of the Association for Computational Linguistics: System Demonstrations, pp. 79–84 (2014)
12. Schwartz, L.: Monolingual post-editing by a domain expert is highly effective for translation triage. In: Proceedings of the Third Workshop on Post-editing Technology and Practice, pp. 34–44 (2014)
13. Smith, J.R., Quirk, C., Toutanova, K.: Extracting parallel sentences from comparable corpora using document level alignment. In: Human Language Technologies: The 2010 Annual Conference of the North American Chapter of the Association for Computational Linguistics, pp. 403–411 (2010)
14. Uszkoreit, J., Ponte, J., Popat, A., Dubiner, M.: Large scale parallel document mining for machine translation. In: Proceedings of the 23rd International Conference on Computational Linguistics (Coling 2010), pp. 1101–1109 (2010)

15. Utiyama, M., Isahara, H.: A Japanese-English patent parallel corpus. In: MT summit XI, pp. 475–482 (2007)
16. Zaidan, O.F., Callison-Burch, C.: Crowdsourcing translation: professional quality from non-professionals. In: Proceedings of the 49th Annual Meeting of the Association for Computational Linguistics: Human Language Technologies, pp. 1220–1229 (2011)
17. Zhang, Y., Uchimoto, K., Ma, Q., Isahara, H.: Building an annotated Japanese-Chinese parallel corpus - a part of NICT multilingual corpora. In: Proceedings of 2nd International Joint Conference on Natural Language Processing, pp. 85–90 (2005)

Text and Message Understanding

Active Learning to Remove Source Instances for Domain Adaptation for Word Sense Disambiguation

Hiroyuki Shinnou[✉], Yoshiyuki Onodera, Minoru Sasaki, and Kanako Komiya

Department of Computer and Information Sciences, Ibaraki University, 4-12-1 Nakanarusawa, Hitachi, Ibaraki, Japan
{hiroyuki.shinnou.0828,14nm705n,minoru.sasaki.01, kanako.komiya.nlp}@vc.ibaraki.ac.jp

Abstract. In this paper, an active learning method of domain adaptation issues for word sense disambiguation is presented. In general, active learning is an approach where data with high learning effect is selected from an unlabeled data set, then labeled manually, and added to the training data. However, data in the source domain can deteriorate classification precision (misleading data), which extends errors to the domain adaptation. When data labeled by active learning is added to training data, an attempt is made to detect misleading data in the source domain and delete it from the training data. In this way, compared to standard learning classification precision is improved.

Keywords: Active learning · Domain adaptation · Word sense disambiguation

1 Introduction

When a natural language processing task is performed, the training and test data are usually in the same domain. However, sometimes the data comes from different domains. Recently, studies into domain adaptation have fine-tuned the classifier by using the training data of a learned domain (source domain) to match the test data of another domain (target domain) [5, 7, 11].

If the subject of the domain adaptation is problematic due to lack of target domain labels, active learning [8, 10] and semi-supervised learning [1] are effective. In this paper, we use active learning for domain adaptation for Word Sense Disambiguation (WSD).

Generally, active learning is an approach that gradually increases the precision of the classifier by selecting data with a high learning effect from an unlabeled data set, labeling the data, and adding it to the training data, thereby increasing the amount of training data monotonically. However, in domain adaptation, there are data that have a negative influence on the target domain due to classification in the source domain training data. Here we refer to such data as

© Springer Science+Business Media Singapore 2016
K. Hasida and A. Purwarianti (Eds.): PACLING 2015, CCIS 593, pp. 97–107, 2016.
DOI: 10.1007/978-981-10-0515-2_7

"misleading data" [3]. In this paper, we detect such data in the source domain training data and delete it to construct training data suitable for the target domain using active learning.

In the experiment, we use three domains: Yahoo! Answers (OC), Book (PB) and newspaper (PN) from the Balanced Corpus of Contemporary Written Japanese (BCCWJ [4]). The data set, which is provided by a Japanese WSD SemEval-2 task [6] has word sense tags attached to parts of these corpora. There are 16 multi-sense words with a certain frequency across all domains, and six patterns of domain adaptation (OCPB, PBPN, PNOC, OCPN, PNPB, and PBOC). We investigate domain adaptation for WSD using the proposed active learning method for $16 \times 6 = 96$ patterns and show the effectiveness of the proposed method.

2   Active Learning with Deleted Misleading Data

2.1   Active Learning

Active learning is an approach that reduces the amount of manual labeling when building effective training data.Using a classifier trained on the current training data, we selected data with as high a learning effect as possible from an unlabeled data set. Then, we manually assign correct labels to the selected data and add it to the training data. Consequently, the amount of labeled data is increased and the classifier is improved.

The key question of active learning is how to choose data with a high learning effect. There are many active learning methods [10]; however, one particularly effective method is widely used. This method selects data with the lowest classification reliability determined by a powerful classifier such as a support vector machine (SVM) classifier [9].

2.2   Detecting and Deleting Misleading Data

The initial labeled data in a general active learning is fixed. This is not problematic because all labeled data is useful. However, the initial pool of labeled data for domain adaptation, i.e., labeled data in the source domain can include harmful data.Here we refer to such data 'misleading data.' When general active learning is applied to domain adaptation, misleading data in the source domain prevents active learning from improving the classifier. Therefore, when we add labeled data to the training data, we detect misleading data and delete it from the labeled training data in the source domain.

Figure 1 shows the algorithm of our method. The initial labeled data in the source domain is denoted D_0, and the labeled data added to training data during the active learning process is denoted A, where initial A is empty. D_1 is the union of D_0 and A, and h_1 is the classifier learned through D_1. By using h_1, we classify D_0; the classification result is denoted L_1. Like general active learning, we classify the unlabeled data set U in the target domain using h_1 and assign a correct label

---

D_0 is set labeled data in source domain
U is set unlabeled data in target domain
$A \leftarrow \{\}$; labeled data added by Active Learning
$D_1 \leftarrow D_0 \cup A$
h_1 is set the classifier learned through D_1
L_1 is set the classification of D_0 by h_1

repeat 10 times do
    b is the labeled data obtained by active learning for U using h_1
    $U \leftarrow U - \{b\}$
    $A \leftarrow A \cup \{b\}$
    $D_2 \leftarrow D_0 \cup A$
    h_2 is set the classifier learned through D_2
    L_2 is set the classification of D_0 by h_2
    z is the misleading data detected through L_1 and L_2
    $D_0 \leftarrow D_0 - \{z\}$
    $D_1 \leftarrow D_0 \cup A$
    $h_1 \leftarrow h_2$
    $L_1 \leftarrow L_2$
done

h_2 is the final classifier

Fig. 1. Our proposed active learning

to identify data b with the lowest classification reliability. Data b is added to A. D_2 is the union of D_0 and A, and h_2 is the classifier learned through D_2. We use h_2 to classify D_0 and denote the classification result as L_2. We detect misleading data z using L_1 and L_2 by following procedure. Using to following cases (a),(b) or (c), we can identify misleading data. (a) There are false classifications in L_2. In this case, we identify the data with the highest classification reliability among the false classifications. (b) There are no false classifications. In this case, by comparing L_1 with L_2, we identify the data with the greatest decrease in reliability from L_1 to L_2. (c) There are no false classifications and no data with decreased reliability. In this case, no misleading data is identified. As shown in Fig. 1, this procedure is repeated 10 times.

In this study, active learning is complete when 10 data have been added to the labeled training data set. The only difference between general active learning and active learning for domain adaptation is the distribution of the initial labeled data set. Thus when labeled data is increased through active learning, there are very few differences. Therefore, we evaluate the proposed method with 10 repetitions of active learning.

3 Experiment

In the experiment, we use three domains: OC, PB and PN from the Balanced Corpus of Contemporary Written Japanese (BCCWJ [4]). As mentioned

Table 1. Target words of experiment

Word	# of meanings in dictionary	OC		PB		PN	
		Freq.	Meanings	Freq.	Meanings	Freq.	Meanings
(Iu)	3	666	2	1114	2	363	2
(Ireru)	3	73	2	56	3	32	2
(Kaku)	2	99	2	62	2	27	2
(Kiku)	3	124	2	123	2	52	2
q (Kodomo)	2	77	2	93	2	29	2
(Jikan)	4	53	2	74	2	59	2
(Jibun)	2	128	2	308	2	71	2
o (Deru)	3	131	3	152	3	89	3
(Toru)	8	61	7	81	7	43	7
(Baai)	2	126	2	137	2	73	2
(Hairu)	3	68	4	118	4	65	3
O (Mae)	3	105	3	160	2	106	4
(Miru)	6	262	5	273	6	87	3
(Motsu)	4	62	4	153	3	59	3
(Yaru)	5	117	3	156	4	27	2
(Yuku)	2	219	2	133	2	27	2
Average	3.35	193.9	2.94	150.6	2.88	75.56	2.69

previously the data set, which was provided by a Japanese WSD SemEval-2 task [6], has word sense tags attached to part of these corpora. There are 16 multi-sense words with some frequency across all domains. These 16 target words are shown in Table 1.[1] There are six direction patterns of (OCPB, PBPN, PNOC, OCPN, PNPB, and PBOC). Consequently $16 \times 6 = 96$ types of domain adaptation of WSD are used in the experiment.

In each direction of domain adaptation (e.g., OCPB), we conducted active learning for 16 target words. We evaluated the active learning method for domain adaptation using the average of these 16 precision.

We tried three methods. The first method is active learning to select added data at random (Random), the second is standard active learning (AL), and the third is our proposed active learning (Our AL). For all methods, the classifier is a SVM. We use the SVM tool 'libsvm'[2] to train the classifier. Using the -b option, we can obtain the reliability of the classification.

We show the result of the experiment in Figs. 3, 4, 5, 6, 7 and 8. Each figure shows the result of each domain adaptation. In this experiment, active learning

---

[1] The word "(Hairu)" has three senses in a dictionary. However, it has four senses in OC and PB domain. The fourth sense is new. In Japanese WSD SemEval-2 task, tagging the new sense was attempted.

[2] http://www.csie.ntu.edu.tw/~cjlin/libsvm/.

Table 2. Average precision of the final classifier (%)

	AL	Our AL	Random
OCPB	78.25	**78.98**	75.94
PBPN	84.06	**84.46**	80.38
PNOC	75.51	**78.41**	75.31
OCPN	79.54	**80.24**	77.04
PNPB	80.81	**81.13**	79.08
PBOC	78.00	**78.52**	76.33
Average	79.36	**80.29**	77.35

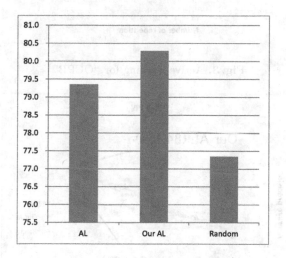

Fig. 2. Comparison of average precisions

stops after 10 repetitions. After 10 repetitions, the current classifier is presented in Table 2 and Fig. 2. Our proposed active learning method outperforms standard active learning in every domain adaptation type.

4 Discussion

4.1 Existence and Detection of Misleading Data

We do not know whether the data as misleading data in the experience are actually misleading data. Here, we use the data labels to determine if the detected data are in fact misleading data, and we examine whether the method for detecting misleading data is effective.

At first, we identify the misleading data individually following a previously proposed method [13]. The labeled data D in S of target word w exists in domain adaptation for fine-tuning the domain S to T. Next we measure the correct answer rate p_0 of the classifier T learned by D, delete data x from D,

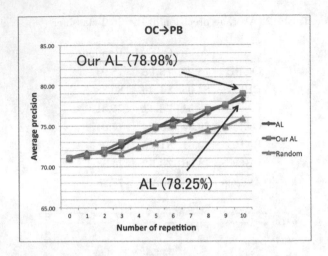

Fig. 3. Active learning for "OCPB"

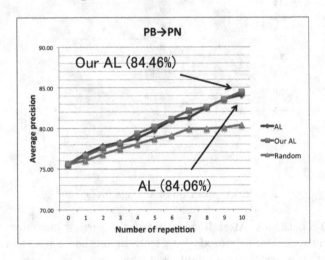

Fig. 4. Active learning for "PBPN"

and measure the correct answer rate p_1 of the classifier T learned by $D - \{x\}$. When $p_1 > p_0$, we consider data x to be misleading data. We perform this procedure for all data across D and find the misleading data of target word w. Table 3 shows the amount of misleading data found by this process. The numerical values in the parentheses are the amount of all data.

From the data presented in Table 3, we investigate whether misleading data detected by the experimental procedure are true or not. The result are shown in Table 4. The numerical values in the parenthesis are the amount of detected data, and the numerical values next to the parenthesis are the amount of the true misleading data. From Table 4, it is evident that the amount of detected data is 959, the amount of true misleading data is 121, and the precision is 0.1262.

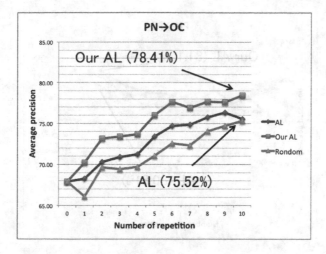

Fig. 5. Active learning for "PNOC"

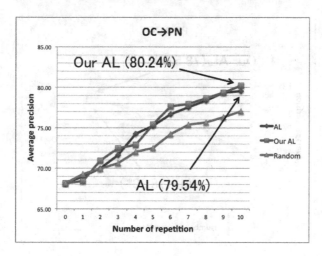

Fig. 6. Active learning for "OCPN"

It is thought that this value is low. However, precision is not always reduced deleting false detected data. Therefore, we believe that the detected data were not related to classification.

4.2 Instance Weight

In domain adaptation tasks, labeled data in the target domain are more important than labeled data in the source domain. Therefore, instance weight learning is effective in domain adaptation [3]. Generally, the weight of the instance is defined by the probability density ratio [12]. Here, we investigate active learning weighting of the detected target domain data. We simply weight detected data

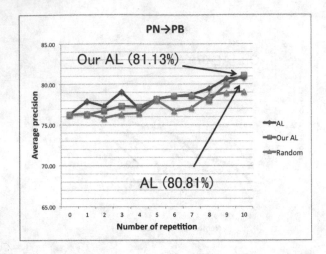

Fig. 7. Active learning for "PNPB"

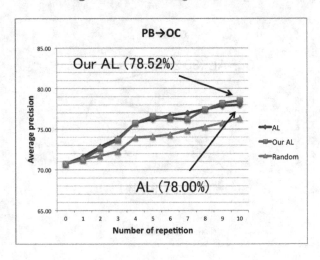

Fig. 8. Active learning for "PBOC"

by doubling the frequency of such data. Table 5 shows the average precision of the final classifier obtained by active learning.

From Table 5, we can confirm the effect of weighting on target domain labeled data. This experiment is simply weighting double heaviness. We intended to investigate the potential for improvement in future work.

4.3   Feature Weight

Because target domain labeled data are added by active learning, we can use the supervised domain adaptation method.

Table 3. Misleading data

Word	OCPB	PBPN	PNOC	OCPN	PNPB	PBOC
(Iu)	159 (666)	75 (1114)	82 (363)	158 (666)	35 (363)	127 (1114)
(Ireru)	6 (73)	15 (56)	3 (32)	28 (73)	1 (32)	19 (56)
(Kaku)	21 (99)	2 (62)	12 (27)	39 (99)	15 (27)	0 (62)
(Kiku)	26 (124)	0 (123)	4 (52)	21 (124)	27 (52)	26 (123)
q (Kodomo)	5 (77)	1 (93)	12 (29)	0 (77)	13 (29)	12 (93)
(Jikan)	1 (53)	0 (74)	0 (59)	8 (53)	5 (59)	0 (74)
(Jibun)	13 (128)	0 (308)	0 (71)	25 (128)	1 (71)	0 (308)
o (Deru)	14 (131)	32 (152)	22 (89)	10 (131)	10 (89)	39 (152)
(Toru)	6 (61)	18 (81)	12 (43)	5 (61)	22 (43)	10 (81)
(Baai)	0 (126)	13 (137)	14 (73)	0 (126)	9 (73)	7 (137)
(Hairu)	36 (68)	27 (118)	27 (65)	11 (68)	42 (65)	38 (118)
O (Mae)	8 (105)	1 (160)	15 (106)	5 (105)	2 (106)	10 (160)
(Miru)	10 (262)	12 (273)	8 (87)	3 (262)	28 (87)	3 (273)
(Motsu)	8 (62)	11 (153)	1 (59)	0 (62)	1 (59)	2 (153)
(Yaru)	0 (117)	0 (156)	0 (27)	0 (117)	0 (27)	0 (156)
(Yuku)	17 (219)	1 (133)	3 (27)	0 (219)	3 (27)	15 (133)

Table 4. Correct answer rates of detection of misleading data

Word	OCPB	PBPN	PNOC	OCPN	PNPB	PBOC
(Iu)	2 (10)	2 (10)	2 (10)	3 (10)	1 (10)	2 (10)
(Ireru)	2 (10)	3 (10)	2 (10)	4 (10)	0 (10)	2 (10)
(Kaku)	1 (10)	1 (10)	5 (10)	3 (10)	5 (10)	0 (10)
(Kiku)	1 (10)	0 (10)	2 (10)	1 (10)	4 (10)	1 (10)
q (Kodomo)	1 (10)	1 (10)	3 (10)	0 (10)	5 (10)	0 (10)
(Jikan)	0 (10)	0 (10)	0 (10)	0 (10)	0 (10)	0 (10)
(Jibun)	0 (10)	0 (10)	0 (10)	2 (10)	0 (10)	0 (10)
o (Deru)	1 (10)	1 (10)	2 (10)	2 (10)	0 (10)	1 (10)
(Toru)	2 (10)	2 (10)	4 (10)	1 (10)	4 (10)	2 (10)
(Baai)	0 (10)	2 (10)	3 (10)	0 (10)	1 (10)	0 (10)
(Hairu)	5 (10)	2 (10)	4 (10)	1 (10)	7 (10)	3 (10)
O (Mae)	0 (10)	0 (10)	1 (10)	1 (10)	0 (10)	1 (10)
(Miru)	0 (10)	1 (10)	0 (10)	0 (10)	1 (10)	0 (10)
(Motsu)	1 (10)	0 (10)	1 (10)	0 (10)	0 (10)	0 (10)
(Yaru)	0 (10)	0 (10)	0 (9)	0 (10)	0 (10)	0 (10)
(Yuku)	1 (10)	0 (10)	0 (10)	0 (10)	1 (10)	1 (10)

Table 5. Active learning with instance weight (%)

	Our AL	Our AL with instance weight
OCPB	**78.98**	77.70
PBPN	84.46	**84.75**
PNOC	**78.41**	78.05
OCPN	**80.24**	80.15
PNPB	81.13	**82.25**
PBOC	78.52	**79.81**
Average	80.29	**80.45**

Table 6. Use of Daumé's method in active learning (%)

	AL	Our AL	AL with Daumé	Our AL with Daumé
OCPB	78.25	**78.98**	77.09	76.24
PBPN	84.06	**84.46**	82.08	79.00
PNOC	75.51	78.41	**78.98**	75.50
OCPN	79.54	**80.24**	79.37	78.75
PNPB	80.81	**81.13**	81.01	74.57
PBOC	78.00	78.52	**80.83**	80.75
Average	79.36	**80.29**	79.89	77.47

Here, we combine Daumé's method [2] with active learning. We convert vector x_s of the source domain into a triple length vector $(x_s, x_s, 0)$, and vector x_t of the target domain into a triple length vector $(0, x_t, x_t)$ using Daumé's method. We classify the target domain data with the standard classification using the tripled vector. This method weights the common (overlapped) features of the source domain and the target domain.

When the Daumé's method is combined with active learning, we only have to convert source domain data x_s into $(x_s, x_s, 0)$, and target domain data x_t into $(0, x_t, x_t)$. The result for ten repetitions are shown in Table 6.

From Table 6, it is evident that using the proposed method with Daumé's method is not effective; however standard active learning combined with Daumé's method is effective. It is thought that the influence of misleading data becomes small with Daumé's method; consequently, the proposed method with Daumé's method was not effective. In future, we intend to investigate this possibility.

5   Conclusion

In this paper, we proposed a new active learning method of domain adaptation for WSD. In standard active learning, labeled training data increases monotonically. However, data in the source domain can deteriorate classification precision (misleading data), which extends errors to the domain adaptation. Our proposed method detects and deletes misleading data in the source domain during the standard active learning process. Through an experiment using three domains (OC, PB and PN) in BCCWJ and 16 common target words, the proposed method outperformed standard active learning. In future, we intend to investigate methods to detect misleading data more accurately and to assign proper weight to instances and features during the active learning process.

References

1. Chapelle, O., Schölkopf, B., Zien, A., et al.: Semi-supervised learning, vol. 2. MIT press, Cambridge (2006)
2. Daumé, III, H.: Frustratingly easy domain adaptation. In: ACL-2007, pp. 256–263 (2007)
3. Jiang, J., Zhai, C.: Instance weighting for domain adaptation in NLP. In: ACL-2007, pp. 264–271 (2007)
4. Maekawa, K.: Design of a balanced corpus of contemporary written Japanese. In: Symposium on Large Scale Knowledge Resources (LKR 2007), pp. 55–58 (2007)
5. Mori, S.: Domain adaptation in natural language processing (in japanese). Jpn. Soc. Artif. Intell. **27**(4), 365–372 (2012)
6. Okumura, M., Shirai, K., Komiya, K., Yokono, H.: SemEval-2010 task: Japanese WSD. In: The 5th International Workshop on Semantic Evaluation, pp. 69–74 (2010)
7. Pan, S.J., Yang, Q.: A survey on transfer learning. IEEE Trans. Knowl. Data Eng. **22**(10), 1345–1359 (2010)
8. Rai, P., Saha, A., Daumé III., H., Venkatasubramanian, S.: Domain adaptation meets active learning. In: NAACL HLT 2010 Workshop on Active Learning for Natural Language Processing, pp. 27–32 (2010)
9. Schohn, G., Cohn, D.: Less is more: Active learning with support vector machines. In: ICML, pp. 839–846 (2000)
10. Settles, B.: Active Learning Literature Survey. University of Wisconsin, Madison (2010)
11. Søgaard, A.: Semi-Supervised Learning and Domain Adaptation in Natural Language Processing. Morgan & Claypool, Milton Keynes (2013)
12. Sugiyama, M., Kawanabe, M.: Machine Learning in Non-Stationary Environments: Introduction to Covariate Shift Adaptation. MIT Press, Cambridge (2011)
13. Yoshida, H., Shinnou, H.: Detection of misleading data by outlier detection methods (in japanese). In: The 5th Japanese Corpus Linguistics Workshop, pp. 49–56 (2014)

Context Representation with Word Embeddings for WSD

Hiromu Sugawara[1], Hiroya Takamura[2], Ryohei Sasano[2(✉)],
and Manabu Okumura[2]

[1] Department of Information Processing, Tokyo Institute of Technology,
Tokyo, Japan
`suga@lr.pi.titech.ac.jp`
[2] Precision and Intelligence Laboratory, Tokyo Institute of Technology,
Tokyo, Japan
`{takamura,sasano,oku}@pi.titech.ac.jp`

Abstract. Word embeddings obtained through neural language models developed recently can capture semantic and grammatical behaviors of words and very capably find relationships between words. Such word embeddings are shown to be effective for various NLP tasks. In this paper, we develop a supervised method for word sense disambiguation (WSD) that employs word embeddings as local context features. Our experiments show the usefulness of word embeddings in the WSD task. We also compare the methods with different vector representations and reveal their effects on the WSD task.

Keywords: Word sense disambiguation · Word representation · Supervised machine learning

1 Introduction

Polysemous words are a major obstacle in many natural language processing (NLP) tasks. To circumvent this obstacle, NLP researchers have been developing methods for word sense disambiguation (WSD) [3,8,12,22]. Supervised learning approaches have performed especially well in many NLP tasks including the WSD task. Since the words in the neighborhood/context of the target polysemous word provide clues to the disambiguation, bag-of-words (BoW) of the context (usually a few words preceding or following the target word) is often used as a basic feature set. In addition to the local context features such as the BoW, there are several features that have been usually used in supervised WSD: topical features, syntactic features, and semantic features [18]. Other features also exist for the WSD task. For example, Agirre et al. [1] used Word-Net [17] as a resource for representing domains in WSD and constructed two domain features: the domain that is the most relevant with the context, and a list of domains the relevance of which is above a predefined threshold. It has been expected that combining these additional features with the local context features will contribute to the improvement of the system performance.

© Springer Science+Business Media Singapore 2016
K. Hasida and A. Purwarianti (Eds.): PACLING 2015, CCIS 593, pp. 108–119, 2016.
DOI: 10.1007/978-981-10-0515-2_8

When we use BoW as local context features, the context words in the test data that do not appear in the training data cannot be effective, even if their synonymous words are found in the training data. One of the approaches which attacks the problem of the sparseness is using concepts of context words rather than the words themselves as features. In this approach, the concepts are usually based on a thesaurus or a knowledge base. The other way is to use vector representation of words as representation of local context features. When we use the vector representation, cosine similarity between two vectors is usually used for calculating similarity between two words. Therefore, we can say that two words are similar when their two vector representations look similar. To solve the above-mentioned problem, in this paper, we attempt to represent the sense of each context word by means of the vector representations of words.

Many researchers have attempted to represent the word meanings as real-valued vectors. Recently, neural language models, such as the feed-forward neural network language model [5] and the recurrent neural network language model [15], have succeeded in obtaining the word representation (or embedding) that captures the semantic and grammatical behaviors of words. There are a number of implementations and variants of those neural language models above. Among them, Mikolov et al. proposed a skip-gram model and a continuous bag-of-words (CBOW) model [14,16]. Both the skip-gram model and the CBOW model are log-linear models without any nonlinear hidden layer. The word embeddings obtained by the skip-gram model and the CBOW model have been shown to be very useful to calculate word similarity. In particular, the word embeddings obtained by the skip-gram model achieved the best performance in their experiments.

The high performance in measuring word similarity suggests that the word embeddings obtained through the neural language models are good candidates for the vector representations of context words for WSD. Therefore, we employ word embeddings obtained by neural language models as features for supervised sense classifiers and confirm the usefulness of word embeddings in a WSD task. To support this claim, we also compare the word embeddings by neural language models with other vector representations in terms of the accuracy of WSD.

2   Background

The skip-gram model is a language model proposed by Mikolov et al. [14,16]. This language model predicts words that appear within a context window of an input word, which consists of N_e word tokens to the left and another N_e tokens to the right.

The skip-gram model differs from the models based on simple co-occurrences of words in the context window, because it assumes that each word in the context window, as well as the word in the center ("walking" in the example below), also has its own embedding and that the co-occurrence is caused by the two embeddings. Therefore, this model learns vector representations of words to assign larger co-occurrence probability to word pairs co-occurring more frequently.

The skip-gram model has two different types of parameters: *input* and *output* vector representations for each word. The first type of vector represents the word w_I in the center of the context window, while the second type of vector represents the other words w_O in the context window. The probability of w_O appearing within a context-window of w_I is defined as follows:

$$p(w_O|w_I) = \frac{\exp(v'_{w_O} \cdot v_{w_I})}{\sum_{w \in W} \exp(v'_w \cdot v_{w_I})} \tag{1}$$

where v_w and v'_w are the vector representations of *input* and *output* of w, and W is the vocabulary. Thus, this model assigns a large conditional probability to word pair w_I and w_O if the inner product of v_{w_I} and v'_{w_O} is large.

Specifically, the model maximizes the average of the logarithm of probability:

$$\frac{1}{T}\sum_{t=1}^{T} \sum_{-N_e \leq j \leq N_e, j \neq 0} \log p(w_{t+j}|w_t) \tag{2}$$

where T is the number of words in the training corpus and w_t is the t-th word in the corpus.

For example, suppose that there are two sentences in the training corpus:
- The cat is walking in the bedroom.
- The cat was running in the room.

If N_e is set to 2, the words in the context window of "walking" are "cat", "is", "in", and "the" in this example. Also, the words in the context window of "running" are "cat", "was", "in", and "the". The skip-gram model increases the probabilities of each pair of the word in the center (e.g., "walking" and "running") and a context word (e.g., "cat" for both examples) by bringing the *input* vector of the word in the center and the *output* vector of the context words close together, i.e. the cosine similarity between these vectors becomes large. Thus, the vector pair ($v_{walking}$ and v'_{cat}) get close to each other. The pair ($v_{running}$ and v'_{cat}) also get close to each other. As a result, *input* vectors of words with similar context ($v_{walking}$ and $v_{running}$) become similar to each other through the *output* vector (v'_{cat}).

Word embeddings are usually used as the input layer of neural network models [10,21]. Collobert and Weston [10] proposed a single convolutional neural network architecture that performs multi-task learning. Their model learns each word embedding as feature representations of each task. Although these (deep) neural network models work very well, the computational cost is mostly high. It is therefore practically important to consider how to represent instances of the data in supervised learning by using word embeddings learned from an unlabeled corpus, because feature representations are fundamental to supervised classifiers that have lower computational cost. Yu et al. [23] employed the feature that represents words by a cluster of embeddings. They used the support vector machines (SVM) and the multilayer perceptron with their features on chunking and named entity recognition tasks.

Some researchers have extended vector space models to deal with polysemous words. Agirre et al. [2] proposed a method of using the inter-word similarity on the basis of latent semantic analysis (LSA). They applied the method to the domain adaptation of word sense disambiguation. Cai et al. [7] used latent Dirichlet allocation (LDA) [6] to create a naive Bayesian classifier, and achieved a high accuracy in the Semeval 2007 coarse-grained lexical sample task [20]. Chen et al. [9] proposed a unified model for joint word sense representation and disambiguation, which assigned a distinct representation for each word sense. Their model achieved state-of-the-art performance on the coarse-grained all-words dataset and domain-specific WSD dataset. Neelakantan et al. [19] also focused on a method for obtaining word sense representation. They proposed two models: one has a fixed number of word senses, and the other automatically determines the number of word senses.

3   Methodology

In this section, we first describe the task definition of WSD and then present the features of the supervised classifier that employ word embeddings.

3.1   Task Definition

The word sense disambiguation is a task to choose appropriate senses of polysemous words in the given context. The possible senses of each word are based on external knowledge, such as WordNet, in most cases. In the lexical sample task of WSD, the corpus annotated with word senses is usually given as the training data, and the WSD task is reduced to a supervised classification task. Since a single polysemous word can have three or more senses, we should construct a multi-class classifier.

3.2   Proposed Feature Representation

For a classifier, we use the support vector machines (SVM) together with the one-versus-rest approach to extend SVMs to a multi-class classifier. In this section, we explain feature representation based on word embeddings and we call it Context Word Embeddings. Since we compare four types of context features in our experiments in the next section, we explain them all in this section. Two are based on BoW, and the others are based on word embeddings.

Bag-of-Words (BoW)
This type of feature indicates whether a word appears within the context window of size N. The dimension of the feature space is equal to the vocabulary size $|W|$.

Position-Bag-of-Words (PosiBoW)
With this feature set, each feature vector is represented as a concatenation of one-of-V representations. One-of-V representation represents each word by a binary vector, in which only the element associated with this word is 1, and the others are 0. The one-of-V representations of words within the

Index	Word	Vector
0	cat	0.1, 0.2, 0.1
1	machine	-0.1, 0.3, 0.5
2	around	0.7, -0.2, 0.1
3	well	0.6, -0.1, 0.5

Data   cat **run** around

Feature

BoW: 1,0,1,0

PosiBoW: 1,0,0,0   0,0,1,0

AveWE: 0.4, 0.0, 0.1

CWE: 0.1, 0.2, 0.1   0.7, -0.2, 0.1

Fig. 1. Example of each feature

context window are concatenated to make a feature vector of $2 \times N \times |W|$. While the simple BoW described above does not contain position information, PosiBoW does. We use this feature for comparison, because the following Context-Word-Embeddings feature takes positions into consideration.

Average-Word-Embeddings (AveWE)

This feature set uses word embeddings, but does not take into account the position of each context word. The feature vector is the average of vector representations of words in the context window. The dimension of the feature space is the same as the dimension of each word embedding.

Context-Word-Embeddings (CWE)

This feature vector is a concatenated vector of the real-valued vectors of the words in the context window. If the window size is N and words appearing in the context window are $w_{-N}, \ldots, w_{-1}, w_{+1}, \ldots, w_{+N}$, this feature vector is a vector concatenating $v_{w_{-N}}, \ldots, v_{w_{-1}}, v_{w_{+1}}, \ldots, v_{w_{+N}}$, where v_w represents an embedding of word w. If the dimension of each word embedding is d, the size of this feature vector is $2 \times N \times d$.

Fig. 1 shows a simple example of each feature representation. Please assume that only four words "cat," "machine," "around," and "well" are in the vocabulary (the vocabulary size $|W|$ is 4). In the top, word embeddings for each word are shown (the dimension of each word embedding d is 3). The instance data to be represented as feature representation is shown in the middle, where the target word is "run" and the window size N is 1. In the bottom, four types of context features are shown.

4   Experiments

We evaluated word embedding based features on an English lexical-sample data set. We also investigated the effect of the difference in word embeddings.

4.1   Experimental Settings

We used the SemEval 2007 lexical sample task (task17) dataset [20]. This dataset contains training and test data for 100 polysemous words. The average numbers of instances are 222 for the training set and 48 for the test set.

We lemmatized each word by using the lemmatizer in the Natural Language Toolkit[1] that is based on WordNet. We chose the skip-gram model [16] to learn embeddings. Mikolov et al. [16] distributed word embeddings learned from news articles containing about 100 billion words[2]. We used this data to compare features based on binary vector and features based on word embeddings. The dimension of these vectors is 300. We also used linear SVM (LIBLINEAR [11]) as a classifier and used five-fold cross validation on the training dataset in order to determine the value of soft-margin parameter C by changing its value from 0.1 to 1 with a step size of 0.1 and from 1 to 10 with a step size of 1.

4.2   Comparison of BoW and CWE

We used four types of features explained in Sect. 3: BoW, PosiBoW, AveWE, and CWE. We also tested their combinations in experiments. Table 1 shows the experimental results.

Table 1. Classification results of each feature and combination of features

Features	Accuracy
BoW	84.72 %
PosiBoW	85.53 %
AveWE	84.56 %
CWE	87.51 % [†] [‡]
PosiBow+CWE	87.18 % [†] [‡]
BoW+CWE	87.80 % [†] [‡]

'†' and '‡' denote significant differences from BoW and PosiBoW, respectively.

We performed McNemar's test [13] at the significance level of 1 % to assess whether two classifiers were performing significantly differently. '†' and '‡' mean

---

[1] http://www.nltk.org/.
[2] https://code.google.com/p/word2vec/.

that the corresponding feature set significantly outperforms BoW and PosiBoW, respectively. This result shows that CWE is better than BoW, PosiBoW, and AveWE in this task. This also shows that PosiBoW outperforms BoW. Therefore, position information of words would be helpful on WSD. However, the system using PosiBoW+CWE performed worse than that using BoW+CWE. We conjecture that PosiBoW+CWE does not work better than BoW+CWE despite the useful information from word positions, because CWE itself contains position information. CWE worked very well, but AveWE did not work well. There are two possible reasons: one is that the size of context window was not enough to represent context, and the other is that simply averaging vectors can not represent context well. Actually, we tried AveWE with broader context windows, but obtained worse results. Thus we consider this is because averaging word-representations obscures information about which words appear in local context. We conclude simple averaging is not enough to represent context from this result. Actually, we tried AveWE with broader context window, but it shows worser result. Thus, we consider this is because averaging word-representations lose information about what words appear in local context. We conclude simple averaging is not enough to represent context from this result.

If many words in an instance data to be classified do not appear in the training dataset, it is difficult to classify the instance correctly, especially when we use BoW. However, when we use word embeddings, information of words that do not appear in the training set is expected to be leveraged for classification. To confirm this assumption, we checked the number of words that do not appear in the context window when we train classifiers for each instance in the test set. Hereinafter, we call such words unknown word (UNKs), and we also examine the correlation between the accuracy and the number of UNKs.

Table 2 shows the number of instances per the number of UNKs and Fig. 2 shows the ratios (%) of correct and incorrect outputs per the number of UNKs. The first figure shows the ratios with BoW only, and the second figure shows the ratios of the system using BoW and CWE.

Table 2. The number of instances per the number of UNKs

0	1	2	3	4	5	6	7	8	9	10
564	765	872	846	766	525	321	109	50	21	12

The first and second rows denote the number of UNKs and the number of instances, respectively.

Vertical and horizontal axes of both graphs are the ratios and the number of UNKs, respectively. Thus, the rightmost bar represents cases in which all words are UNKs, and the leftmost bar represents cases in which neither words are UNKs. Right cases are expected to be more difficult to classify than left cases. When we used only BoW, the ratio of incorrect outputs increased as we had assumed. Next, we focus on bars representing the ratios of cases whose result

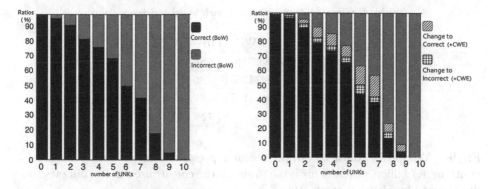

Fig. 2. Effect of UNKs on accuracy

Table 3. The relationships between the accuracy and the sizes of training sets

Feature	The size of training set			
	100 %	75 %	50 %	25 %
PosiBoW	85.53 %	83.67 %	82.81 %	80.64 %
CWE	87.51 %	86.94 %	86.44 %	84.85 %
diff.	1.98 %	3.27 %	3.63 %	4.21 %

became correct when we used BoW and CWE (bars with blue slash). These ratios did not monotonically decrease even if the number of UNKs increased. These results show that CWE can utilize of UNKs, while BoW cannot.

The feature set based on word embeddings would alleviate the sparseness problem. Thus, we next examined how the performance of the classifier changed depending on the size of training data. The size of test data was the same as in the above experiment, although we changed the size of training data in this experiment. We randomly divided each piece of training data of each word into quarters and then gradually removed quarters from training data. Each piece of divided data has almost the same amount of data for each sense. Table 3 shows the relationships between the accuracy and the number of the training instances. The row *diff.* shows the accuracy differences between PosiBoW and CWE. Table 3 shows that the difference between two systems is large when the number of training instances is small. This result suggests that the CWE feature is useful, especially when only a small training data set is available.

4.3 Effect of the Methods for Constructing Vector Representations

A method for constructing vector representation is crucial for a high performance of WSD. To investigate how the choice of vector representation affects the performance of WSD, we used the singular value decomposition (SVD) and word2vec[3] (skip-gram model) to obtain vector representation. We also used

---

[3] https://code.google.com/p/word2vec/.

Table 4. Classification results of each word representation

	CWE	BoW + CWE
EnWiki SVD	83.54 %	86.15 %
EnWiki w2v	86.45 %	86.58 %
Google w2v	87.51 %	87.80 %
(BoW)	84.72 %	

English Wikipedia[4] data to obtain vector representations of words. This data contains 1.7 billion words. This is 0.5 % size of the corpus used in learning vectors distributed by Mikolov et al. [16].

We chose a method using SVD following Baroni et al. [4]. We regarded two word tokens as having co-occurred when their distance was less than N_e. We then made the co-occurrence matrix by using their method and factorized the matrix as $X = U\Sigma V^T$. In this study, X represents the co-occurrence matrix. We assume that each row of U represents the vector of the word associated with the row. When we used word2vec, we chose the skip-gram with negative-sampling as a model and set the number of negative-samples to 10. We also set the dimension of vectors to 300 both for skip-gram and SVD.

We compared three vector representations: vectors obtained by SVD from English Wikipedia (EnWiki SVD), vectors obtained by word2vec from English Wikipedia (EnWiki w2v), and vectors distributed by Mikolov et al. that are trained on part of the Google News dataset (Google w2v). Table 4 shows the experimental results.

With the word representation by SVD, the system using both BoW and CWE (BoW+CWE) outperformed BoW, although CWE did not outperform BoW. On the other hand, with the word representation by word2vec, both CWE and BoW+CWE outperformed BoW even when using English Wikipedia data to obtain the vector representation. This result suggests that the word embeddings obtained by the skip-gram model contain very helpful information for WSD.

4.4 Examples of Word Embeddings Affecting the Results

Table 5 shows instances, for which BoW predicted the wrong sense and BoW+CWE with Google w2v predicted the correct sense. The blue italicized words in the table represent UNKs, and the red bold words are the target words. In the examples of the sense 2 of the noun "management", which means *the people who direct a business*, there are some UNKs that are names of companies or organizations: "Younkers", "swift", and "Wedtech". Well-learned embeddings would capture the similarity between these names appearing in training data and test data, resulting in a high performance of CWE for "management".

UNKs could also be clues for predicting the sense in the examples of the verb "begin". Senses shown in the examples of "begin" are all sense 2, i.e., *take*

---

[4] We accessed the Wikipedia dataset in August 2014.

Table 5. Examples improved by using CWE

Word	Sense	Examples improved by using CWE
management.n	2	*Younkers* management is likely to buy a 10 % to 20 % interest in the chain in January , said Fred S. Hubbell , Equitable 's president and chief executive officer .
	2	Subcontractors will be offered a settlement and a *swift transition* to new management is *expected* to *avert* an exodus of skilled workers from Waertsilae Marine 's two big shipyards , government officials said .
	2	*Wedtech* management *used* the *merit* system .
	2	New management at *Kentucky Fried Chicken*, a unit of PepsiCo Inc. , has fought back with new medium and large chicken sandwiches for the lunch crowd .
begin.v	2	If the investor does n't put up the extra cash to satisfy the call , the *brokerage* firm *may* begin *liquidating* the *securities* .
	2	General Motors Corp. said it had discussed the possibility of a joint *venture* with *Jaguar* before *Ford* began *buying* shares .
	2	Precision Castparts Corp. , *Portland* , *Ore.* , will begin trading with the *symbol PCP* .

the first step or steps in carrying out an action. In these examples, two gerunds ("buying" and "liquidating") are UNKs. However, since "trading" appears in the training data and the cosine similarities between the embeddings of "trading" and those gerunds are large, these examples were correctly disambiguated by means of CWE. Note that although these words are not synonyms, they are given a high similarity by CWE because they are semantically related and have the same type of inflection (i.e., -ing). We thus consider the system outputs of these instances changed to correct answers because CWE captured the similarity of these words.

5 Conclusion

In this paper, we investigated the effects of features based on word embeddings on a WSD task. We confirmed that the classifier based on the word embeddings feature set outperforms those based on bag-of-words features. Our experiments also confirmed that the feature set based on word embeddings was more robust to the sparseness problem than features based on binary representation. We expect that the features that we used will contribute to the performance of a supervised classifier by being combined with other features. Although the feature sets that take word positions into account (CWE and PosiBoW) outperformed those that do not, they also have a downside: they are sensitive to the slight difference in positions of context words. A better way to handle the positions of context words would improve the performance of WSD.

References

1. Agirre, E., de Lacalle, O.L.: UBC-ALM: Combining k-NN with SVD for WSD. In: Proceedings of the 4th International Workshop on Semantic Evaluations (Semeval) pp. 342–345 (2007)
2. Agirre, E., de Lacalle, O.L.: Supervised domain adaption for WSD. In: Proceedings of the 12th Conference of the European Chapter of the Association for Computational Linguistics (EACL), pp. 42–50 (2009)
3. Banerjee, S., Pedersen, T.: An adapted lesk algorithm for word sense disambiguation using wordnet. In: Gelbukh, A. (ed.) CICLing 2002. LNCS, vol. 2276, pp. 136–145. Springer, Heidelberg (2002)
4. Baroni, M., Dinu, G., Kruszewski, G.: Don't count, predict! A systematic comparison of context-counting vs. context-predicting semantic vectors. In: Proceedings of the 52nd Annual Meeting of the Association for Computational Linguistics (ACL), pp. 238–247 (2014)
5. Bengio, Y., Ducharme, R., Vincent, P., Janvin, C.: A neural probabilistic language model. J. Mach. Learn. Res. **3**, 1137–1155 (2003)
6. Blei, D.M., Ng, A.Y., Jordan, M.I.: Latent dirichlet allocation. The Journal of Machine Learning Research **3**, 993–1022 (2003)
7. Cai, J.F., Lee, W.S., Teh, Y.W.: NUS-ML: improving word sense disambiguation using topic features. In: Proceedings of the 4th International Workshop on Semantic Evaluations. Association for Computational Linguistics (SemEval-2007), pp. 524–531 (2007)
8. Carpuat, M., Wu, D.: Improving statistical machine translation using word sense disambiguation. In: Proceedings of the 2007 Joint Conference on Empirical Methods in Natural Language Processing and Computational Natural Language Learning (EMNLP-CoNLL), pp. 61–72 (2007)
9. Chen, X., Liu, Z., Sun, M.: A unified model for word sense representation and disambiguation. In: Proceedings of the 2014 Conference on Empirical Methods in Natural Language Processing (EMNLP), pp. 1025–1035 (2014)
10. Collobert, R., Weston, J.: A unified architecture for natural language processing: deep neural networks with multitask learning. In: Proceedings of the 25th International Conference on Machine Learning (ICML), pp. 160–167 (2008)
11. Chang, K.W., Hsieh, C.J., Wang, X.R., Lin, C.J., Fan, R.E.: LIBLINEAR: a library for large linear classification. J. Mach. Learn. Res. **9**, 1871–1874 (2008)
12. Ide, N., Vronis, J.: Word sense disambiguation: The state of the art. Computational Linguistics **24**, 1–40 (1998)
13. McNemar, Q.: Note on the sampling error of the difference between correlated proportions or percentages. Psychometrika **12**(2), 153–157 (1947)
14. Mikolov, T., Chen, K., Corrado, G., Dean, J.: Efficient estimation of word representations in vector space. In: Workshop at International Conference on Learning Representations (ICLR) (2013)
15. Mikolov, T., Karafiát, M., Burget, L., Cernocký, J., Khudanpur, S.: Recurrent neural network based language model. In: 11th International Conference of the International Speech Communication Association (INTERSPEECH), pp. 1045–1048 (2010)
16. Mikolov, T., Sutskever, I., Chen, K., Corrado, G., Dean, J.: Distributed representations of words and phrases and their compositionality. Advances in Neural Information Processing Systems 26 (NIPS), pp. 3111–3119 (2013)

17. Miller, G.A.: Wordnet: a lexical database for english. Commun. ACM **38**(11), 39–41 (1995)
18. Navigli, R.: Word sense disambiguation: a survey. ACM Comput. Surv. **41**(2), 10:1–10:69 (2009)
19. Neelakantan, A., Shankar, J., Passos, A., McCallum, A.: Efficient non-parametric estimation of multiple embeddings per word in vector space. In: Proceedings of the 2014 Conference on Empirical Methods in Natural Language Processing (EMNLP), pp. 1059–1069 (2014)
20. Pradhan, S.S., Loper, E., Dligach, D., Palmer, M.: SemEval-2007 task 17: English lexical sample, SRL and all words. In: Proceedings of the 4th International Workshop on Semantic Evaluations (SemEval-2007), pp. 87–92 (2007)
21. Socher, R., Huang, E.H., Pennington, J., Ng, A.Y., Manning, C.D.: Dynamic pooling and unfolding recursive autoencoders for paraphrase detection. In: Proceedings of Advances in Neural Information Processing Systems 24 (NIPS), pp. 801–809 (2011)
22. Yarowsky, D.: Unsupervised word sense disambiguation rivaling supervised methods. In: Proceedings of the 33rd Annual Meeting on Association for Computational Linguistics (ACL), pp. 189–196 (1995)
23. Yu, M., Zhao, T., Dong, D., Tian, H., Yu, D.: Compound embedding features for semi-supervised learning. In: Proceedings of the 2013 Conference of the North American Chapter of the Association for Computational Linguistics: Human Language Technologies (NAACL-HLT), pp. 563–568 (2013)

Information Extraction
and Text Mining

Location Mention Detection in Tweets and Microblogs

Shervin Malmasi[(✉)] and Mark Dras

Centre for Language Technology, Macquarie University, Sydney, NSW, Australia
{shervin.malmasi,mark.dras}@mq.edu.au

Abstract. The automatic identification of location expressions in social media text is an actively researched task. We present a novel approach to detection mentions of locations in the texts of microblogs and social media. We propose an approach based on Noun Phrase extraction and n-gram based matching instead of the traditional methods using Named Entity Recognition (NER) or Conditional Random Fields (CRF), arguing that our method is better suited to noisy microblog text. Our proposed system is comprised of several individual modules to detect addresses, Points of Interest (e.g. hospitals or universities), distance and direction markers; and location names (e.g. suburbs or countries). Our system won the ALTA 2014 Twitter Location Detection shared task with an F-score of 0.792 for detecting location expressions in a test set of 1,000 tweets, demonstrating its efficacy for this task. A number of directions for future work are discussed.

Keywords: Location detection · Location identification · Twitter · Tweet · Microblog · Social media

1 Introduction

Locations are a key piece of information in social media discourse, often linked to specific events or news that are being discussed. In this context, the identification of location expressions in social media has attracted the attention of researchers and the extraction of this data from Twitter messages, called tweets, is actively researched [7,18].

The specific goal of this task is to identify all mentions of locations in the text of tweets. A *location* can be defined as any specific mention of a country, region, city, suburb, street address, or other POI (Point of Interest). A POI can be a library, such as "Central Library" or the name of an airport such as "Manchester Airport". These location expressions can appear in the text itself, or in hashtags (e.g. #china) and mentions (e.g. @Visit_Japan). Some example tweets and their identified locations are shown in Fig. 1. Some tweets can contain multiple locations, as shown in Fig. 2. Applications of such systems include the early detection of emergencies, crises and natural disasters in real time [12,15,19]. They could also be employed for targeted advertising purposes [17].

The overarching aim of the present work is to propose and evaluate a methodology for the detection of such location mentions in microblogs and social media.

© Springer Science+Business Media Singapore 2016
K. Hasida and A. Purwarianti (Eds.): PACLING 2015, CCIS 593, pp. 123–134, 2016.
DOI: 10.1007/978-981-10-0515-2_9

Tweet	Location
France and Germany join the US and UK in advising their nationals in Libya to leave immediately http://bbc.in/1rVmrDJ	France, Germany, US, UK, Libya
Dutch investigators not going to MH17 crash site in eastern Ukraine due to security concerns, OSCE monitors say	MH17 crash site, eastern Ukraine
Seeing early signs of potential flash flooding with stationary storms near St. Marys, Tavistock, Cambridge #onstorm pic.twitter.com/BtogIxgQ5G	St. Marys, Tavistock, Cambridge

Fig. 1. Several example tweets and the location expressions that they contain. Reproduced from [13].

2   Related Work

Researcher have been actively working on detecting such location mentions in both social media data as well as formal texts. In this section we briefly look at some previous approaches to this task.

One approach to this task has been based on Named Entity Recognition (NER), which is the process of identifying names, locations and organizations within texts. When applied to our target problem, this can be viewed as a subtask of NER where we are only interested in locations.

A set of tools for performing tasks such as NER specifically on Twitter was developed by [16]. The system, known as *T-NER*, was designed to also perform geo-location detection in tweet data. This system augmented the Stanford NER system with information from Freebase [3] to improve performance and achieved an F-score of 0.77 in detecting locations.

Another approach proposed by [6] has a 2-stage architecture and makes use of Conditional Random Field (CRF) modelling. Furthermore, they also used gazetted resources from Wikipedia to augment their system.

The authors of [5] also applied NER to the task and compared various tools with the standard models as well as NER models trained only on Twitter data. They conclude that existing NER tools should be re-trained on microblog data before being applied to Twitter data.

Fig. 2. An example tweet which contains more than one distinct location expression. Reproduced from [13].

We should also note that such content-based approaches are not limited to English data or Twitter; other researchers have also tested them on other languages and microblogs such as Weibo [1].

3 Data

Data for the task included a training set of 2,000 tweets with manually annotated location information and 1,000 test tweets to be processed. To ensure a blind evaluation, the location annotations for the test tweets were not made available until after testing. This data was collected as part of the research presented by [5] and more details can be found in their work.[1]

4 Methodology

In contrast with the work described in Sect. 2, we take a different approach to this problem. Instead, we opt to use syntactic parse trees to identify potential location information. Parse trees have been used in other NLP tasks such as Native Language Identification [9–11] and other tree representations such as parent-annotated trees [8] have also been tested.

It is well known that microblog data is noisy and contains large proportions of non-standard words which pose challenges for most NLP systems trained on well-formed text. These include misspellings, hashtags, abbreviations, malformed sentences and other slang and colloquial terms. Although NER methods are highly effective in detecting locations in formal texts, they do not perform as well for Twitter data [5]. It is most likely this noisy nature of tweets and microblog data that makes it more challenging to distinguish the syntactic environments that predict locative arguments.

Yet another disadvantage of supervised NER systems is the requirement for sufficient amounts of annotated training data, preferably sourced from microtext sources if they are to be trained specifically for such target texts.

---

[1] Requests for the data should also be directed to the authors of [5].

Given the above reasoning, we opt to develop an *unsupervised* approach based on a combination of syntactic parse trees and gazetteer information.

During the last decade, there has been growing interest and work in the development of geo-information databases and resources which could be utilised for such tasks. These *gazetteers* are usually made available in machine-readable format or web services. GeoNames[2] is one such data source and we use it in the present work.

The GeoNames geographical database[3] contains over 10 million geographical names and consists of over 9 million unique features of 2.8 million populated places and 5.5 million alternate names. The database is updated regularly and the information is sourced from dozens of unique sources.[4]

The remainder of this section focuses on describing how we achieve this through the various components of our system.

4.1   Preprocessing

As a first step, non-English tweets are detected using a dictionary-based language identification approach and discarded.

The tweets are then processed to normalize mentions and hashtags within the text by removing the @ and # symbols. These tokens are also stored separately in the original form for further processing in later stages. URLs are also stripped from the text and we do no process them.

4.2   Syntactic Parsing

Next, the Stanford CoreNLP[5] suite of NLP tools and the provided pre-trained English models are used to tokenize, POS tag and parse each tweet. This information is stored on separate annotation layers from the original tweet text. This is so that we can recover the untokenized strings in the original tweet.

4.3   Noun Phrase Extraction

The extraction of noun phrases is a critical component of our system. This is due to the fact that locative information is generally expressed through nouns and we can exploit this by discarding tokens that have been identified as other phrase types, such as verbs. After parsing, we use the generated constituency parses to extract the noun phrases (NPs) from within each tweet.

Many of the NPs found in the data can be considered complex NPs,[6] and in these cases we only extract the constituent NPs they contains. This is achieved through a rule-based tree splitting method that breaks the tree at certain

---

[2] http://www.geonames.org/.

[3] Available for download free of charge under a creative commons attribution license.

[4] http://www.geonames.org/data-sources.html.

[5] http://nlp.stanford.edu/software/corenlp.shtml.

[6] A noun phrase that contains other NPs, for example, within prepositions.

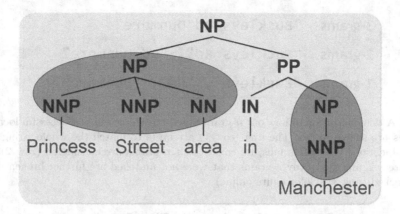

Fig. 3. An example of a complex noun phrase (NP) which contains additional NPs embedded within it. In such cases it may not be possible to match the entire NP as a single location since it contains constituent NPs with different locations.

branches. Our method works by recursively breaking down the NP at non-NP branches, such as prepositions, in order to extract only the simpler constituent NPs. Figure 3 shows an example of a complex NP and its constituent NPs.

One important advantage of this approach is that the parser will tag any words that it does not recognize (such slang), or tokens that are not part of a sentence (e.g. a trailing list of tags after a post) or incomplete text fragments as NPs. These tokens may contain locations that would likely not be identified by NER or CRF systems due to the lack of appropriate syntactic context.

4.4 *N*-gram Based Location Matching

The extracted noun phrases may still contain more than one location or other non-location tokens – *e.g.* "Christchurch New Zealand earthquake" or "Bangkok residents" – making it difficult to precisely match the locations. We resolve this by using an *n*-gram based matching approach. Here, we first attempt to match the whole NP as a single location, and if no exact match is found, we consider all of its *n*-gram subsets. For an NP of N tokens, this include all *n*-grams of order $N - 1$ through to unigrams. It is important to process the subsets in this descending in order to match maximal subsets of the NPs. If an *n*-gram is matched as a location, its subsets will not be considered.

Let us illustrate this with an example noun phrase "Buckleys Rd Dunmore", as shown in Fig. 4. This NP contains two location mentions (Buckleys Road in the suburb of Dunmore) within a single phrase. As a first step we attempt to match the entire NP as a location, but no precise match can be found. Consequently, we then consider the subset 2-grams and 1-grams, as shown in the second and third rows of Fig. 4. These two location mentions are then matched by two separate components of our system: the address matching and geographic lookup modules, respectively. These components are described later this section.

3-grams	"Buckleys Rd Dunmore"
2-grams	"Buckleys Rd", "Rd Dunmore"
1-grams	"~~Buckleys~~", "~~Rd~~", "Dunmore"

Fig. 4. A demonstration of how our n-gram based matching works. Successful location matches are shown in red. The first (row 1) attempts to match the whole string as a unique location. When this fails, its constituent n-grams are considered (row 2) and an address is matched. Any n-grams that were not matched are further broken down and checked (row 3) (Color figure online).

Greater Manchester Fire Service
Dandenong train crash
Queensland flood report
Guatemala Earthquake

Fig. 5. Some examples of how our partial matching method can detect the location tokens (shown in red) within noun phrases. Without using an n-gram based matching approach, some of the non-location tokens may be erroneously detected as locations, increasing the detector's false positive rate (Color figure online).

In our experiments, not processing the phrases via this n-gram matching procedure leads to a higher false positive rate as some extra parts of NPs may be matched as locations.

This procedure is also helpful when processing noun phrases with partial location information, e.g. "China earthquake report". Only one noun in the NP is a location expression here. Some examples of how this method can capture the location-relevant subsets of NPs is shown in Fig. 5.

We now describe several subcomponents of our system that are used to determine if these n-gram candidates are location expressions.

Address Matching. Addresses are a crucial piece of location information. The generally structured format of addresses makes them suitable for matching via regular expressions. To this end we developed a set of regular expressions to capture NPs containing address expressions using a wide array of street types along with their abbreviations. Examples of such road types include Arcade, Avenue, Boulevard, Road, Street, Highway, Overpass, *etc.* The regular expressions are also designed to capture street numbers. Some sample addresses extracted by our system are listed in Table 1.

Point of Interest Matching. Another type of location we are interested in are Points of Interest (POIs). A POI can be, *inter alia*, a hospital, airport, river,

Table 1. Some example addresses matched by our regular expressions.

Orchard Rd	Yanilla Ave
Warrego Hwy	Hawkesbury River Bridge
Forge Creek Rd	North West Coastal Highway
Wedderburn-brenanah Rd	Kaban Rd
School Rd overpass	Princess Street
333 Manly Road	Batemans Bay

Table 2. Some example Point Of Interest (POI) locations matched by our regular expressions.

Kumbarilla State Forest	Nudgee Golf Club
Princess Alexandra Hospital	Melbourne Airport
Wong Wong bakery	Thomas Jefferson University Hospital
Navigator College	Khartoum arms factory

university, park or shopping center. We compiled a list of such locations and created a set of regular expressions to match NPs that contain them. Some example results are shown in Table 2.

Location Name Matching. We employ the above-described GeoNames database to match non-address locations, such as suburbs, countries and other landmarks. To do this, we utilize the advanced search features offered by the web service, including fuzzy matching to help address misspellings.[7] The location candidates are sent via the API and they are marked as locations if a match is reported.

Some example locations matched by GeoNames include Guatemala, Wahroonga, Syria, Ultimo, Greece, Brisbane, New Jersey, and Manchester.

Distance and Direction Marker Matching. The final component of our system matches distance and direction markers, which were also annotated in our training data. This type of information, *e.g.* "*25 km North of* Beijing", is often found within complex locative NPs.

We compiled a list of such directional and distance markers and created a rule-based module to match them, again using regular expressions. Some example of markers found in our data are shown in Fig. 6.

4.5   Hashtag and Mention Matching

In developing the above-described components we discovered that these methods could not match locations that were embedded within hashtags and mentions

---

[7] The web service offers a number of advanced features that can help increase search specificity.

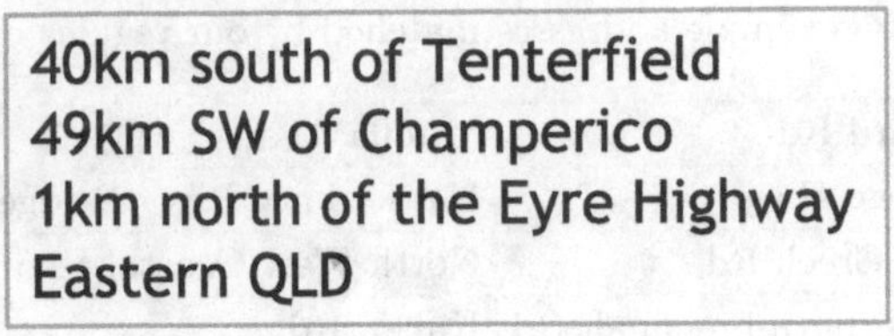

> 40km south of Tenterfield
> 49km SW of Champerico
> 1km north of the Eyre Highway
> Eastern QLD

Fig. 6. Some example of various distance and direction markers, highlighted in red, as matched by our matching module. These segments provide important info for pinpointing a specific location within a broad geographical area (Color figure online).

that included multiple concatenated words, *e.g.* "#ChinaFlooding". The key issue here is the concatenation of the words which prevent our modules from detecting the location words [2]. To address this, these compound word tokens need to be segmented to decompose them into the constituent words. An example of this segmentation is shown in Fig. 7.

We attempt to address this issue by applying a word segmentation method. More specifically, we employ an approach based on language models, as described by [14]. Using this method a segmenter is built using unigram and bigram models of word frequency and attempts to find the word boundaries using a naive Bayes approach. We augment our language models with additional location information from GeoNames and other tokens that have been detected by our system.

We apply this method in our system to process hashtags and mentions before passing them to our detection modules. Some example segmentation results extracted from our data are shown in Fig. 8.

4.6   Caching

Optionally, the matched locations can be cached for faster lookups in processing future entries. There are many common location mentions that appear with great frequency and storing a cached mapping of NPs/hashtags/mentions to their particular location mentions can provide a significant improvement in processing large amounts of data.

5   Evaluation Method

Evaluation for this task is usually performed using the F1 score. This is a metric based on precision – the ratio of true positives (tp) to predicted positives (tp + fp) – and recall – the ratio of true positives to actual positives (tp + fn). The F1 metric is calculated as:

$$F1 = 2\frac{pr}{p+r} \quad \text{where} \quad p = \frac{tp}{tp+fp}, \quad r = \frac{tp}{tp+fn}$$

Here p refers to precision and r is a measure of recall.[8] Results that maximize both will receive a higher score since this measure weights both recall and

---

[8] See [4] for more details about these metrics.

Fig. 7. An example of applying word segmentation to a Twitter hashtag. The aim here is to find the perfect segmentation boundaries to recover the intended words in a concatenated hashtag. In this example the hashtag has been correctly segmented into the three words and it refers to a location.

```
eyrepeninsula  → eyre peninsula
southaustralia → south australia
sunshinecoast  → sunshine coast
774melbourne   → 774 melbourne
abcsouthqld    → abc south qld
livetrafficnsw → live traffic nsw
```

Fig. 8. Some examples of hashtags/mentions and their segmentations on the right. This is an important step in finding tokens that are location expressions, particularly those that are contained in tags with multiple words, such as "nsw".

precision equally. It is also the case that average results on both precision and recall will score higher than exceedingly high performance on measure but not the other.

Furthermore, the evaluation here is conducted on a per-token basis and partial location mentions are also included. This means for a text with a location mention "Northern Canada", annotating just "Canada" would receive a precision of $\frac{1}{1}$ and recall of $\frac{1}{2}$.

6   Experiment and Results

Our system was used to enter the Twitter Location Detection competition at the 2014 Australasian Language Technology Association (ALTA) Workshop [13]. We run our system on the test set of the data which contains $1,000$ tweets. The location annotations were not made available to us. Our described system achieved an F-score of 0.792 on the test set, ranking first among the shared task entries and winning the competition.

We believe that this is a good result which proves the efficacy of our proposed system in a demonstrable manner.

An analysis of our system results shown that all components contribute to the system. The GeoNames components is one of the most important modules and responsible for much of the performance.

We also want to emphasize the important of hashtag segmentation for this task; our results improved by around 0.05 through the addition of the compound word decomposition functionality, making it an important component.

7   Discussion and Conclusion

We presented a novel unsupervised approach for detecting location mentions in microblogs and social media texts.

A key contribution here is the definition of various location expression types and methods to detect them independently. The inclusion of hashtag segmentation was also found to be a key factor in maximizing performance.

There are a number of directions for future work. The application of lexical tweet normalization techniques could help improve the parsing results which could in turn improve the accuracy of our NP extraction.

Information from other services such as Yahoo BOSS Geo Services[9] could also be incorporated into the system. Data sourced from more granular gazetteers that include street-level information, such as OpenStreetMap[10] could help improve the accuracy of the location expression matching. This can help overcome some limitations of our address matching modules. The following tweet is a particular example which highlights a weakness of this module:

> "The road to **Easy Street** goes through the sewer. It is a **rough road** that leads to the heights of greatness."

Here the tokens in bold have been erroneously marked as location expressions, even though they are only figurative expressions. Having street level data could help reduce these false positives.

We also note that conducting a comprehensive error analysis could also provide to be a fruitful line of future inquiry. This analysis could provide valuable insights about the most common errors being committed by the current system — similar to the above example — thus helping guide future efforts in this area.

Displaying the locations on a map, in conjunction with an interactive system, is an interesting idea for future work which can help users find tweets pertaining to a specific geographic space. Such methods are also useful for visualization and can help find trends within the data.

Acknowledgments. We would like to thank our three anonymous reviewers for their valuable comments. The data and the task's original idea is from John Lingad's Honours project (The University of Sydney) co-supervised with Jie Yin (CSIRO). The shared task prize was sponsored by IBM Research.

---

[9] https://developer.yahoo.com/boss/geo/.
[10] http://www.openstreetmap.org/.

References

1. Ao, J., Zhang, P., Cao, Y.: Estimating the locations of emergency events from twitter streams. Procedia Comput. Sci. **31**, 731–739 (2014)
2. Berardi, G., Esuli, A., Marcheggiani, D., Sebastiani, F.: ISTI@ TREC microblog track 2011: exploring the use of hashtag segmentation and text quality ranking. In: TREC (2011)
3. Bollacker, K., Evans, C., Paritosh, P., Sturge, T., Taylor, J.: Freebase: a collaboratively created graph database for structuring human knowledge. In: Proceedings of the 2008 ACM SIGMOD International Conference on Management of Data, pp. 1247–1250. ACM (2008)
4. Grossman, D.A.: Information Retrieval: Algorithms and Heuristics, vol. 15. Springer, Dordrecht (2004)
5. Lingad, J., Karimi, S., Yin, J.: Location extraction from disaster-related microblogs. In: Proceedings of the 22nd International Conference on World Wide Web Companion, pp. 1017–1020. International World Wide Web Conferences Steering Committee (2013)
6. Liu, X., Zhang, S., Wei, F., Zhou, M.: Recognizing named entities in tweets. In: Proceedings of the 49th Annual Meeting of the Association for Computational Linguistics: Human Language Technologies, vol. 1, pp. 359–367. Association for Computational Linguistics (2011)
7. Mahmud, J., Nichols, J., Drews, C.: Where is this tweet from? inferring homelocations of twitter users. In: ICWSM (2012)
8. Malmasi, S., Cahill, A.: Measuring feature diversity in native language identification. In: Proceedings of the Tenth Workshop on Innovative Use of NLP for Building Educational Applications, pp. 49–55. Association for Computational Linguistics, Denver, June 2015. http://aclweb.org/anthology/W15-0606
9. Malmasi, S., Dras, M.: Chinese native language identification. In: Proceedings of the 14th Conference of the European Chapter of the Association for Computational Linguistics (EACL 2014), pp. 95–99. Association for Computational Linguistics, Gothenburg, April 2014. http://aclweb.org/anthology/E14-4019
10. Malmasi, S., Dras, M.: Large-scale native language identification with cross-corpus evaluation. In: Proceedings of NAACL-HLT 2015, pp. 1403–1409. Association for Computational Linguistics, Denver, June 2015. http://aclweb.org/anthology/N15-1160
11. Malmasi, S., Wong, S.M.J., Dras, M.: NLI shared task 2013: MQ submission. In: Proceedings of the Eighth Workshop on Innovative Use of NLP for Building Educational Applications, pp. 124–133. Association for Computational Linguistics, Atlanta, June 2013. http://www.aclweb.org/anthology/W13-1716
12. Middleton, S., Middleton, L., Modafferi, S.: Real-time crisis mapping of natural disasters using social media (2014)
13. Molla, D., Karimi, S.: Overview of the 2014 ALTA shared task: identifying expressions of locations in tweets. In: Proceedings of the Australasian Language Technology Workshop (ALTA), pp. 151, Melbourne, Australia (2014)
14. Norvig, P.: Natural language corpus data. In: Beautiful Data, pp. 219–242 (2009)
15. Núñez-Redó, M., Díaz, L., Gil, J., González, D., Huerta, J.: Discovery and integration of web 2.0 content into geospatial information infrastructures: a use case in wild fire monitoring. In: Tjoa, A.M., Quirchmayr, G., You, I., Xu, L. (eds.) ARES 2011. LNCS, vol. 6908, pp. 50–68. Springer, Heidelberg (2011)

16. Ritter, A., Clark, S., Etzioni, O., et al.: Named entity recognition in tweets: an experimental study. In: Proceedings of the Conference on Empirical Methods in Natural Language Processing, pp. 1524–1534. Association for Computational Linguistics (2011)
17. Tuten, T.L.: Advertising 2.0: social media marketing in a web 2.0 world. Greenwood Publishing Group, New York (2008)
18. Vieweg, S., Hughes, A.L., Starbird, K., Palen, L.: Microblogging during two natural hazards events: what twitter may contribute to situational awareness. In: Proceedings of the SIGCHI Conference on Human Factors in Computing Systems, pp. 1079–1088. ACM (2010)
19. Yin, J., Lampert, A., Cameron, M., Robinson, B., Power, R.: Using social media to enhance emergency situation awareness. IEEE Intell. Syst. 27(6), 52–59 (2012)

Recognizing and Normalizing Temporal Expressions in Indonesian Texts

Paramita Mirza[✉]

Fondazione Bruno Kessler, University of Trento, Trento, Italy
paramita@fbk.eu

Abstract. In this work we present a rule-based system for recognizing and normalizing temporal expressions in Indonesian documents. We adapt an existing temporal expression normalizer for English, TimeNorm, for Indonesian language. We then build a finite state transducer based on the crafted TimeNorm grammar for Indonesian, to recognize temporal expressions in texts. The system yields good results of 92.87 % F1-score and 85.26 % F1-score for recognizing and normalizing temporal expressions respectively.

Keywords: Temporal expression tagging · Temporal expression normalization · TIMEX3 · TimeML

1 Introduction

Research on temporal processing has been gaining a lot of attention from the NLP community in the recent years. The goal is to automatically extract temporal entities from texts in natural language. TimeML [1] annotation format is specifically designed for this purpose. The main goal is to automatically extract temporal entities to support a question answering system in answering temporally-based questions.

One of the main tasks in TempEval-3 [2], which is the most recent evaluation campaign in temporal and event processing, is the automatic extraction of temporal expressions. The task includes recognizing the extents of temporal expressions in TimeML documents and determining their types and values (normalization). Recognizing and normalizing temporal expressions is the crucial steps in order to time-stamp events and ordering events (in a timeline) with respect to one another.

For English, the current state-of-the-art temporal expression tagging systems achieve around 90 % F1-score (relaxed matching) and around 82 % F1-score (strict matching) for recognizing the extents, and around 81 % F1-score for normalizing the values of temporal expressions.

Unfortunately, there exists no temporal expression tagging system, which annotates documents in TimeML specification, for Indonesian language yet.

We propose a rule-based system for recognizing and normalizing temporal expressions for Indonesian documents. For normalizing temporal expressions,

© Springer Science+Business Media Singapore 2016
K. Hasida and A. Purwarianti (Eds.): PACLING 2015, CCIS 593, pp. 135–147, 2016.
DOI: 10.1007/978-981-10-0515-2_10

we extend an existing normalizer for English, TimeNorm [3]. We report some modifications of the tool required for Indonesian language, with respect to the different characteristics of Indonesian temporal expressions compared with English.

For recognizing (and determining the types of) temporal expressions, we build a finite state transducer heavily influenced by the crafted TimeNorm's time grammar for Indonesian. Even though it is shown that the machine learning approach can be as good as rule-engineering for recognizing temporal expressions, since there is no available Indonesian TimeML corpus yet, we resort to the rule-based approach. We believe that annotating sufficient data for the machine learning approach is more time-consuming than hand-crafting a transducer.

The evaluation is done on 25 news articles, containing 9,549 tokens (comparable with the TempEval-3 evaluation corpus with 9,833 tokens). The system yields 92.87 % F1-score in recognizing temporal expressions and 85.26 % F1-score in normalizing them.

2   Related Work

TempEval-3 [2], being the most recent shared task (with published results) focused on temporal and event processing, defined three main tasks:

1. Task A: Temporal expression extraction and normalization
2. Task B: Event extraction and classification
3. Task ABC: Annotating temporal relations (which entails performing tasks A and B)

The best performing systems participating in Task A can be perceived as the current state-of-the-art systems for the automatic extraction of temporal expressions in English documents.

For recognizing the extents of temporal expressions (including determining the types), the statistical-based system ClearTK [4] performed best at strict matching with 82.71 % F1-score, and the rule-based systems NavyTime [5], SUTime [6] and HeidelTime [7] performed best at relaxed matching with 90.32 %, 90.32 % and 90.3 % F1-scores respectively.

While rule-engineering and machine learning are equally good at the temporal expression recognition task, normalization is currently done best by rule-engineered systems. The best performing system for normalizing temporal expressions at TempEval-3 is HeidelTime [7] with 77.61 % F1-score. However, apart from TempEval-3, there are some other systems for the temporal expression normalization, such as TIMEN [8] and TimeNorm [3]. TimeNorm is shown to be better than HeidelTime and TIMEN for most evaluation corpora, specifically with 81.6 % F1-score on the TempEval-3 evaluation corpus [3].

Regarding multilinguality, HeidelTime is perhaps the temporal expression tagging system covering the most languages. HeidelTime currently understands documents in 11 languages, including English, German, Dutch, Vietnamese, Arabic, Spanish, Italian, French, Chinese, Russian, and Croatian. Unfortunately, Indonesian is not yet included.

The recent work on temporal expression tagging for Indonesian documents [9] only covers temporal expressions of DATE type. Moreover, the annotated documents are not in the TimeML annotation format, which is the widely used annotation format for temporal expression tagging. As far as we know, we are the first to implement a system for annotating temporal expressions in Indonesian documents with the TimeML format.

3   TimeML and TIMEX3 Annotation

TimeML [1] is a language specification for *events* and *temporal expressions*, which was developed in the context of TERQAS workshop[1] supported by the AQUAINT program. The main purpose is to identify and extract events and their temporal anchoring from a text, such that it can be used to support a question answering system in answering temporally-based questions like "In which year did Iraq finally pull out of Kuwait during the war in the 1990s?".

The design of TimeML is primarily based on the TIDES TIMEX2 annotation effort [10], which introduces a *value* attribute whose value is an ISO time representation of the ISO 8601 standard, and the temporal annotation language presented in Andrea Setzer's thesis [11].

There are four major data structures that are specified in TimeML: EVENT, TIMEX3, SIGNAL, and LINK. The EVENT tag is used to annotate a term for situations that *happen* or *occur*, or predicates describing *states* or *circumstances*. The TIMEX3 tag, which is compliant with the TIMEX2 tag in TIDES(02) guidelines [10] but introduces some more extensions, is used to annotate temporal expressions. The SIGNAL tag is used to annotate terms (typically function words) indicating how temporal entities are related to each other, e.g. *before*, *during*. Finally, one of the major innovations introduced in TimeML is the LINK tag, falling under three categories: *(i)* TLINK for specifying temporal relationships between two events or between an event and a temporal expression; *(ii)* SLINK for specifying subordinate relationships between events; and *(iii)* ALINK for representing relationships between an aspectual event and its argument event.

We are particularly interested in the TIMEX3 tag for annotating temporal expressions in texts. According to the TimeML Annotation Guidelines version 1.2.1 [12], the attributes (and the attribute values) for the TIMEX3 tag are defined as follows:

- *tid* (non-optional), a unique ID number to identify each TIMEX3 expression.
- *type* (non-optional), which can be DATE (e.g. *the summer of 1964*), DURATION (e.g. *24 h*), TIME (e.g. *half past noon*), or SET (e.g. *twice a week*).
- *value* (non-optional), which is exactly as specified in TIDES(02) [10] Sects. 3.2 and 3.3, adopting the ISO 8601 standard.
- *mod* (optional), representing modifiers such as APPROX (*about three years ago*), MID (*mid-February*), etc.

---

[1] http://www.timeml.org/site/terqas/index.html.

- *temporalFunction*, a binary value representing whether a temporal expression needs to be evaluated through a function (e.g. *last week*) or not (e.g. *Saturday, January 10, 2015*).
- *anchorTimeID* (optional), the *tid* of another temporal expression to which the TIMEX3 is temporally anchored.
- *functionInDocument*, which can be CREATION_TIME, MODIFICATION_TIME, PUBLICATION_TIME, RELEASE_TIME, RECEPTION_TIME, EXPIRATION_TIME or NONE.
- *beginPoint* and *endPoint*, which is used when a temporal expression of DURA-TION type is anchored by another temporal expression, hence, the value is the *tid* of the anchor.
- *quant* and *freq*, which is used when a temporal expression is of SET type, e.g. *3 days each week* (quant = EACH, freq = 3d).

In this work, we focus on annotating a TimeML document with TIMEX3 tags for temporal expressions, and completing the TIMEX3 tags with the non-optional attributes, i.e. *tid*, *type* and *value*.

4   Temporal Expression Tagging

The actual steps in temporal expression tagging are *(i)* recognizing the extent of a temporal expression, *(ii)* determining its type, then *(iii)* normalizing the temporal expression (resolving its value). However, during the development phase, we first develop the system to normalize temporal expressions based on an existing system for English. Then, based on the created time grammar, we develop a finite state transducer to do both recognizing temporal expressions' extents and determining their types in one step.

4.1   Normalizing Temporal Expressions

Temporal expressions in Indonesian language are quite similar with the ones in English. Therefore, for normalization, we decided to extend TimeNorm [3] to cover Indonesian temporal expressions. TimeNorm is a tool for normalizing temporal expressions based on a synchronous context free grammar, developed in Scala. Given an anchor time, TimeNorm parses time expressions and returns all possible normalized values of the expressions. A temporal expressions is parsed with an extended CYK+ algorithm, then converted to its normalized form by applying the operators recursively. The normalization value is determined as specified in TIDES(02).

The time grammar in TimeNorm, based on a synchronous context free grammar formalism, allows two trees (one in the source language and one in the target language) to be constructed simultaneously. Figure 1 shows a synchronous parse for *tiga hari yang lalu* [three days ago], where Fig. 1a is the source side (an Indonesian expression), Fig. 1b is the target side (a temporal operator expression), and the alignment is shown via subscripts.

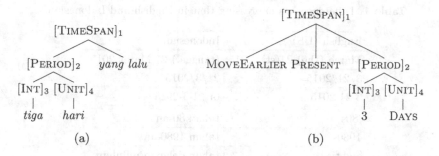

Fig. 1. The synchronous parse from (a) the source language *tiga hari yang lalu* [three days ago] to (b) the target formal time representation MoveEarlier(PRESENT, Simple(3, Days)). Subscripts on non-terminals indicate the alignment between the source and target parses.

Extending TimeNorm for a new language is very straightforward, we just need to translate the existing time grammar for English into Indonesian. However, there are some differences on expressing time in American English and Indonesian, as shown in Table 1; in particular the order of numbers in dates (e.g. *3/21/2015* vs *21/3/2015*) and the punctuations used (e.g. *5:30* vs *05.30*, *2.5* vs *2,5*). Therefore, several adjustments are required to cope with those differences, as well as to comply with the TIDES(02) standard:

- Dates are always in the Day-Month-Year order.
- Roman numerals are added since they are used in describing century (e.g. *abad XVII* [17th century]).
- The expression for time is written with dot (.) instead of colon (:), and the same applies for time duration.
- The 'am/pm' expression is not used since hours range from 0 to 24.
- Comma (,) is used as the decimal separator instead of dot (.).
- There is no distinction between plural and singular time units following quantifiers (e.g. *tahun* [year] denotes both *year* and *years*).
- There are three time zones in Indonesia, namely *WIB* (UTC+07:00), *WITA* (UTC+08:00) and *WIT* (UTC+09:00). In normalizing the temporal expression, we decided to ignore the time zones even though they are included in the extents.
- Indonesia has only two seasons, *musim hujan* [rainy season] and *musim kemarau* [dry season], which are not available in the standard. Hence, we normalize *musim hujan* and *musim kemarau* as Winter and Summer respectively.
- *Sore* and *petang* could mean both 'afternoon' and 'evening'. We decided to normalize *sore* as Afternoon, while *petang* as Evening.
- The 'DayOfWeek *malam*' [DayOfWeek night] expression, can also be expressed with '*malam* DayOfWeek-after', e.g. *malam Minggu* [night (of) Sunday] means *Sabtu malam* [Saturday night]. A special rule is needed to handle this case, which is quite similar with the rule for 'Christmas Eve' or 'New Year's Eve'.

Table 1. Differences on expressing time in English and Indonesian.

English (US)	Indonesian
March (the) 21(st), 2015	(tanggal) 21 Maret 2015
3/21/2015	21/3/2015
3-21-2015	or 21-3-2015
'80s	tahun 80-an
1980s	tahun 1980-an
eighties	tahun delapan puluhan
21st century	abad ke-21
	abad XXI
5:30 (am)	(pukul) 05.30
5:30 (pm)	(pukul) 17.30
1 h 34' 56"	1.34.56 jam
2.5 h	2,5 jam
a year	setahun
5 years	5 tahun
few years	beberapa tahun
years	bertahun-tahun

Apart from the grammar, there are several modifications of the TimeNorm code in order to support Indonesian temporal expressions:

- In Indonesian language, being an agglutinative language, some temporal expressions contain affixes. In the numerals, the prefix *se-* when attached to a UNIT (e.g. *tahun* [year]) or a PARTOFDAY (e.g. *pagi* [morning]) means one. Hence, *setahun* denotes a year and *sepagian* (with suffix -*an*) a whole morning. Moreover, to make a UNIT become plural, the prefix *ber-* is added to the reduplicated UNIT, e.g. *berjam-jam* [hours]. In order to have a concise grammar, we need to isolate the affixes from the root expressions before giving the temporal expressions to the parser.
- The term *minggu* is ambiguous, which could mean 'week' (a UNIT) or 'Sunday' (a DAYOFWEEK). However, as in English, a DAYOFWEEK is always capitalised. Therefore, we disambiguate the term according to this rule before giving it to the parser.

4.2   Recognizing Temporal Expressions and Determining the Types

Based on the time grammar for TimeNorm, we construct regular expression rules to label tokens with [INT], [UNIT] or [FIELD], e.g. *hari* → UNIT. The defined labels are as follows:

- [INT:NUMERAL], e.g. *satu* [one], *puluh* [(times) ten]
- [INT:DIGIT], e.g. *12*, *1,5*, *XVII* [17]

- [INT:ORDINAL], e.g. *ke-2* [2nd], *ketiga* [third], *ke XVII* [17th]
- [UNIT], e.g. *hari* [day], *musim* [season]
- [UNIT:DURATION], e.g. *setahun* [a year], *berjam-jam* [hours]
- [FIELD:YEAR], e.g. *'86, 2015*
- [FIELD:DECADE], e.g. *70-an* [70's], *limapuluhan* [fifties]
- [FIELD:TIME], e.g. *08.30, WIB*
- [FIELD:DATE], e.g. *10/01/2015*
- [FIELD:PARTOFDAY], e.g. *pagi* [morning]
- [FIELD:DAYOFWEEK], e.g. *Selasa* [Tuesday]
- [FIELD:MONTHOFYEAR], e.g. *Januari* [January]
- [FIELD:SEASONOFYEAR], e.g. *kemarau* [dry], *gugur* [autumn]
- [FIELD:NAMEDDAY], e.g. *Natal* [Christmas]

In expressing TIME and DATE, some tokens are commonly used preceding the temporal expression, which by themselves cannot be considered a temporal expression (e.g. *pukul 08.30* [08:30], *tanggal 10 Januari* [January 10]). Hence, we define labels for those tokens as follows:

- [PRE:TIME], i.e. *pukul*
- [PRE:DATE], i.e. *tanggal*

Apart from [INT], [UNIT] and [FIELD], some tokens can be considered a single temporal expression. Moreover, some tokens preceding or following [INT], [UNIT] and [FIELD] can be included in the temporal expression extent to further define the expression. Such tokens are labelled as follows:

- [DATE:SOLO], e.g. *dulu* [in the past], *kini* [now]
- [DATE:BEGIN], e.g. *masa* [period], *zaman* [times] (they are usually combined with other tokens, e.g. *masa lalu* [the past], *zaman sekarang* [nowadays])
- [DURATION:SOLO], e.g. *sebentar* [for a while]
- [QUANTIFIER], e.g. *beberapa* [a few]
- [MODIFIER], e.g. *sekitar* [around], *penghujung* [the end of]
- [CURRENT], e.g. *ini* [this], *sekarang* [now]
- [EARLIER], e.g. *kemarin* [yesterday], *lalu* [last]
- [LATER], e.g. *besok* [tomorrow], *mendatang* [next]
- [SET], e.g. *setiap* [each], *sehari-hari* [daily]

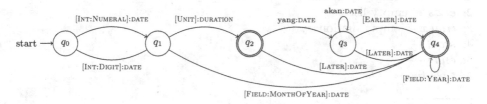

Fig. 2. Part of the FST's transition diagram used to recognize *tiga hari yang lalu* [three days ago] as a temporal expression of DATE type.

We then build a deterministic finite state transducer (FST) to recognize a temporal expression and to label it with one of the TIMEX3 types, i.e. DATE, DURATION, TIME and SET. We define the FST $T = (Q, \Sigma, \Gamma, \delta, \omega, q_0, F)$ such that:

- Q is a finite set of states;
- Σ as the *input alphabet* is a finite set of previously defined token labels $\{[\text{INT:NUMERAL}], [\text{INT:DIGIT}], ..., [\text{LATER}], [\text{SET}]\} \cup \{yang, ke, akan, dan\}$ (i.e. function words that are often used in temporal expressions);
- Γ as the *output alphabet* is a finite set of temporal expression types $\{$DATE, DURATION, TIME, SET$\}$;
- $\delta : Q \times \Sigma \rightarrow Q$ is the transition function;
- $\omega : Q \times \Sigma \rightarrow \Gamma$ is the output function;
- $q_0 \in Q$, is the start state;
- $F \subseteq Q$, is the set of final states;

Figure 2 shows a small part of the developed FST's transition diagram that is used to recognize the temporal expression *tiga hari yang lalu* [three days ago] as of DATE type, with *tiga* is initially labelled as [INT:NUMERAL], *hari* as [UNIT] and *lalu* as [EARLIER] using the regular expression rules.

We used *OpenFST*[2] to minimize the built FST, resulting in a deterministic FST with 26 states (of which 8 are final states) and 177 arcs. The complete FST is specified in a text file using the AT&T FSM format[3], and visualized as a transition diagram using OpenFST[4].

4.3 Temporal Expression Tagging System

Given a document in the TimeML annotation format, we first parse the document creation time (DCT) inside the DCT tag and the document content inside the TEXT tag. The content is further tokenized following a simple splitting rule with white-spaces and punctuations as delimiters, except for tokens containing digits (e.g. *08.30*, *'86*, *ke-2*, *70-an*, *10/01/2015*).

Given a list of tokens and the document creation time, the tagging algorithm goes as follows:

Input: list of tokens *tok*, DCT *dct*, FST *T*
Output: string *out* of text annotated with TIMEX3 tags
    Recognizing temporal expressions
1: *starts* ← empty dictionary
2: *ends* ← empty list
3: *timex* ← empty dictionary
4: *start* ← −1
5: *end* ← −1
6: *tmx_type* ← O

[2] http://www.openfst.org.
[3] http://github.com/paramitamirza/IndoTimex/blob/master/lib/fst/timex.fst.
[4] http://github.com/paramitamirza/IndoTimex/blob/master/lib/fst/timex.pdf.

```
 7: i ← 0
 8: while i < length of tok do
 9:     tlabel ← token label of tok[i] based on regex
10:     if start is −1 then
11:         if tlabel is in input labels of T.initial then
12:             start ← i
13:             (q, type) ← T.transition(q₀, tlabel)
14:             if q is in T.final then
15:                 end ← i
16:                 tmx_type ← type
17:             end if
18:         end if
19:     else
20:         if T.transition(q, tlabel) is not null then
21:             (q, type) ← T.transition(q, tlabel)
22:             if q is in T.final then
23:                 end ← i
24:                 tmx_type ← type
25:             end if
26:         else
27:             if start > −1 and end > −1 then
28:                 starts[start] ← tmx_type
29:                 Add end to ends
30:                 timex[start] ← tok[start...end]
31:             end if
32:             start ← −1
33:             end ← −1
34:             tmx_type ← O
35:         end if
36:     end if
37:     i ← i + 1
38: end while
    Normalizing temporal expressions
39: timex_norm ← empty dictionary
40: for key in timex do
41:     timex_norm[key] ← normalize(timex[key], dct)
42: end for
    TIMEX3 tagging
43: out ← empty string
44: tid ← 1
45: for i = 0 to length of tok do
46:     if i in keys of starts then
47:         timex_id ← tid
48:         timex_type ← starts[i]
49:         timex_value ← timex_norm[i]
```

50:      $out \leftarrow out$ + TIMEX3 opening tag (with $timex\_id$, $timex\_type$ and
          $timex\_value$) + $tok[i]$ + space
51:      $tid \leftarrow tid + 1$
52: **else if** i in $ends$ **then**
53:      $out \leftarrow out + tok[i]$ + TIMEX3 closing tag + space
54: **else**
55:      $out \leftarrow out + tok[i]$ + space
56: **end if**
57: **end for**
58: **return** out

The complete system, called *IndoTimex*[5], is implemented in Python and made available for download[6]. The system takes as input a TimeML document (or a collection of TimeML documents) and gives as output a TimeML document (or a collection of TimeML documents) annotated with temporal expressions (TIMEX3 tags).

Table 2. Corpora used in development and evaluation phases.

Corpus	# of docs	# of tokens
Development	50	17,026
Evaluation	25	9,549

5   Evaluation

5.1   Dataset

The dataset comprises 75 news articles taken from www.kompas.com, and is made available for download[7]. The preparation of the dataset includes cleaning the HTML files and converting the text into the TimeML document format. As shown in Table 2, during the development phase only 50 news articles are used to develop the time grammar and the transducer. The rest 25 articles are used for the evaluation phase.

5.2   Results

Table 3 shows the performance results of each task in temporal expression tagging, including temporal expression recognition and normalization. As there is no gold standard available yet for Indonesian TimeML, the results are obtained through manual observations.

There are 211 temporal expressions identified by our method in the evaluation data. With 189 correctly identified entities, 22 false positives and 7 false

---

[5] http://paramitamirza.ml/indotimex/.
[6] http://github.com/paramitamirza/IndoTimex.
[7] http://github.com/paramitamirza/IndoTimex/tree/master/dataset.

Table 3. Performance results on temporal expression recognition and normalization tasks on Indonesian documents, in terms of precision (P), recall(R), F1-score (F1) and accuracy (Acc).

Task	P	R	F1	Acc
Timex recognition	89.57 %	96.43 %	92.87 %	-
Timex normalization	88.04 %	82.65 %	85.26 %	85.71 %

negatives, the system yields 89.57 % precision, 96.43 % recall and 92.87 % F1-score.

Among the false positives, 11 entities which are actually flight numbers (e.g. *8501*) are tagged as DATE, while 5 entities which are part of a geographic coordinate (e.g. *08 derajat 50 menit 43 detik selatan* [08 degrees 50 minutes 43 seconds south] or *03.22.46 Lintang Selatan* [3° 22' 46" South]) are tagged as DURATION or TIME. There are 6 entities identified incorrectly due to the ambiguous nature of *dulu/dahulu*, which could mean 'in the past' or 'first' (as in "John wants to say goodbye *first* before leaving") depending on the context.

Registering an assumption on the reasonable maximum year number that could appear in a text (e.g. year 3000) will decrease the number of falsely extracted flight numbers (e.g. 8501) because it is in the same format as a year. It might also help to include temporal signals such as *pada* [on/at] or *selama* [during] in the transducer, to ensure that the following tokens are indeed temporal expressions.

We could also include in the transducer the expressions that can rule out the following tokens to be part of temporal expressions. For example, if we find *derajat* [degree], we can make sure that even though the following tokens are usually part of temporal expressions (i.e. *menit* [minutes] and *detik* [seconds]), the transducer will end up in a non-final state. The same strategy could be applied if the following tokens denote geographical directions such as *Lintang Selatan* [South] or *Bujur Timur* [East].

The false negatives include *esok hari* [tomorrow] and *setengah hari* [half a day], which are due to the incomplete transducer. Another cases are *jauh-jauh hari sebelumnya* [many days before] and *2–3 menit* [2–3 min], which are due to the incomplete regular expressions to recognize indefinite quantifiers for expressing durations (i.e. *jauh-jauh* [many] and 2–3).

In determining the temporal expression types (i.e. DATE, TIME, DURATION and SET), the system achieves a perfect accuracy. Meanwhile, for normalizing the correctly identified temporal expressions, the system achieves 85.71 % accuracy, resulting in 85.26 % F1-score.

Most incorrect cases in the normalization task are because of the wrong anchor time, since we always use the document creation time as the anchor time in resolving the values. For example, in the documents, the expressions *saat itu* [that moment] mostly refer to the previously mentioned temporal expressions of TIME type.

There are 3 temporal expressions of which TimeNorm failed to normalize, including *saat yang sama* [the same moment], *tanggal 24 kemarin* [24th yesterday] and *pukul 13.25 kemudian* [13:25 later].

6   Conclusion

We have developed a rule-based system for recognizing and normalizing temporal expressions in Indonesian documents. For recognizing temporal expressions, the built framework can be easily extended to accommodate other low resource languages, requiring only modifications of the regular expression rules and the finite state transducer.

Similarly, for normalizing temporal expressions, the adaptation of the existing tool for English, i.e. TimeNorm, is quite straightforward, with few modifications in order to deal with the characteristics of Indonesian temporal expressions.

Even though the system could still be improved, particularly by completing the regular expression rules and the finite state transducer for recognizing temporal expressions, the system achieves good results of 92.87 % F1-score and 85.26 % F1-score for recognizing and normalizing temporal expressions respectively.

For the future work, including temporal signals (e.g. *pada* [on/at], *selama* [during]) in the transducer to make sure that the following tokens are indeed part of temporal expressions, as well as including expressions that rule out the following or preceding tokens to be part of temporal expressions (e.g. *derajat* [degree], *Lintang Selatan* [South]), might be useful to reduce the number of false positives.

Furthermore, we could implement some strategies to select the correct anchor time for some temporal expressions, in order to correctly resolve their values. The best approximation would be to use the preceding temporal expressions of the same type (if any) as the anchor time.

References

1. Pustejovsky, J., Castaño, J., Ingria, R., Saurí, R., Gaizauskas, R., Setzer, A., Katz, G.: TimeML: robust specification of event and temporal expressions in text. In: Proceedings of the Fifth International Workshop on Computational Semantics (IWCS-5) (2003)
2. UzZaman, N., Llorens, H., Derczynski, L., Allen, J., Verhagen, M., Pustejovsky, J.: Semeval-2013 task 1: tempeval-3: evaluating time expressions, events, and temporal relations. In: Proceedings of the Seventh International Workshop on Semantic Evaluation, ser. SemEval 2013, Atlanta, Georgia, USA, pp. 1–9 (2013). http://www.aclweb.org/anthology/S13-2001
3. Bethard, S.: A synchronous context free grammar for time normalization. In: Proceedings of the 2013 Conference on Empirical Methods in Natural Language Processing, Seattle, Washington, USA, pp. 821–826 (2013). http://www.aclweb.org/anthology/D13-1078
4. Bethard, S.: Cleartk-timeml: a minimalist approach to tempeval 2013. In: Proceedings of the Seventh International Workshop on Semantic Evaluation, ser. SemEval 2013, Atlanta, Georgia, USA (2013). http://www.aclweb.org/anthology/S13-2002

5. Chambers, N.: Navytime: event and time ordering from raw text. In: Proceedings of the Seventh International Workshop on Semantic Evaluation, ser. SemEval 2013, Atlanta, Georgia, USA, pp. 73–77 (2013). http://www.aclweb.org/anthology/S13-2012
6. Chang, A.X., Manning, C.D.: SUTIME: a library for recognizing and normalizing time expressions. In: 8th International Conference on Language Resources and Evaluation (LREC 2012), May 2012. http://nlp.stanford.edu/pubs/lrec2012-sutime.pdf
7. Strötgen, J., Zell, J., Gertz, M.: Heideltime: tuning english and developing spanish resources for tempeval-3. In: Proceedings of the Seventh International Workshop on Semantic Evaluation, ser. SemEval 2013, Atlanta, Georgia, USA, pp. 15–19 (2013). http://www.aclweb.org/anthology/S13-2003
8. Llorens, H., Derczynski, L., Gaizauskas, R., Saquete, E.: Timen: an open temporal expression normalisation resource. In: Proceedings of the Eight International Conference on Language Resources and Evaluation (LREC 2012), Istanbul, Turkey (2012)
9. Simamora, A.: Temporal entity tagging untuk dokumen bahasa Indonesia (2013). http://repository.ipb.ac.id/handle/123456789/64661
10. Ferro, L., Mani, I., Sundheim, B., Wilson, G.: Tides temporal annotation guidelines. Version 1.0.2, MITRE Technical report, MTR 01W0000041 (2001)
11. Setzer, A.: Temporal information in newswire articles: an annotation scheme and corpus study (2001). http://www.andrea-setzer.org.uk/PAPERS/thesis.pdf
12. Saurí, R., Littman, J., Gaizauskas, R., Setzer, A., Pustejovsky, J.: TimeML Annotation Guidelines, Version 1.2.1 (2006)

Named Entity Recognizer Trainable from Partially Annotated Data

Tetsuro Sasada[1]([✉]), Shinsuke Mori[1], Tatsuya Kawahara[1], and Yoko Yamakata[2]

[1] Academic Center for Computing and Media Studies, Kyoto University,
Yoshidahonmachi, Sakyo-ku, Kyoto 606-8501, Japan
`sasada@ar.media.kyoto-u.ac.jp`, {`forest,kawahara`}`@i.kyoto-u.ac.jp`
[2] Graduate School of Informatics, Kyoto University, Yoshidahonmachi, Sakyo-ku,
Kyoto 606-8501, Japan
`yamakata@dl.kuis.kyoto-u.ac.jp`

Abstract. In this paper we propose a named entity recognizer (NER) which we can train from partially annotated data. As the natural language processing is getting to be applied to diverse texts, there arise high demands for the NER for new named entity (NE) definition in different domains. For these special NE definitions, only a small annotated corpus is available in the beginning, and a rapid and low-cost development of an NER is needed in practice. To satisfy the needs, we propose the use of partially annotated data, which is a set of sentences in which only a limited number of words are annotated with NE tags. Our NER method uses two-pass search for sequential labeling of NE tags: (1) enumerate NE tags with confidences for each word independently from the tags for other words and (2) the best NE tag sequence search referring to the tag-confidence pairs by CRFs. For the first-pass module, our method uses partially annotated data to improve the accuracy in the target domain. By this two-pass search framework, our method is expected to incorporate tag sequence statistics and to outperform state-of-the-art NERs based on a sequence labeling while keeping the high domain adaptability. We conducted several experiments comparing state-of-the-art NERs in various scenarios. The results showed that our method is effective both in the normal case and in adaptation cases.

Keywords: Partial annotation · Incomplete data · Named entity recognition · Pointwise prediction · Sequence labeling · Recipe

1 Introduction

One of the important natural language processing (NLP) is to recognize spans of words in a text corresponding to the real world and classify them into one of the classes defined in advance. In newspaper articles, which were the main target of NLP for long time, the classes are person names, company names, amount of money, etc. as defined in [5]. In the researches they are called named entities (NEs) and the task of automatically recognizing them is called the NE

© Springer Science+Business Media Singapore 2016
K. Hasida and A. Purwarianti (Eds.): PACLING 2015, CCIS 593, pp. 148–160, 2016.
DOI: 10.1007/978-981-10-0515-2_11

recognition (NER). NERs are useful for information retrieval from newspaper articles, question and answering about the world knowledge, and others. The NER task can be considered as a sequence labeling and tried many methods such as hidden markov model, conditional markov model, support vector machine (SVM) with dynamic programming (DP), conditional random fields (CRFs), etc. [3,7,12].

As the NLP is getting to be used more and more widely, the NER is applied to various texts in many languages. In addition, NLP users started to notice that task dependent definitions of NEs are useful for a special purpose instead of the general definition. Famous one is medical NE [1]. Obviously body part names, disease names, and protein names are important for information retrieval or text mining in medical texts. Nowadays there are many applications of NLP. For the reputation analysis of a company it is important to distinguish the product names of the company from those of its competitors. For recipe search it is important to recognize food name correctly in a certain context. For example, a recipe entitled "hamburger of steak house" is not a steak recipe. So we want to figure out that "steak" in this context is not a food. For these special NE definitions in the beginning only a small annotated corpus is available and a rapid and low cost development of an NER is called for.

In this background we propose an NER which we can train from partially annotated data. In NER case partially annotated data is a set of sentences in which only some words are annotated with NE tags and others are not. In practical cases they may be new NEs not appearing in a small fully annotated data. Our method is composed of two modules: (1) Enumerate NE tag with confidence for each word independently from the tags for other words and (2) NE tag sequence search referring to the tag-confidence pairs. We conducted several experiments comparing state-of-the-art NERs in various scenarios. The results showed that our method is effective both in the normal case and in adaptation cases.

2   Related Work

The task we solve in this paper is NER. NER is a sequence labeling problem and many solutions have been proposed [3, 21, *inter alia*]. To our best knowledge one of the state-of-the-art methods is based on CRFs [10]. In this method first they convert the training corpus annotated with NE tags into so-called extended BIO system. B, I, and O stand for begin, intermediate, and other, respectively. Let us assume that there are NE types T_1, T_2, ..., T_J, they annotate a word sequence w_1, w_2, ..., w_n of an NE of type T_j as w_1/T_j-B, w_2/T_j-I, $\cdots$, w_n/T_j-I and a word not included in any NE as w/O. In the BIO system, there are $2J+1$ tags and a word is annotated with one of them. The problem is similar to POS tagging which assign a grammatical category tag to each word, but in NER there are constraints on tag sequence. For example, $(w_i/O, w_{i+1}/T_j$-I$)$, $(w_i/T_j$-B$, w_{i+1}/T_k$-I$)$ and $(w_i/T_j$-I$, w_{i+1}/T_k$-I$)$ $(j \neq k)$, are illegal and we cannot interpret them. The NER based on CRFs automatically captures these constraints and outputs a legal sequence for an input word sequence. Some researches use a pointwise (PW) classifier such as a SVM or a logistic regression (LR) combined with a tag sequence search module based on dynamic programing (DP).

These NERs based on SVM+DP or LR+DP has an advantage that they can use a partially annotate data for training, in which only some words are annotated with BIO tags and many other words are not. This advantage is very beneficial especially in resource-poor situations such as NER for a new NE definition or a new language. As it is well known, the coverage has a strong relationship with the NER accuracy. And the trainability from partial annotations allows annotators to focus on new NEs or an active learning [4,22,23,25,26] to select annotation unit smaller than a sentence. These methods help us to build an NER for short time and lower cost. This advantage may also allow researchers to try to devise an NER method for using natural annotations like HTML tags in Wikipedia, which is a hot topic in the word segmentation research recently [11,30]. Our method extends these pointwise NERs with a reranker based on CRFs. Our BIO tag sequence search is more accurate than DP, so our method is expected to be better than the pointwise NERs without losing their advantage, trainability from partially annotate data.

As the input of our NER we assume a word sequence but not tagged with a part-of-speech (POS) tag. So when we apply our method to languages without obvious word boundary we need a word segmenter [18,24]. The reason why we do not assume POS tagger results is that some research has reported a severe degradation in the POS tagger accuracy on texts in a new domain [8]. By assuming a word sequence as the input, we can skip an adaptation of a POS tagger to the target domain. As a result we can avoid that an entire NLP system including our NER loses its domain adaptability in real use.

The domain in which we test our NER in the experiment is cooking recipe. In the past the main target of NLP was newspaper articles but nowadays NLP is used in various texts. For example, a special definition of NE for medical texts has been defined and medical NER had a great success [1,19]. Our application, recipe texts, is one of the user generated contents and have many potential applications ranging from researches to real uses: recipe search [29], procedural text understanding [13], computer vision [15,20], cooking robot [2], etc. The recipe NER has not been as mature as the medical NER and only small training data is available. So it is a good test bet for an NER trainable from various types of training data, which is important in resource-poor domain and/or language. The NER method which we propose in this paper is not limited to this domain but is applicable to others.

3   Recipe Named Entity

The test data we use in the experiment is named entity specially defined for recipe texts (r-NE) [14]. Their structure is the same as the general NE [5]. An r-NE is a span of one or more words without overlap. No NE boundary occurs in the middle of a word. So a word in a sentence belongs to at most one r-NE. An r-NE has one type

Table 1. r-NE tags.

r-NE tag	Meaning
F	Food
T	Tool
D	Duration
Q	Quantity
Ac	Action by the chef
Af	Action by foods
Sf	State of foods
St	State of tools

label listed in Table 1. So we can say that only the type definition is different from the general NE. The types for the general NE are designed to be useful for information retrieval from the newspaper articles. Contrary r-NE types are useful to recognize actions, objects, and their status in the recipe texts. They are important for recipe text search [29], its understanding [2], and symbol grounding for cooking videos [15, 20]. Similar to NER for the general NE, NER for r-NE can be formalized as a sequence labeling problem and many solutions for the general NE [3, 21, *inter alia*] are applicable.

The reason why we use r-NE instead of the general NE is that we want to solve a practical problem, in which some NLP application is under development and we want to increase the NER accuracy in a resource-poor situation. Our NER method is, however, applicable to the general NE and other NE such as medical NE etc.

4   2-Step Named Entity Recognition

The NER method which we propose in this paper is composed of two modules:

1. Enumerate BIO tag with confidence for each word independently from the tags for other words,
2. BIO tag sequence search referring to the tag-confidence pairs.

In this section we explain these one by one.

4.1   Tag-Confidence Pair Enumeration

Given an input word sequence, the first module provides pairs of a tag and its confidence for each word to the second module. In order to make this module trainable from partially annotated data, we propose to use a pointwise classifier which refers, as features, only to the information contained in the input word sequence but not to the estimation results (so-called dynamic features).

Table 2. Feature set of the LR.

Type	Feature templates
Character n-gram	$x^{-1}, x^{+1},$
	$x^{-2}x^{-1}, x^{-1}x^{+1}, x^{+1}x^{+2}$
	$x^{-2}x^{-1}x^{+1}, x^{-1}x^{+1}x^{+2}$
Character type n-gram	$c(x^{-1}), c(x^{+1}),$
	$c(x^{-2})c(x^{-1}), c(x^{-1})c(x^{+1}), c(x^{+1})c(x^{+2}),$
	$c(x^{-3})c(x^{-2})c(x^{-1}), c(x^{-2})c(x^{-1})c(x^{+1}),$
	$c(x^{-1})c(x^{+1})c(x^{+2}), c(x^{+1})c(x^{+2})c(x^{+3})$

Table 3. Feature set of the CRFs.

Type	Feature templates
Word n-gram	$w^{-1}, w^{+1},$
	$w^{-2}w^{-1}, w^{-1}w^{+1}, w^{+1}w^{+2}$
Word type n-gram	$c(w^{-1}), c(w^{+1}),$
	$c(w^{-2})c(w^{-1}), c(w^{-1})c(w^{+1}),$
	$c(w^{+1})c(w^{+2}),$
	$c(w^{-2})c(w^{-1})c(w^{+1}),$
	$c(w^{-1})c(w^{+1})c(w^{+2})$
Tag-confidence pair (LR+CRF only)	$\langle t_1, s_{i,1} \rangle, \langle t_2, s_{i,2} \rangle, \cdots, \langle t_{2J+1}, s_{i,2J+1} \rangle$

As it is clear from the above design, this module is trainable from partially annotated data, because we can just use only the annotated words and its context as the training data. The following example:

ex.) Sprinkle black/F-B pepper/F-I and salt,

where only two words are annotated with BIO tags, is converted into the training data as follows:

Left context	Word	Right context	Tag
$\langle BOS \rangle$	Sprinkle	black pepper	–
$\langle BOS \rangle$ Sprinkle	black	pepper and	F-B
Sprinkle black	pepper	and salt	F-I
black pepper	and	salt $\langle EOS \rangle$	–
pepper and	salt	$\langle EOS \rangle$	–

We train a pointwise classifier such as SVM or LR [6], which estimate the tag for a word.

$P_{LR}(t\|w)$	w				
	Sprinkle	black	pepper	and	salt
F-B	0.00	**0.40**	0.37	0.00	**0.80**
F-I	0.00	0.10	**0.63**	0.00	0.20
Ac-B	**0.99**	0.00	0.00	0.00	0.00
t Ac-I	0.01	0.00	0.00	0.00	0.00
T-B	0.00	0.50	0.00	0.00	0.00
$\vdots$	$\vdots$	$\vdots$	$\vdots$	$\vdots$	$\vdots$
O	0.00	0.00	0.00	**1.00**	0.00

Fig. 1. DP search for the most likely tag sequence.

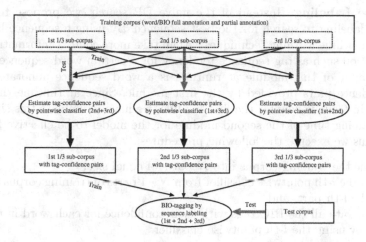

Fig. 2. Procedure for generating the training corpora for BIO tagging by the sequence labeling ($N = 3$).

At runtime, different from the normal classification task, the classifier enumerates all the possible tags and their confidence. As the confidence we can use the margin from the separation hyper-plain in the SVM case or probability in the LR case. In this paper we use an LR as the classifier and the confidence $s_{i,j}$ for each tag t_j for a word w_i in the context of $\boldsymbol{x}^-, w_i, \boldsymbol{x}^+$ is calculated as follows:

$$s_{i,j} = P_{LR}(t_j|\boldsymbol{x}^-, w_i, \boldsymbol{x}^+). \tag{1}$$

The features are listed in Table 2. $c(\cdot)$ is a function, which maps the character type of a word or a character (Chinese character, *hiragana*, Arabic number, etc.). So we have $(\langle t_1, s_{i,1}\rangle, \langle t_2, s_{i,2}\rangle, \cdots, \langle t_{2J+1}, s_{i,2J+1}\rangle)$, where $2J + 1$ is the size of the BIO tag set and $s_{i,j}$ is the confidence of BIO tag t_j for word w_i.

4.2 Search for the Best Sequence

The second module is to search the best tag sequence given a word sequence annotated with tag-confidence pairs provided by the first module.

DP Search. We can use a DP search to select the most likely tag sequence, where the likelihood can be defined the product of the probabilities as follows:

$$\hat{t}_1^m = \operatorname*{argmax}_{t_1, t_2, ..., t_m} \prod_{j=1}^{m} s_{i,j}. \tag{2}$$

Figure 1 illustrates this DP search. The numbers in the bold face indicate the selected node. In the search, we take the constraints on the BIO tag sequence into consideration. For example, as shown in Fig. 1, "black/T-B pepper/F-I" is illegal. This is one of the baselines and we test this in the experiments.

Sequence Labeling. Instead of the naive DP search, we propose to use a sequence labeling to search for the best sequence. By using a sequence labeling based on machine learning techniques we can take more context information into consideration such as tag sequence tendency for a certain word sequence, etc.

The input of this module at runtime is a word sequence annotated with tag-confidence pairs provided by the first module. Since at runtime the word sequence in focus is new for the first module, we have to emulate this situation at the training time of the second module for the model to be effective for new texts. Thus we execute the following procedures:

(i) Divide the training corpus into N parts of equal size,
(ii) Build the i-th pointwise classifier from $N-1$ parts of training corpus excluding the i-th part, and
(iii) Enumerate all the BIO tags with their confidence for each word in the i-th part by using the i-th pointwise classifier.

Figure 2 shows these procedures. As a result we can annotate the words in the training corpus with tag-confidence pairs $(\langle t_1, s_{i,1} \rangle, \langle t_2, s_{i,2} \rangle, \cdots, \langle t_{2J+1}, s_{i,2J+1} \rangle)$ estimated by a pointwise classifier built from training data not containing the words in focus[1]. That is to say, we can successfully emulate the runtime situation.

Now we are ready to train the second module. This part is formulated as a sequence labeling. The training data is a set of word sequences annotated with tag-confidence pairs provided by the first module. The training data is similar to Fig. 1 except that the correct tags for each word (label sequence) are attached in addition. As the sequence labeling we use CRFs [10], but we can use any other sequence labeling methods such as structured SVM [27]. Table 3 lists the features referred to by the second module. Note that in many NER researches POSs of the word in focus or in the context are also referred to as features, but we do not do it to keep the domain adaptability of our method in the entire system as we stated in Sect. 2. If we assumed the POS as the input, we would have to spend time and cost to adapt a POS tagger to the target domain in order to build a practically valuable NER system.

---

[1] We can also use so-called leaving-one-out technique [9], but it is computationally too costly because we have to build as many models as the number of words in the training data.

Table 4. Corpus specification.

Usage	#recipes	#sentences	#r-NEs	#words	#characters
Train	386	2,946	17,243	54,470	82,393
Test	50	371	1,996	6,072	9,167
(Total)	436	3,317	19,239	60,542	91,560

Table 5. Experimental settings about training corpus.

Training corpus set	#sentences	#r-NEs	#BIO tags
1/2 FULL	1,473	8,543	27,119
1/2 FULL + 1/2 PART	2,946	10,810	31,770
1/1 FULL	2,946	17,243	54,470

5 Evaluation

As evaluations of our NER, we measured the accuracies of our NER and other methods under various settings. In this section we present the results and evaluate our NER.

5.1 Experimental Settings

The domain in the experiments below is cooking recipe. The NE definition is described in Sect. 3 which is different from the general one for newspaper articles [5]. So we test our method mainly in a relatively resource-poor situation. The corpus we used is procedural text sentences fully annotated with r-NE [14]. Table 4 shows the specifications of the corpus. We see in this paper that the number of sentences, 2,946 + 371, is much smaller than the corpus annotated with general domain NE (normally more than 10,000 sentences). In addition the sentences tend to be much shorter than newspaper articles, thus the number of annotated NE instances is much smaller that the general NER case. For a detailed description about the NE definition and the corpus the readers may refer to [14].

In the experiments we divided the training data into two parts in order to test our NER and others simulating resource-poor situations, or the beginning of a project which NLP is applied to. The concrete settings are as follows:

- 1/2 FULL: The first half of training data is available as fully annotated corpus,
- 1/2 FULL + 1/2 PART: In addition to the first half, the second half is available as a partially annotated corpus,
- 1/1 FULL: The entire training data is available as fully annotated corpus, that is the training data size is twice as large as the 1/2 FULL case.

Table 5 shows the numbers of r-NEs and those of BIO tags in the above settings. In the partially annotated corpus, 1/2 PART, we emulated the situation

Table 6. Result:1/2 full annotaion corpus.

Method	BIO Accu.	Precision	Recall	F-measure
CRF	0.8949	0.8491	0.8372	0.8438
LR	0.8930	0.8441	0.8407	0.8424
LR+DP	0.8951	0.8397	0.8477	0.8437
LR+CRF (proposed)	**0.8989**	**0.8591**	0.8402	**0.8495**

Table 7. Result: 1/2 full and 1/2 partial annotaion corpus.

Method	BIO Accu.	Precision	Recall	F-measure
CRF	0.8990	0.8612	0.8452	0.8531
LR	0.8995	0.8559	0.8452	0.8505
LR+DP	0.9012	0.8539	0.8552	0.8546
LR+CRF (proposed)	**0.9112**	**0.8773**	**0.8632**	**0.8702**

where new r-NEs not contained in 1/2 FULL are annotated three times (if the frequency is less than 3, that number of times).

The methods we compared are as follows:

- **CRF:** Sequence labeling by conditional random fields trainable from partially annotated data [28],
- **LR:** Pointwise classification by a logistic regression [6] without DP search,
- **LR + DP:** LR with DP search,
- **LR + CRF:** LR with the best tag sequence search by conditional random fields trained from the fully annotate data only (proposed method; see Sect. 4).

In **LR + CRF**, we divided the fully annotate training into 3 to create the corpus containing sentences of words with tag-confidence pairs (see Sect. 4.2 and Fig. 2).

As the implementation of CRFs which we can train from partially annotated data [28] we used partial-crfsuite toolkit[2] [11]. As an LR classifier we adopt KyTea toolkit[3] [18]. Tables 2 and 3 show the feature sets of **CRF** and **LR**, respectively. The 2nd module of **LR + CRF** uses the tag-confidence pairs as features in addition.

5.2 Evaluation Criterion

We adopt two criteria. The first one is the tag accuracy, the percentage of the BIO tags correctly estimated by the NER system. The second is F-measure, which is the standard criterion for the NER task. The F-measure is the harmonic mean

---

[2] https://github.com/ExpResults/partial-crfsuite.
[3] http://www.phontron.com/kytea/.

Table 8. Result: 1/1 full annotaion corpus.

Method	BIO Accu.	Precision	Recall	F-measure
CRF	0.9065	0.8759	0.8627	0.8693
LR	0.9056	0.8713	0.8582	0.8647
LR+DP	0.9069	0.8696	0.8652	0.8674
LR+CRF (proposed)	**0.9157**	**0.8853**	**0.8742**	**0.8798**

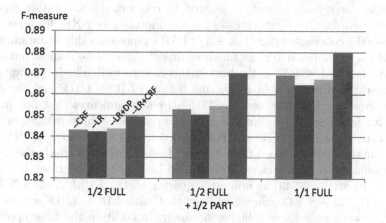

Fig. 3. NER accuracies.

of precision and recall. Let N_{sys}, N_{ref}, and N_{int} be the number of the estimated NEs, the gold standard NEs, and their intersection, respectively. Then precision $= N_{int}/N_{sys}$, recall $= N_{int}/N_{ref}$, and F-measure $= 2N_{int}/(N_{ref} + N_{sys})$, the harmonic mean of them.

5.3 Evaluation

We compared our method **LR + CRF** with three methods: **CRF**, **LR**, and **LR + DP** under three settings, 1/2 FULL, 1/2 FULL + 1/2 PART, and 1/1 FULL. Tables 6, 7, and 8 show the results. And Fig. 3 shows the F-measures of the same results in graph form. As we see in Fig. 3, the proposed method, **LR + CRF**, outperforms the other three methods, **CRF**, **LR**, and **LR + DP**) in all the cases. Below we discuss the results in detail.

When a large full annotation corpus is available, that is the case of Table 8, **CRF** is better than **LR**, and **LR + DP**. This is the reason why CRF is used as the state-of-the-art method for NER task in recent researches [16]. However, in case where the size of the full annotation corpus is small (Table 6) or a partially annotated corpus is available additionally (Table 7), **LR + DP** is better than **CRF**. **LR + DP** is simple and not so bad because the machine learning part is pointwise, not sequence labeling, thus its training time is much shorter than **CRF** especially when a partially annotated corpus is available. As we see in the paper [28], training CRF from a partially annotated corpus requires a number of iterations calculating the expected values of the possible tags for each words without annotation and the time needed for training tends to be long. Contrary **LR** is based on a pointwise classifier and we can train it for short time just by using the annotated words [17]. Thus we can say that in the beginning of an NE tagging project with a new NE definition, **LR + DP** is suitable allowing frequent model updates especially when use an active learning technique [18,23].

In real situations, we want to maximize the accuracy for a certain annotation cost. As we have pointed out, it is good to concentrate annotation work on informative words. One simple strategy is to annotate new r-NEs for a few times to increase the coverage. 1/2 FULL + 1/2 PART represents this situation, where new r-NEs are annotated at most for three times[4]. As we have pointed out above, our method, **LR + CRF**, is the best in this case as well. The important point is, however, the differences in F-measure between **LR + CRF** and the others are very large in this case (see Fig. 3). This result indicates that our method is effective for constructing an NE recognizer in real situations. Surprisingly Fig. 3 clearly shows that **LR + CRF** trained from 1/2 FULL + 1/2 PART is better than the others trained from 1/1 FULL. As shown in Table 5, the number of additional r-NE annotations for 1/2 FULL + 1/2 PART from 1/2 FULL $(2,267 = 10,810 - 8,543)$ is around a quarter of 1/1 FULL from 1/2 FULL $(8,700 = 17,243 - 8,543)$. So we can say that with **LR + CRF** we need less annotation work to achieve a higher accuracy. In addition the time needed for training **LR + CRF** from a partially annotated corpus is as short as **LR** and **LR + DP**, and much shorter than **CRF**, because we only need to update the first part, the pointwise classifier which is the same as those in **LR** and **LR + DP**. Therefore we can say that after development of a small fully annotated corpus it is a good strategy to annotate new NEs providing a partially annotated corpus and to use our method, **LR + CRF**, which is trained from that partially annotated corpus.

6   Conclusion

In this paper we have proposed a method for recognizing named entities. Our method is trainable from partially annotated data and we have experimentally shown that our method is better than extisting ones in both the situations where only fully annotated data is available and where partially annotated data is additionally available. Thus our method is useful not only for the normal setting but also for resource-poor domains and/or languages.

An interesting research direction is to try to improve NER by using partially annotated texts converted from wikipedia or other hyper texts. Active learning is another good research direction. Our method allows more flexible units to be annotated selection to make active learning more effective.

---

[4] This is a simulation and does not include real annotation work. An experiment with the real annotation time is a future work.

Acknowledgments. This work was supported by JSPS Grants-in-Aid for Scientific Research Grant, and JSPS Grant-in-Aid for Young Scientists Grant. We are grateful to the annotators for their contribution to the design of the guidelines and the annotation effort.

References

1. Ben Abacha, A., Zweigenbaum, P.: Medical entity recognition: a comparaison of semantic and statistical methods. In: Proceedings of BioNLP 2011 Workshop, pp. 56–64. Association for Computational Linguistics, Portland, June 2011. http://www.aclweb.org/anthology/W11-0207
2. Bollini, M., Tellex, S., Thompson, T., Roy, N., Rus, D.: Interpreting and executing recipes with a cooking robot. In: Desai, J.P., Dudek, G., Khatib, O., Kumar, V. (eds.) Experimental Robotics, Part VII. STAR, vol. 88, pp. 481–495. Springer, Heidelberg (2013)
3. Borthwick, A.: A Maximum Entropy Approach to Named Entity Recognition. Ph.D. thesis, New York University (1999)
4. Chan, Y.S., Ng, H.T.: Domain adaptation with active learning for word sense disambiguation. In: Proceedings of the 45th Annual Meeting of the Association for Computational Linguistics, pp. 49–56 (2007)
5. Chinchor, N.A.: Overview of muc-7/met-2. In: Proceedings of the Seventh Message Understanding Conference (1998)
6. Fan, R.E., Chang, K.W., Hsieh, C.J., Wang, X.R., Lin, C.J.: LIBLINEAR: a library for large linear classification. J. Mach. Learn. Res. **9**, 1871–1874 (2008)
7. Finkel, J.R., Grenager, T., Manning, C.: Incorporating non-local information into information extraction systems by gibbs sampling. In: Proceedings of the 43rd Annual Meeting of the Association for Computational Linguistics, pp. 363–370 (2005)
8. Kevin, G., Nathan, S., Brendan, O., Dipanjan, D., Daniel, M., Jacob, E., Michael, H., Dani, Y., Jeffrey, F., Smith, N.A.: Part-of-speech tagging for twitter: annotation, features, and experiments. In: Proceedings of the ARPA Workshop on Human Language Technology, pp. 42–47 (2011)
9. Kneser, R., Ney, H.: Improved clustering techniques for class-based statistical language modelling. In: Proceedings of the Third European Conference on Speech Communication and Technology, pp. 973–976 (1993)
10. Lafferty, J., McCallum, A., Pereira, F.: Conditional random fields: probabilistic models for segmenting and labeling sequence data. In: Proceedings of the Eighteenth ICML (2001)
11. Liu, Y., Zhang, Y., Che, W., Liu, T., Wu, F.: Domain adaptation for crf-based chinese word segmentation using free annotations. In: Proceedings of the 2014 Conference on Empirical Methods in Natural Language Processing, pp. 864–874 (2014)
12. McCallum, A., Li, W.: Early results for named entity recognition with conditional random fields, feature induction and web-enhanced lexicons. In: CoNLL 2003 (2003)
13. Momouchi, Y.: Control structures for actions in procedural texts and pt-chart. In: Proceedings of the Eighth International Conference on Computational Linguistics, pp. 108–114 (1980)

14. Mori, S., Maeta, H., Yamakata, Y., Sasada, T.: Flow graph corpus from recipe texts. In: Proceedings of the Nineth International Conference on Language Resources and Evaluation, pp. 2370–2377 (2014)
15. Naim, I., Song, Y.C., Liu, Q., Kautz, H., Luo, J., Gildea, D.: Unsupervised alignment of natural language instructions with video segments. In: Proceedings of the 28th National Conference on Artificial Intelligence (2014)
16. Neelakantan, A., Collins, M.: Learning dictionaries for named entity recognition using minimal supervision. In: Proceedings of the Fourteenth European Chapter of the Association for Computational Linguistics, pp. 452–461 (2014)
17. Neubig, G., Mori, S.: Word-based partial annotation for efficient corpus construction. In: Proceedings of the Seventh International Conference on Language Resources and Evaluation (2010)
18. Neubig, G., Nakata, Y., Mori, S.: Pointwise prediction for robust, adaptable japanese morphological analysis. In: Proceedings of the 49th Annual Meeting of the Association for Computational Linguistics, pp. 529–533 (2011)
19. Ratinov, L., Roth, D.: Design challenges and misconceptions in named entity recognition. In: Proceedings of the 13th Conference on Computational Natural Language Learning, pp. 147–155. Association for Computational Linguistics, Boulder, June 2009. http://www.aclweb.org/anthology/W09-1119
20. Rohrbach, M., Qiu, W., Titov, I., Thater, S., Pinkal, M., Schiele, B.: Translating video content to natural language descriptions. In: Proceedings of the 14th International Conference on Computer Vision (2013)
21. Sang, E.F.T.K., Meulder, F.D.: Introduction to the conll-2003 shared task: language-independent named entity recognition. In: Proceedings of the Seventh Conference on Computational Natural Language Learning, pp. 142–147 (2003)
22. Sassano, M.: An empirical study of active learning with support vector machines for japanese word segmentation. In: Proceedings of the 40th Annual Meeting of the Association for Computational Linguistics, pp. 505–512 (2002)
23. Settles, B., Craven, M., Friedland, L.: Active learning with real annotation costs. In: NIPS Workshop on Cost-Sensitive Learning (2008)
24. Sproat, R., Chang, N., Shih, C., Gale, W.: A stochastic finite-state word-segmentation algorithm for chinese. Comput. Linguist. 22(3), 377–404 (1996)
25. Tang, M., Luo, X., Roukos, S.: Active learning for statistical natural language parsing. In: Proceedings of the 40th Annual Meeting of the Association for Computational Linguistics, pp. 120–127 (2002)
26. Tomanek, K., Hahn, U.: Semi-supervised active learning for sequence labeling. In: Proceedings of the 47th Annual Meeting of the Association for Computational Linguistics, pp. 1039–1047 (2009)
27. Tsochantaridis, I., Joachims, T., Hofmann, T., Altun, Y.: Large margin methods for structured and interdependent output variables. Mach. Learn. 6, 1453–1484 (2005)
28. Tsuboi, Y., Kashima, H., Mori, S., Oda, H., Matsumoto, Y.: Training conditional random fields using incomplete annotations. In: Proceedings of the 22nd International Conference on Computational Linguistics (2008)
29. Wang, L., Li, Q., Li, N., Dong, G., Yang, Y.: Substructure similarity measurement in chinese recipes. In: Proceedings of the 17th International Conference on World Wide Web, pp. 978–988 (2008)
30. Yang, F., Vozila, P.: Semi-supervised chinese word segmentation using partial-label learning with conditional random fields. In: Proceedings of the 2014 Conference on Empirical Methods in Natural Language Processing, pp. 90–98 (2014)

Relation Extraction Using Semantic Information

Jian Xu, Qin Lu[✉], and Minglei Li

The Hong Kong Polytechnic University, Hung Hom, Hong Kong
{csjxu,csluqin,csmli}@comp.polyu.edu.hk

Abstract. Research works on relation extraction have put a lot of attention on finding features of surface text and syntactic patterns between entities. Much less work is done using semantically relevant features between entities because semantic information is difficult to identify without manual annotation. In this paper, we present a work for relation extraction using semantic information as we believe that semantic information is the most relevant and the least noisy for relation extraction. More specifically, we consider entity type matching as one of the additional feature because two entities of a relation must be confined to certain entity types. We further explore the use of trigger words which are semantically relevant to each relation type. Entity type matching controls the selective preference of arguments that participate in a relation. Trigger words add more positive evidences that are closely related to the target relations, which in turn help to reduce noisy data. To avoid manual annotation, we develop an automatic trigger word identification algorithm based on topic modeling techniques. Relation extraction is then carried out by incorporating these two types of semantic information in a graphical model along with other commonly used features. Performance evaluation shows that our relation extraction method is very effective, outperforming the state-of-the-art system on the CoNLL-2004 dataset by over 13 % in F-score and the baseline system without using these semantic information on Wikipedia data by over 12 %.

Keywords: Relation extraction · Semantic information · Trigger word · Entity type

1 Introduction

Relation extraction plays an important role in information acquisition from web text and such information can be useful in a wide range of applications such as Question Answering, bio-informatics etc. [12, 14, 16, 18]. Some algorithms use hand-written extraction patterns [1, 3, 7]. Others apply supervised methods, such as tree kernel methods [4, 21], maximum entropy model [8], and joint modeling approach [9, 18]. Unlike these supervised methods that rely heavily on annotated training data, distant supervision approaches are particularly attractive because supervised relation extractors can be learned from a large amount of facts in some available knowledge base [8, 15, 17]. Most feature selections for relation extraction focus more on lexical words in the context with additional features such as lexical order, word capitalization/place, syntactic patterns, POS tags and path of a parse tree between entities [5, 8, 9, 15, 17, 22]. Because of the difficulty in obtaining semantic information, much less work is done using semantically relevant features between entities.

© Springer Science+Business Media Singapore 2016
K. Hasida and A. Purwarianti (Eds.): PACLING 2015, CCIS 593, pp. 161–176, 2016.
DOI: 10.1007/978-981-10-0515-2_12

In this paper, we propose a relation extraction method using two pieces of simple semantic based information to improve relation extraction performance. The first semantic information requires that two entities in question must have matching entity types for a given relation type. The second is the presence of a set of trigger words (in lexical form) that are semantically relevant to a given relation type. To address the issue of manual annotation, trigger words are automatically learned through a topic modeling method for each relation type [2]. Relation extraction is then carried out using a graphical model that can add the proposed semantic information to an existing set of features. When no annotated training data is available, we use distant supervision based approach to obtain training data from some existing knowledge base.

The rest of this paper is organized as follows. Section 2 describes related works. Section 3 gives algorithm design. Section 4 is performance evaluation. Section 5 concludes this paper.

2   Related Works

Relation extraction targets at mining knowledge from free text. Relation in this paper refers to a semantic link between two entities of a given relation type. For example, Sibling is a relation type that can exist between two persons. Relation extraction refers to the analysis of text at the sentence level to identify the relation given in the text through the use of explicit text features and implicit knowledge through annotation or other means. Given an example of a running text:

"Mona Shaito is a Lebanese international fencer, who along with her brother Zain Shaito, will represent Lebanon in foil at the 2012 Olympic/Games held in London", it describes the Sibling relation between two entities whose name are "Mona Shaito" and "Zain Shaito", mentioned in the text. Note that the literal strings in the text, such as "Mona Shaito" and "Zain Shaito" are referred to as name mentions or entity mentions in relation extraction.

Different approaches have been proposed to extract relations between entities for certain relation types. Earlier systems are more likely to use hand crafted rules [1, 3, 7] which require a lot of expertise and often use very strict patterns. They have a generalization issue over heterogeneous data. Supervised approaches treat relation extraction as a classification problem [5, 9, 22]. Kambhatla [9] used a maximum entropy classifier with lexical and syntactic features including words and path of a parse tree between entities. Culotta, McCallum, and Betz [5] presented a conditional random field model to extract relations on biographical text using features such as neighboring words, syntactic information and hand crafted relation deductions (e.g., cousin = father's sister's son). To make use of the rich features to represent text data, kernels are used to define similarity between entities in a high dimensional space. Tree kernels and shortest path dependency kernels are designed to calculate similarity based on shallow parse tree of text and have been used with SVMs and Voted Perceptron to extract relations [4, 21].

These supervised methods work in a pipeline manner by extracting entities first and then predicting relations between entities. Another line of supervised methods jointly extract entity and relations. Kate and Mooney [10] took a joint approach to extract entities and relations simultaneously using a card-pyramid parsing technique. Features used include part-of-speech (POS) tags of words, context words, capitalization, suffix, and alphanumeric pattern of characters. Roth and Yih [19] used separate classifiers for entities and relations, and then compute a most likely globally consistent set of entities and relations using linear programming. Features used include capitalization, suffix, bigram, number of words and geo-names. The difficulty of these approaches lies in the fact that manually annotated data are expensive to obtain.

For this reason, distant supervision approach has attracted more attention in recent years because distant supervision makes use of relational facts in an existing knowledgebase so as to minimize annotation efforts [1, 8, 17]. In distant supervision based algorithms, relations of known types are first obtained from a knowledgebase such as Freebase[1]. Then, training data are automatically obtained by extracting sentences containing the relevant entity mentions from some reliable language resource such as Wikipedia articles. Lexical features, lexical order, and syntactic features of these extracted sentences are used to learn a model without any annotation. The main issue in the distant supervision approach is how to eliminate noises from a language resource to reduce the mismatch of automatically obtained training data to the truths in the knowledgebase used.

3   Algorithm Design

In this paper, we take the pipeline approach for relation extraction so we assume that entities and their entity types such as locations, person names, etc. are already available. The task is then to extract relations between entities of some given types. We propose a relation extraction method which makes use of two additional semantics based information to improve the performance of relation extraction. The first semantic information requires that the two entities in question to have matching entity types for a given relation type. For instance, for the Birthplace relation type, the first entity should be a Person and the second should be a Location. Since for each relation type, the matching of entity types is fixed and thus can be manually prepared as static knowledge to serve as a semantic feature.

The second semantic information is the presence of a set of trigger words (in lexical form) that are semantically relevant to a given relation type. Manual supply of a list of trigger words is ad-hoc and would be subjected to question on their relevance. A systematic approach is to develop an automatic method to extract trigger words for each given relation type.

3.1   LDA Based Trigger Word Extraction

In this work, we apply the Latent Dirichlet Allocation algorithm (LDA) used in topic modeling [2] to identify trigger words of a given set of relation types. The LDA originally works at the document level to capture topics through word co-occurrence patterns.

---

[1] http://www.freebase.com/.

It cannot be applied directly in relation extraction because training data are a collection of sentences and applying LDA at sentence level will suffer from data sparseness issue. To solve this problem, we randomly split n training sentences of a given relation type to m groups and aggregate the sentences in each group into one document. On the basis of m documents, the topic model using LDA is then trained to find the best topic for each document. The LDA algorithm will identify a ranked list of topics (each will contain a set of words associated with that topic). We then choose the most frequent top-ranked topic as the topic of the document set associated with one relation type.

Since there are different ways to group training sentences, for robustness reason, we introduce an algorithm parameter, MaxIter, to do random grouping MaxIter times to obtain MaxIter number of topics (and thus MaxIter groups of topic words). Among the different topics of the document set, only the most frequent appeared K topic words will be selected as the trigger words. Details of the algorithm are given as follows.

Input: n sentences for a relation type R, m (m≪n), i=1, MaxIter, l (l m), K

- Step 1: Randomly split n sentences into m groups
- Step 2: Aggregate sentences in m groups to form m documents
- Step 3: Train the LDA (l) model over m documents to identify the topic distribution for each document
- Step 4: Select the most frequent top-ranked topic Ti (and the TWordi topic words) among m documents
- Step 5: i++, if i < MaxIter, go back to Step 1

Output: Select the top K frequent topic words from TWord1 to TWordMaxIter

---

Given MaxIter as the algorithm parameter, the algorithm iterates from Step 1 to Step 5. Each time, the training data is randomly grouped before running the LDA Algorithm l is the LDA parameter that fixes the number of topics[2]. K is another algorithm parameter for selecting the total number of K trigger words.

Table 1 shows the trigger words automatically extracted for the five relations. These trigger words are informative and semantically relevant for their corresponding relations and can be used as features in relation extraction.

3.2   Relation Extraction by Graphical Model

The two semantic information entity type matching and relation-specific trigger words need to be incorporated into an existing relation extraction model. Generally speaking, to verify the usefulness of the semantic information, we can use different learning methods to see which learning method is more effective. In this work, we have conducted some experiments using different methods (as will be shown later in the experiment), and the conditional random field (CRF) using undirected probabilistic graphical model [10] gives the best result. So, we briefly introduce how the model works with the two additional semantic features added.

---

[2] Other parameters used in LDA are not listed here.

Table 1. Trigger word examples.

Relation type	Trigger words
Organization.founders	founded, founder, leader, ...
Organization.parent_child	subsidiary, acquisition,...
Organization.headquarter	headquarter, based,...
People.education	degree, professor, graduate, ...
People.sibling	brother, sister, younger, ...
Person.place_lived	living, moved, grew, residing, ...
Kill	assassin, shot, convicted, killing, ...

In a factor graph, factors are usually formulated as an exponential function of weighted features, that is, $\varphi(x, y) = \exp\left(\theta \cdot \overrightarrow{\mathbf{f}(x, y)}\right)$, where $\vec{\mathbf{f}}$ is a vector of feature functions and θ is a vector of model parameters, x is a list of features and y is a hidden variable. To incorporate semantic information into this model, we treat the general bias of the model towards a particular relation for two entities as factor φ_1 and the additional semantic information and their related observations as factor φ_2. The conditional probability distribution over these hidden and observation variables is defined as the product of φ_1 and φ_2, formulated by,

$$p\left(r_{ij} | x\right) \propto \varphi_1\left(m_i, m_j, r_{ij}\right) \varphi_2\left(m_i, m_j, t_i, t_j, w_{r_{ij}}, r_{ij}, x\right) \tag{1}$$

where, as a feature value, refers to the words before the first entity mention, after the second entity mention or between the two entity mentions; m_i and m_j are the ith and j^{th} entity mentions used by φ_1 and φ_2; t_i and t_j are the newly introduced entity types used in φ_2, and $w_{r_{ij}}$ are the newly introduced trigger words for relation r_{ij} in φ_2. To differentiate the triggers from other words used in the feature set, we concatenate the relation label with the trigger word, for example, *"professor"* + *employment_tenure*.

In this model, factor φ_1 assesses the general bias of the model towards a particular relation for two entities. Take this sentence for example, "Robert Rynasiewiez is a professor of Philosophy at Johns Hopkins University ...", "Robert Rynasiewics" and "Johns Hopkins University" should participate in the employment_tenure relation. It is defined over the relation variable r_{ij} and its corresponding entity mentions m_i and m_j, as formulated by,

$$\varphi_1(m_i, m_j, r_{ij}) = e^{\sum_k \lambda_k f_k(m_i, m_j, r_{ij})} \tag{2}$$

where λ_k is the weight for the kth feature function $f_k\left(m_i, m_j, r_{ij}\right)$. The following shows a feature function,

$$f_k(m_i, m_j, r_{ij}) = \begin{cases} 1, \text{if } r_{ij} = employment \text{ and } m_i = Robert\ Rynasiewics \\ 0, otherwise \end{cases} \tag{3}$$

This example feature returns 1 only if r_{ij} is employment_tenure and two entity mentions matches: "Robert Rynasiewics" and "Johns Hopkins University".

Factor φ_2 examines the compatibility between entity mentions, entity types and trigger words. It is defined by,

$$\varphi_2(m_i, m_j, t_i, t_j, w_{r_{ij}}, r_{ij}, x) = e^{\sum_l u_l g_l(m_i, m_j, t_i, t_j, w_{r_{ij}}, r_{ij}, x)} \tag{4}$$

where μ_1 is the weight for the lth feature function g_1. Here is an example feature function,

$$g_l(m_i, m_j, t_i, t_j, w_{r_{ij}}, r_{ij}, x) = \begin{cases} 1, & \text{if } r_{ij} = employment \text{ and } m_i.Type = PER \text{ and} \\ & m_j.Type = ORG \text{ and } tw = professor \text{ in } w_{r_{ij}} \\ 0, & otherwise \end{cases} \tag{5}$$

This feature fires when the first entity is a Person and the second entity is an Organization. And the word "professor" is a trigger for the target relation type.

Figure 1 shows some details of an instantiated factor graph for the employment_tenure relation between two entity mentions ("Robert Rynasiewicz" & "Johns Hopkins University"), their types (person and organization), and trigger word ("professor"). In general, the hidden variables encode various relationships among the entities: for example, r_{ij} indicates the most likely relation between two entity mentions m_i and m_j and.

In this model, factors φ_1 and φ_1 compute the inner product of the vectors of features (f_k, g_1) and parameters $(\{\lambda_k\}, \{\mu_1\})$. In the two factor templates, higher positive

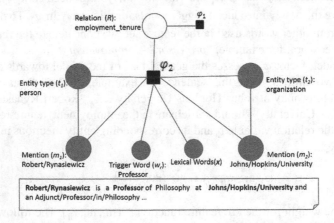

Fig. 1. Factor graph that measures the compatibility between entities, entity types and trigger words.

weights $\left(\lambda_k \text{ or } \mu_1\right)$ imply the corresponding features contribute more to the target relation whereas the negative weights will downgrade the contribution of the feature function for that relation.

Given these observation variables m_i, m_j, t_i, t_j and $w_{r_{ij}}$, the inference procedure is to compute the marginal distribution $p(r_{ij}|m_i, m_j, t_i, t_j, w_{r_{ij}})$ or find the most likely relation assignment

$$\hat{r} = \arg \max_{r_{ij}} p(r_{ij}|m_i, m_j, t_i, t_j, w_{r_{ij}}). \tag{6}$$

Maximum a posterior inference (MAP) is used to predict relations for a new pair of entities. In this task, Gibbs sampling is used. The Gibbs sampling method, as a Markov chain Monte Carlo algorithm, randomly selects a relation variable, r_{ij} and samples the relation value conditioned on all the remaining observation variables. At test time, the temperature of the sampler is decreased to find an approximation of the MAP estimate, thus assigning larger weights to higher probable relation variable.

The goal of learning is to find a configuration to the parameters $\Lambda = \left\{\lambda_k, \mu_l\right\}$ that yields the highest prediction for $\hat{r}$. However, learning parameters in complex factor graphs is a very challenging task because computing gradients requires inferences over the full dataset before the parameters are updated. The SampleRank method remedies this problem by performing parameter updates within each step of the MCMC inference [20]. It computes gradients between neighboring configurations in an MCMC chain. Parameters are updated when the model's ranking of any pair of neighboring configurations disagrees with the ranking by the objective function (the ground truth function). Suppose at the current time step t, we have the sample r_t and let the previous sample be $r_{(t-1)}$ at time step (t - 1) in the chain, a perceptron-style update of model parameters is taken in case of disagreement of objective function and model ranking,

$$\Lambda = \{\lambda_k, u_l\} \quad \hat{r} \quad t \quad r_t \quad r_{t-1} \quad t-1 \qquad \Lambda^t = \Lambda^{t-1} + \eta \left(\Phi\left(r_t, x\right) - \Phi\left(r_{t-1}, x\right)\right) \tag{7}$$

where $\emptyset: Y \times X \rightarrow \mathbb{R}^{|\Lambda|}$ refers to feature functions between relations and a sequence of inputs. η is the learning rate. In this work parameter estimation is done by running the SampleRank in Gibbs sampler using AdaGrad updates with Hamming loss [6].

4   Features

We now describe the set of features we use in this CRF based graphic model. For the factor φ_1, we used two features:

1. **Surface text of entity mentions,** for example, the person *"Robert Rynasiewics"*, we will have two surface features extracted: *Robert* and *Rynasiewics*.

2. **Part of speech of the entity mentions,** for the person "*Robert Rynasiewics*", entity mentions are labeled as NNP as their Part-of-Speech tag for "*Robert*" "*Ryna-siewics*" generated by the Stanford CoreNLP tool[3].

For the factor φ_2, we use the following features. Some features are semantic as new ones introduced by this paper and these new semantic features are marked by underscores.

1. **Entity type:** entity type feature, for example, "*London*" is a *Location*, "*Defense/ Ministry*" is an *Organization*, and "*Carlos/Santana*" is a *Person*.
2. **Trigger word:** we assign the corresponding relation to a trigger word, for example, we can have "*married*" linked to *person.marriage* and "*capital*" to *location.capital_of*, if they are in the sentences where the two entity mentions are located in.
3. **Entity type+trigger word:** we combine the entity type with trigger words. If a sentence with the two entities has trigger word (s), we will associate the entity types with the trigger word (s), for example, LOCATION + born, PERSON + brothers and so on.
4. **Entity mention+part of speech:** we link the entity mentions with their corresponding part of speeches, for example, Reagan + NNP and Normandy + NNP.
5. **First entity type+token+second entity type:** this feature allows one token in-between two entities and only entity types are used in order to have a wide coverage of entity mentions. This feature is introduced because we observe that in terms of the *location.capital_of* relationship, most of these sentences contain no trigger words such as "*capital*", yet these entities are separated by a token, such as a comma. Below is an example of a very common type of sentences:

Marc/Laurick, born August/20/,/1963 in Trenton, New/Jersey, is a Seattle-based bass player, songwriter, singer, and producer.

We can see that between "Trenton" and "New Jersey", there is the comma symbol and we know that "Trenton" is the capital city of "New Jersey". We have randomly sampled 500 sentences from the training data, and found that 301 (60.2 %) sentences are expressed in this way. For example, Austin, Texas; Warsaw, Poland; Harbin, Heilongjiang all have the pattern LOCATION_, _LOCATION and the first entities are capital cities of the second entities.

In CoNLL-2004 dataset, the Located_In relation between two locations is expressed in this way, for example,

It is roughly bounded by Ostined COMMA Lesny and Liberec in Czechoslovakia and Gmund in Austria.

Moreover, this feature will cover the pattern LOCATION_[in/at]_ LOCATION in which the prepositions can be inserted between two entities. "Liberec in Czechoslovakia" is an example.

6. **Context features:** we use the contextual features around the entity mentions, cases are:

---

[3] http://nlp.stanford.edu/software/corenlp.shtml.

Tokens or POS tags before the first entity
Tokens or POS tags after the second entity
Tokens or POS tag between the first and second entities
Examples for contextual features can be,
real, JJ; acquired, VBN
Attacks, NNS; Database, NNP; begin, VB

In addition to these features, we also use the regular expression patterns for the context tokens between two entities, before the first entity and after the second entity. They are prefixes, punctuations, all capitals.

7. **Distance value:** we employ the distance value between two entities. Distance between entities is an integer. For these distance features, we apply a method to bin the features and convert them into categorical values.

It is noteworthy that we did not incorporate parsing features in our model. In other words, we did not use the dependency path features which are used in previous researches [8, 15, 17].

Regular Expression feature: we also use the regular expression patterns for the context tokens between two entities, before the first entity and after the second entity. They are given in Table 2 below.

Table 2. Regular expression features

Features	Regular expressions
All capitals	Token matches [A–Z]+
Numeric number	Token matches [0–9]+
Punctuation	Token matches [-,\\.;:?!()]+
Prefix	Length of token prefix is 3

Table 3. Evaluation of individual semantic information on the CoNLL-2004 dataset

Systems	P (%)	R (%)	F (%)
PolyU14 $_{-ET-TW}$	59.46	73.84	65.59
PolyU14 $_{+ET-TW}$	64.25	79.73	70.92
PolyU14 $_{-ET+TW}$	69.67	76.77	72.81
PolyU14 $_{+ET+TW}$	76.46	83.31	79.49

5   Performance Evaluation

For evaluation, experiments are conducted on two datasets: (1) CoNLL-2004[4] with 7,254 sentences from the TREC corpus; (2) Wikipedia Data from 1.052 million sentences extracted based on relation facts in Freebase. Precision (**P**), recall (**R**) and a harmonic mean F-score (**F**) are used as performance measures.

For trigger word identification, we set m = 20 for CoNLL-2004 and m = 50 for Wikipedia data because Wikipedia dataset is much larger. The number of topics used in LDA is l = 50[5]. To generate a robust set of trigger words, we use MaxIter = 20. We then take K = 10 to extract only 10 trigger words for each relation type. To predict relations using the graphical model, we rank the test examples by sampling 20 iterations with a low temperature of 0.0001 in the Gibbs sampler using the Factorie tool [13].

5.1   Evaluation on CoNLL-2004 Dataset

In the CoNLL-2004 dataset, five relations are given: Located_In (406), Work_For (394), OrgBased_In (451), Live_In (521) and Kill (268). The average number of sentences per relation is 408. For a sentence that does not contain any of the five predefined relations, we introduce an additional relation NONE. We then run 5-fold stratified cross-validations for each relation.

The first experiment is to examine the individual contribution of the two types of semantic information. The results are shown in Table 3. Our proposed algorithm is labeled as PolyU14 and we use the subscripts ET and TW to indicate the use of Entity Type and Trigger Words as features. The positive (+) sign and the negative (–) sign indicate if such features are being used or not. The baseline system, PolyU14 – ET – TW, uses all the features listed in Sect. 4 except those four features marked by underscores because they are related to the additional two types of semantic information in our work. These are very common features used in other works too. Table 3 shows that the combination of the entity type and the trigger words gives the best overall performance. Note that the use of any single semantic information can improve both the precision and recall. But their effect on precision and recall are slightly different. Among the three variations, the use of trigger words (PolyU14 – ET + TW) has a larger increase in precision (10.21 %), and the use of Entity type (PolyU14 + ET – TW) has a larger increase to recall (5.89 %). It should also be noted that these two types of semantic information are not closely correlated, and are thus quite complementary to each other because PolyU14 + ET + TW gives 21.19 % improvement in F-score, much better than the use of a single type of information.

---

[4]   http://cogcomp.cs.illinois.edu/Data/ER/conll04.corp.
[5]   Other parameter values of LDA are $\alpha = 0.1$, $\beta = 0.1$ with 100 iterations.

Table 4. Performance for overall system and indivial five relations

Systems	Overall			Located_In			Work_For			OrgBased_In			Live_In			Kill		
	P	R	F	P	R	F	P	R	F	P	R	F	P	R	F	P	R	F
RY07 Pipeline	64.60	54.88	57.24	52.50	56.40	50.70	60.80	44.40	51.20	77.80	42.10	54.30	58.90	50.00	53.50	73.00	81.50	76.50
RY07 Joint	68.46	54.02	58.14	53.90	55.70	51.30	72.00	42.30	53.10	**79.80**	41.60	54.30	59.10	49.00	53.00	77.50	81.50	79.00
KM10 Pipeline	75.08	60.20	66.28	71.50	57.00	62.30	**74.10**	66.00	69.70	70.60	60.20	64.60	68.10	56.60	61.70	91.10	61.20	73.10
KM10 Joint	73.04	62.66	66.36	67.50	56.70	58.30	73.50	68.30	70.70	66.20	64.10	64.70	66.40	60.10	62.90	91.60	64.10	75.20
PolyU14	**76.46**	**83.31**	**79.49**	58.04	**73.64**	**64.68**	71.10	**78.07**	**74.31**	79.74	**83.83**	**81.54**	**81.70**	**88.10**	**84.75**	**91.74**	**92.91**	**92.17**

To compare to other systems, we made a detailed listing of our work with two other state-of-art systems in Table 3. The first reference system is by Roth and Yih [18], labeled as RY07 Pipeline and RY07 Joint, respectively. The second reference system is by Kate and Mooney [9], labeled as KM10 Pipeline and KM10 Joint, respectively.

Table 4 shows both the overall system performance as well as that of the individual relation types. Table 4 shows that PolyU14 has the best performance achieving 79.49 % average F-score, an increase of 13.13 % when compared to the state-of-the-art system KM10 Joint (66.36 %) which translates to an improvement of 19.8 %. A more detailed examination shows that our algorithm can give cross-the-board improvement in recall. However, precision is improved in only two relation types: Kill and Live_In. Through the analysis of data, we find that entity type matching is more related to recall and trigger words are more related to precision. By examining the automatically extracted trigger words, we find that trigger words for Kill are: "assassination", "death", "killing" etc., and for Live_In are: "native", "home", "born" etc. These trigger words are quite relevant and specific enough to the corresponding relation types. But, for the Located_In relation, the trigger words such as "officials", "government", "state" etc., do seem to be more general words, and their relevance to Located_In is not as specific to this particular

Table 5. Relation types on wikipedia data

Person.birthplace	Person.deathplace
Person.sibling	Person.place_lived
Organization.parent_child	Person.marriage
Person.parents_children	Person.education
Organization.founders	Person.nationality
Organization.headquarters	Location.capital_of
Administrative_divisions	Employment_tenure
Organization.membership	Location.contains
Location.partially_contains	Location.neighborhood

relation type. Similarly, it is harder to find relation specific trigger words for the Work_For and OrgBased_In relations. Take the Located_In relation for example and take the following testing data:

"Officials in Perugia in Umbria province said five people were arrested there Tuesday night after police stopped their car and found 1 million in bogus bills in trunk".

The relation Located_In ("Perugia", "Umbria") is not explicitly expressed with a preposition in.

5.2 Evaluation on Wikipedia Dataset

Supervised methods for relation extraction need human tagged training data, which is costly and labor intensive. To examine how our system can be applied to automatically obtain training data as what was done in [8, 15, 17], we also take distant supervised approach to obtain labeled training and testing data automatically using facts from Freebase. We use a snapshot of Freebase dated June 23, 2013. Out of the 27,538 relations, we took the 39 most frequent relations from Freebase, and mapped them into 18 predefined relation types as listed in Table 5. This additional mapping process is needed because some of the relation types in Freebase are equivalent. Others might simply be variations of the same relation due to rotation of the entities.

To find the training sentences, we use the Wikipedia dump of April 03, 2013. Out of the 4,064,234 articles from this dump, we use the Stanford CoreNLP tool to preprocess articles including POS tagging, named entity recognition. Then we associate these mentions with Freebase entities by simple string matching and then extract sentences containing entity mentions sharing a relation in Freebase to obtain a total of 1.052 million sentences. The extracted data is split into separate training and testing sets with a ratio at about 2.33. To evaluate the performance without annotated gold answers, we made the assumption that all facts in Freebase are correct; the training data extracted using these facts are correct and correspond to the relational facts in Freebase similar to what are done in other works [8, 15, 17][6].

Table 6. Evaluation of individual semantic information on wikipedia data

Systems	P (%)	R (%)	F (%)
PolyU14$_{-ET-TW}$	84.95	80.64	82.32
PolyU14$_{+ET-TW}$	87.69	84.34	85.69
PolyU14$_{-ET+TW}$	91.88	89.08	90.31
PolyU14$_{+ET+TW}$	**95.82**	**94.29**	**95.00**

Table 6 shows the performance evaluation of these 18 relation types showing the different use of the two types of semantic information. Comparing to the baseline system

---

[6] To test this hypothesis, we manually examined 100 actual sentences for each relation type and found the margin of error to be within 15 %.

PolyU14 – ET – TW, using either entity type information (PolyU14 + ET – TW) alone or trigger words (PolyU14 – ET + TW) alone can improve both precision and call. Unlike the CoNLL-2004 dataset, where trigger words contribute more to precision improvement and entity type contributes more to recall. Trigger words give the best improvement for both precision and recall. In other words, trigger words are more effective as a single semantic feature for this dataset. Compared to CoNLL-2004 where triggers words are only extracted from about 7 K sentences, this dataset has more than one million sentences as training data, and thus the trigger words extracted for each relation type are more relevant. For example, "based", "headquarters", "headquartered" are extracted for the Organization.headquarters relation; "son", "daughter", "father" are detected for the Person.parents_children relation; "founded", "founder" are learned for the Organization.founders relation and so on. It should be noted that we did not include the performance of any systems which also used the same type of resources under the distant supervision approach [8, 15, 17]. Even though our performance is better compared to their works in the literature using similar approaches, it is not fair to compare with them because distant supervision relies on knowledge base which is evolved over time and Freebase now contains more facts than it had in 2009 where the previous works were based on.

Note that in the evaluation of Wikipedia data, we have not included the NONE class as what is done for the CoNLL-2004 data. This is because some of the relation that exists in Wikipedia may not be covered in Freebase. So the NONE result may not mean the relation does not exist. Take the following sentences in Wikipedia as examples:

"Wierzyca/Pelpin is a football club based in Pepin, Poland.",

"He also had a daughter Chrysie, who married Dardanus and brought the Palladium to Troy.",

"Grayven is the third son of Darkled, born of an unknown mother, younger brother to Kalibak and Orion",

The three relations Organization.headquarters, Person.marriage, and Person.parents_children do hold. But Freebase contains no record for these relation instances.

We also found that training sentences in Wikipedia may contain relations of two or more types. But our algorithm can only select one relation type. Take a look at the following example:

Table 7. Probability rankings for an entity pair

Rank	Relation type	Probability
1	Organization.founders	0.6866
2	Busness.employment_tenure	0.3128
3	Person.education	5.25E-4

Table 8. Comparison of classifiers on CoNLL-2014 dan wikipedia data

CoNLL-2004 Data

Systems	Without SemInfo			With SemInfo		
	P(%)	R(%)	F(%)	P(%)	R(%)	F(%)
NB	44.40	63.83	52.37	59.06	78.54	67.42
KNN	51.61	48.62	50.07	66.84	55.48	60.63
VP	54.11	51.71	52.88	74.44	72.82	73.63
SVM	74.29	40.75	52.63	93.30	65.64	77.07
PolyU14	59.46	**73.84**	**65.59**	76.46	**83.31**	**79.49**

Wikipedia Data

Systems	Without SemInfo			With SemInfo		
	P(%)	R(%)	F(%)	P(%)	R(%)	F(%)
NB	57.01	60.13	58.53	77.20	78.13	77.66
KNN	72.29	60.13	65.65	86.48	75.87	80.83
VP	85.46	74.21	79.44	93.97	91.69	92.82
SVM	77.69	63.42	69.83	90.65	82.70	86.49
PolyU14	**84.95**	**80.64**	**82.32**	**95.82**	**94.29**	**95.00**

"It is known for the involvement of Gulfstream Aerospace founder Allen Paulson, who was CEO from 1994 to 2000, and former Chrysler chairman Lee Iacocca, who has been a major investor in the company since 1995".

This sentence contains the Organization.founders relation because "Allen Paulson" is the founder of the "Gulfstream Aerospace" organization; it also contains the Business. employment_tenure relation because of the trigger word "CEO" after the second argument "Allen Paulson". In other words, if you look at an entity pair, they have different probabilistic distribution over different relation types. Table 7 shows the probability rankings for the entity pair (Gulfstream Aerospace, Allen Paulson).

Among the 18 relation types, we found that the second relation Business.employment_tenure has a high enough probability that we cannot ignore. However, in our current system, only the top ranked relation will be identified as the result. Investigation in the future can be explored to identify multiple relations at sentence level.

5.3   Comparison with Other Learning Methods

To evaluate the effectiveness of our graphical model as machine learning method with respect to the use of the two semantic information, we also show in Table 8 and the results of several commonly used learning algorithms: Naive Bayesian classifier (NB), K-Nearest Neighbors (KNN, K = 5 in this paper), Voted Perceptron (VP, iterations = 500) implemented in the Weka tool[7], multiclass Support Vector Machines (SVM)[8] with default parameters on the CoNLL-2004 data. The first group of data on the left column does not use any of the semantic information proposed in this work. So, the performance results on the left serve as the baseline for comparison. The basic sets of features are stemmed word surface form, part-of-speech of words, word prefix, capitalization, punctuation or numerical value of a word.

In Table 8, we evaluate the use of semantic features using different classifiers. We can see that all classifiers have shown quite significant improvement in both precision and recall when the two types of semantic information (SemInfo) are used. This further

---

[7] http://www.cs.waikato.ac.nz/ml/weka/.
[8] http://www.cs.cornell.edu/people/tj/svm_light/svm_multiclass.html.

confirms that these two semantic features are effective. Out of the five classifiers, NB has no algorithm parameter, and its performance is the worst. Among the four learning algorithms which require parameter tuning, our system, PolyU14, which uses the graphical model, outperforms all the other three classifiers in F-scores. Furthermore, relation extraction using the graphical model is a good fit to model relations between two entities because the additional semantic information can be easily incorporated into the model and parameter learning allows it to make good use of different features and to capture the correlations between latent and observable variables in an explicit fashion.

6   Conclusion and Future Works

In this paper, we present a novel approach to improve relation extraction using two additional semantic features of entity type matching and trigger words in a graphical model. Entity type matching controls the selective preference of arguments that participate in a relation. Trigger words add more positive evidences that are closely related to target relations, which in turn help to reduce noisy data. In the evaluation of the CoNLL-2004 dataset, we obtained a 79.49 % average F-score, an increase of 13.13 % compared to the state-of-the-art system. In the evaluation of Wikipedia data, we obtained a 95 % average F-score, an increase of 12.68 % compared to the baseline system.

A major advantage of our approach is its extensibility because trigger words from any domain can be learned automatically and be added into the graphical model for various relation types. This is particularly effective in distant supervision based relation extraction which extracts relations from a large knowledgebase. Our approach, however, is currently restricted to only the three major entity types. The extension to other entity types, for example Date, Movie Names, etc., can be very helpful in extracting date/time for a person's activity (birthdate, death date or date of marriage), and also extending relations that can help answer more type of internet queries.

References

1. Banko, M., Cafarella, M. J., Soderland, S., Broadhead, M., Etzioni, O.: Open information extraction from the web. In: Proceedings of the 20th International Joint Conference on Artifical Intelligence, pp. 2670–2676 (2007)
2. Blei, D., Ng, A., Jordan, M.: Latent Dirichlet Allocation. J. Mach. Learn. Res. **3**, 993–1022 (2003)
3. Brin, S.: Extracting patterns and relations from the world wide web. In: Atzeni, P., Mendelzon, A.O., Mecca, G. (eds.) WebDB 1998. LNCS, vol. 1590, pp. 172–183. Springer, Heidelberg (1999)
4. Bunescu, R., Mooney, R.J.: A shortest path dependency kernel for relation extraction. In: Proceedings of the Conference on HLT-EMNLP, pp. 724–731 (2005a)
5. Culotta, A., McCallum, A., Betz, J.: Integrating probabilistic extraction models and data mining to discover relations and patterns in text. In: Proceedings of the main Conference on Human Language Technology Conference of the North American Chapter of the Association of Computational Linguistics, pp. 296–303 (2006)

6. Duchi, J., Hazan, E., Singer, Y.: Adaptive subgradient methods for online learning and stochastic optimization. J. Mach. Learn. Res. **12**, 2121–2159 (2011)
7. Etzioni, O., Cafarella, M., Downey, D., Popescu, A.M., Shaked, T., Soderland, S., Weld, D.S., Yates, A.: Unsupervised named-entity extraction from the web: an experimental study. Artif. Intell. **165**(1), 91–134 (2005)
8. Hoffmann, R., Zhang, C., Ling, X., Zettlemoyer, L., Weld, D.S.: Knowledge-based weak supervision for information extraction of overlapping relations. In: Annual Meeting of the Association for Computational Linguistics (ACL), pp. 541–550 (2011)
9. Kambhatla, N.: Combining lexical, syntactic, and semantic features with maximum entropy models for extracting relations. In: Proceedings of the ACL 2004 (2004)
10. Kate, R.J., Mooney, R.J.: Joint entity and relation extraction using card-pyramid parsing. In: Proceedings of the Fourteenth Conference on Computational Natural Language Learning, pp. 203–212 (2010)
11. Lafferty, J.D., McCallum, A., Pereira, F.C.N.: Conditional random fields: probabilistic models for segmenting and labeling sequence data. In: Proceedings of the Eighteenth International Conference on Machine Learning, pp. 282–289 (2001)
12. Liu, Y., Shi, Z., Sarkar, A.: Exploiting rich syntactic information for relation extraction from biomedical articles. In: The Conference of the North American Chapter of the Association for Computational Linguistics, pp. 97–100 (2007)
13. McCallum, A., Schultz, K., Singh, S.: Factorie: probabilistic programming via imperatively defined factor graphs. In: Bengio, Y., Schuurmans, D., Lafferty, J., Williams, C.K.I., Culotta, A. (eds.) Advances in Neural Information Processing Systems, vol. 22, pp. 1249-1257 (2009)
14. McDonald, R., Pereira, F., Kulick, S., Winters, S., Jin, Y., White, P.: Simple algorithms for complex relation extraction with applications to biomedical IE. In: Proceedings of the 43rd Annual Meeting on Association for Computational Linguistics, pp. 491–498 (2005)
15. Mintz, M., Bills, S., Snow, R., Jurafsky, D.: Distant supervision for relation extraction without labeled data. In: Proceedings of the Joint Conference of the 47th Annual Meeting of the ACL and the 4th International Joint Conference on Natural Language Processing of the AFNLP (2009)
16. Ravichandran, D., Hovy, E.: Learning surface text patterns for a question answering system. In: Proceedings of the 40th Annual Meeting on Association for Computational Linguistics (2002)
17. Riedel, S., Yao, L., McCallum, A.: Modeling relations and their mentions without labeled text. In: Balcázar, J.L., Bonchi, F., Gionis, A., Sebag, M. (eds.) ECML PKDD 2010, Part III. LNCS, vol. 6323, pp. 148–163. Springer, Heidelberg (2010)
18. Rosario, B., Hearst, M.A.: Classifying semantic relations in bioscience text. In: ACL 2004 (2004)
19. Roth, D., Yih, W.: Global inference for entity and relation identification via a linear programming formulation. In: Getoor, L., Taskar, B. (eds.) Introduction to Statistical Relational Learning. MIT Press (2007)
20. Wick, M., Rohanimanesh, K., Culotta, A., McCallum, A.: Samplerank: learning preferences from atomic gradients. In: Neural Information Processing Systems (NIPS), Workshop on Advances in Ranking (2009)
21. Zelenko, D., Aone, C., Richardella, A.: Kernel methods for relation extraction. J. Mach. Learn. Res. **3**, 1083–1106 (2003)
22. Zhao, S., Grishman, R.: Extracting relations with integrated information using kernel methods. In: Proceedings of the 43rd Annual Meeting on Association for Computational Linguistics, pp. 419–426 (2005)

Incorporating Tweet Relationships into Topic Derivation

Robertus Nugroho[1(✉)], Diego Molla-Aliod[1], Jian Yang[1], Youliang Zhong[1], Cecile Paris[2], and Surya Nepal[2]

[1] Department of Computing, Macquarie University, Sydney, Australia
robertus.nugroho@students.mq.edu.au,
{diego.molla-aliod,jian.yang,youliang.zhong}@mq.edu.au
[2] CSIRO, Sydney, Australia
{cecile.paris,surya.nepal}@csiro.au

Abstract. With its rapid users growth, Twitter has become an essential source of information about what events are happening in the world. It is critical to have the ability to derive the topics from Twitter messages (tweets), that is, to determine and characterize the main topics of the Twitter messages (tweets). However, tweets are very short in nature and therefore the frequency of term co-occurrences is very low. The sparsity in the relationship between tweets and terms leads to a poor characterization of the topics when only the content of the tweets is used. In this paper, we exploit the relationships between tweets and propose *intLDA*, a variant of Latent Dirichlet Allocation (LDA) that goes beyond content and directly incorporates the relationship between tweets. We have conducted experiments on a Twitter dataset and evaluated the performance in terms of both topic coherence and tweet-topic accuracy. Our experiments show that *intLDA* outperforms methods that do not use relationship information.

Keywords: Topic derivation · Twitter · Tweets relationship

1 Introduction

With around 350 thousands Twitter messages (tweets) per minute at the time of writing[1], Twitter has become one of the best places on the Internet to get an understanding of what is happening in the world. With such rapidly-changing information, the ability to derive the most important topics from Twitter data is critical to provide an effective way to navigate through the data and explore the information.

In this paper we aim to determine the most important topics of a Twitter dataset by performing topic derivation. For the purposes of this paper, *topic derivation* of a collection of tweets is the process of determining the main topic

---

[1] http://www.internetlivestats.com/twitter-statistics/.

© Springer Science+Business Media Singapore 2016
K. Hasida and A. Purwarianti (Eds.): PACLING 2015, CCIS 593, pp. 177–190, 2016.
DOI: 10.1007/978-981-10-0515-2_13

of every tweet and characterizing the main topics of the collection of tweets by listing their most important words.

Unlike traditional documents with lengthy and structured content, a tweet is limited to 140 characters. Additionally, a tweet could include expressions in informal language, such as emoticons, abbreviations, and misspelled terms. Given their short-text nature, deriving topics from tweets is a challenging problem. The very low co-occurrences between terms will heavily penalize the topic derivation process. Because of this sparsity problem, conventional methods for topic derivation such as Latent Dirichlet Allocation (LDA) [2], PLSA [7] or NMF [10] do not work well in the Twitter environment, as they focus only on content.

Several studies in the literature address the sparsity problem on microblogging environments. For example, [1,17] presented a content expansion method based on an external document collection. Relying on external resources, this approach would become difficult to deal with a highly dynamic environment like Twitter. The study of [19] exploited the semantic features of Twitter content by building the term correlation matrix, but this still potentially suffers from the sparsity problem since the term co-occurrences in Twitter are very low.

The limitations of those methods have inspired us to go beyond content to address the sparsity problem. We investigate the possibility of incorporating the social interaction features in Twitter. Studies by [9,14] show that social interaction features in Twitter play an important role on both topic quality and credibility.

We propose a new method, *intLDA*, that uses the contents of tweets *and* specific relationships between tweets to perform topic derivation. In this paper, we define the relationships between tweets as the interactions based on users (*mentions*), actions (*reply* and *retweet*) and content similarity. Our analysis and experimental results show that our proposed method can significantly outperform other advanced methods and configurations in terms of topic coherence and cluster quality. The main contribution of the paper can be summarized as follows:

- We observe that tweets are related to each other through both interactions and content features. Our analysis reveals that a matrix of tweet relationships have a higher density than one based on term-to-term or tweet-to-term relationships.
- We develop a novel extension of the LDA method, *intLDA*, which incorporates the tweet relationships into topic derivation. Our proposed *intLDA* method can effectively determine and characterize the main topic of each tweet.
- We conduct comprehensive experiments on a Twitter dataset, using widely accepted topic derivation metrics. The experimental results demonstrate significant improvements over popular methods such as LDA, Plink-LDA [18] and NMF. We also discuss an implementation of a simple variation to LDA that takes into account tweets relationships (*eLDA*) and show that *intLDA* is still far better in comparison to this simpler method.

The rest of the paper is organized as follows. Section 2 presents the task of topic derivation and justifies its use for characterizing the most important topics of a collection of tweets. Section 3 introduces the relationships that exist between tweets based on their interactions and content. Section 4 describes how to incorporate the tweet relationships into LDA. Details of the experiments and evaluation are presented in Sect. 5. We discuss the related work in Sect. 6 and conclude in Sect. 7.

2   Topic Derivation

Social media in general, and Twitter in particular, are being used by a large community of people worldwide to post short pieces of information on any matters that are directly relevant to them. People might post for a wide range of reasons, such as to state someone's mood in the moment, to advertise one's business, or to report an accident or disaster. The widespread and continuous use of Twitter by such a large community makes it a desirable source for information sharing. In this paper, we aim to characterize the most salient topics being discussed in Twitter at any point in time by detecting the most important topics and listing their most representative words. This is useful for a wide range of applications. For example, in emergency relief agencies (*e.g.,* fires, floods and other disasters), detection of possible burst of epidemics by health monitoring institutions, and marketing studies to identify possible trends in large communities of potential users.

Topic modeling methods such as Latent Dirichlet Allocation (LDA) [2] model a document as a bag of words drawn from a mixture of topics. LDA has been used to determine the most likely distribution of words per topic, and the most likely distribution of topics in documents. After performing LDA, it is straightforward to determine the most salient topics in a document and the most salient words in a topic. However, since a document is considered as a mixture of topics, it is not trivial to determine the most important topics in the collection.

We have performed LDA on the first 500 tweets of our collection (see Sect. 5.1 for details of our dataset) and observed a marked predominance of one topic per tweet, as we describe below. For any tweet, let t_1 be the topic with the highest probability (p_1) and t_2 the next ranking topic (with probability p_2), as determined by performing LDA on the 500 tweets. We call the ratio of $p1/p2$ the "Prominent Factor" or PF. If t_1 is much more prominent than t_2, PF will be high. Figure 1 shows the prominent factor for each tweet, after performing LDA with 20 topics. The ratio of the prominent factor in this figure is sorted in ascending order. The values are clipped at a factor of 8, but we observed a maximum factor of 2000. Furthermore, 271 tweets (54 %) have a prominent factor over 100. The figure shows that 85 % of the tweets have a prominent factor of 1.4 or higher. A factor higher than 1.4 (e.g.: 0.418 for the highest probability and 0.279 for the next ranking) or higher means that one topic is relatively predominant for this tweet. The larger the factor, the more predominant the topic.

Given the marked preference of one topic in each tweet for most tweets, it is sensible to characterize a tweet by its most salient topic. By establishing this

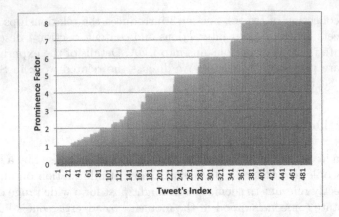

Fig. 1. Topic prominence in the tweets of a collection of 500 tweets, sorted by prominence factor (ratio between the highest and the second highest topic probability for
each tweet). The values are clipped at a factor of 8.

one-to-one mapping from tweets to topics, we can determine the importance of
a topic in the collection of tweets by counting how many tweets are mapped
to the topic. We therefore perform *topic derivation* of a collection of tweets by
determining the main topic of every tweet by grouping tweets on the same topic
and by characterizing the most important topics of the collection of tweets by
listing their most important words.

3   Observing the Relationships Between Tweets

Topic derivation by straight LDA suffers from the fact that the tweets are very
short. Directly applying LDA on Twitter data may produce a poor characterization of the topics due to the sparse relationship between the tweets and the
terms [5]. Several studies in the literature address the sparsity problem that
occurs when dealing with short text. For example, [1] presented a query expansion method based on an external document collection. Relying on external
resources, this approach would become difficult to predict what relevant content
will be relevant to add in a highly changing environment like Twitter. Yan and
his colleagues in [19,20] exploited the semantic features of a document content
to build the term correlation matrix, but this still potentially suffers from the
sparsity problem since the term co-occurrences in Twitter are very low.

A number of researchers have investigated the possibility of incorporating
social interactions in Twitter. For example, studies by [9,14] show that social
interaction features in Twitter play an important role on the determination of
both topic quality and its credibility. In the approach presented here, we use the
interactions between tweets as means to address the sparsity problem to achieve
better topic coherence and higher topic quality.

Owing to the social networking nature of Twitter, there are various relationships on the Twitter platform. Twitter provides a *following-follower* mechanism

to connect users, so that all followed users' tweets will be shown on a user's home page. In addition, Twitter offers several interactive features enabling users to interact with each other through tweets, such as *mention, reply, retweet* and *hashtag*. These features have made Twitter a network of not only people but also information. In this paper, we define the relationships between tweets as the interactions based on users (*mentions*), actions (*reply* and *retweet*) and content similarity.

Mention and *reply* are helpful methods for initiating or joining a conversation in Twitter. Intuitively, all tweets belonging to the same conversation have a high probability of sharing the same or similar topic even if no terms co-occur in their content. A *mention*, denoted as '@' followed by a user name, directly refers to another user. In contrast, a *reply* is used to send out a message in reply to a specific tweet. In a *reply* tweet, the user name of the original tweet's author is included in the message.

Different from the *mention* and *reply* relations, a *retweet* is a re-posting of someone else's tweet. This can be used to further disseminate a tweet, for example to ensure one's followers see it. Since a *retweet* has many words in common with the original tweet, the term co-occurrence between the two tweets (original and retweet) will be high, and both tweets are likely to share a topic.

To capture the interactions in Twitter, we classify the interactions based on people $po(i, j)$ and on actions $act(i, j)$. Let p_i be the number of people mentioned in tweet i. Then, $po(i, j)$ uses the *mention* relationship and is defined as the number of common mentioned people in tweets i and j, normalized by the number of people involved in both tweets.

$$po(i, j) = \frac{|p_i \cap p_j|}{|p_i \cup p_j|}. \tag{1}$$

$act(i, j)$ is determined by the *retweet* and *reply* relations between two tweets. If tweet i is a *retweet* or *reply* of tweet j or vice-versa, or if both tweets are replying or retweeting the same tweet, the $act(i, j)$ value will become 1, otherwise 0. Generally speaking, an $act(i, j)$ value of 1 means that two tweets have a strong relationship with each other, and most likely they share the same topic.

$$act(i, j) = \begin{cases} 1, (rtp_i = j) \ or \ (i = rtp_j) \ or \ (rtp_i = rtp_j) \\ 0, \ otherwise \end{cases} \tag{2}$$

where rtp_i stands for the *retweet* or *reply* information in a tweet i.

There are many *self-contained* tweets in the Twitter platform, where a tweet does not have any references (*mention, reply* or *retweet* relation) to another tweet [13]. We thus also include content based interactions in the relationship between tweets for the purposes of topic derivation. We use *content similarity* ($sim(i, j)$) between two tweets i and j to measure the content based interaction. In this paper we will simply use the word overlap between i and j. Thus, if W_i denotes the set of words of tweet i after preprocessing the text as described in Sect. 5.1, then:

$$sim(i, j) = |D_i \cap D_j|. \tag{3}$$

We can now formalize the relationship between tweets i and j (R_{ij}) based on their interactions (based on people, actions and content), as shown in Eq. 4:

$$R_{ij} = \begin{cases} 1 & \text{if } po(i, j) > 0 \text{ or } act(i, j) > 0 \\ & \text{or } sim(i, j) > 0 \\ 0 & \text{otherwise.} \end{cases} \tag{4}$$

Table 1. Comparison of the density between the relationships of tweet-to-tweet (R), term-to-term (T), and tweet-to-term (W)

# of tweets	# of terms	R	T	W
5K	6119	32.93 %	0.37 %	0.13 %
10K	9103	32.07 %	0.29 %	0.09 %
15K	11973	32.88 %	0.24 %	0.07 %
20K	14283	32.67 %	0.22 %	0.06 %
25K	16121	32.64 %	0.21 %	0.05 %

Table 1 compares the density between the relationships of tweet-to-tweet (R), term-to-term (T), and tweet-to-term (W) from a Twitter dataset. The table shows that the relationship between tweets has the highest density by a large margin. Adding information about tweet relationships can thus dramatically decrease the sparsity of information.

4   Incorporating Tweet Relationships into LDA

In this section, we discuss our method of incorporating the tweet relationships into the LDA process. We present two LDA implementations which directly incorporate the relationships. We first discuss the basic LDA method, then a simple method we call *eLDA*, our naïve way of expanding the tweet content by adding the new content from the related tweets. We then present our proposed method *intLDA*, another variant of LDA that directly incorporates the relationships between tweets.

4.1   Latent Dirichlet Allocation (LDA)

Latent Dirichlet Allocation (LDA) was presented by Blei et al. [2]. This method is used to automatically discover the topics from a collection of documents, with the intuition that every document exhibits multiple topics. LDA models the words of a document as generated randomly from a mixture of topics where each topic has a latent distribution of word probabilities. The documents and their words are generated according to the following generative process:

1. For each document d, draw a topic distribution θ_d, which is randomly sampled from a Dirichlet distribution with hyperparameter α. ($\theta_d \sim Dir(\alpha)$)
2. For each topic z, draw a word distribution ϕ_z, which is randomly sampled from a Dirichlet distribution with hyperparameter β. ($\phi_z \sim Dir(\beta)$)
3. For each word n in document d:
   (a) Choose a topic z_n sampled from the topic distribution θ_d. ($z_n \sim Cat(\theta_d)$)
   (b) Choose a word w_n from $p(w_n|z_n,\beta)$, a multinomial probability conditioned on the topic z_n. ($w_n \sim Cat(\phi_{z_n})$)

4.2   *eLDA:* Expanding Tweet Content Based on Tweet Relationship

From the generative process shown in previous subsection, we can see that LDA works solely on the tweet content, without incorporating the relationships that may exist between tweets. It has a "bag of words" assumption where the order of the words in the documents does not have any effect on the topic derivation process. When dealing with short texts such as tweets, term co-occurrences amongst tweets can be low, which hurts the topic derivation process. A naïve way of improving the LDA method is to augment the tweet content to increase the term co-occurrences. While expanding the content of the tweets using external documents seems to be ideal [1], the method would become difficult to deal with Twitter's highly dynamic environment, as already mentioned. Furthermore, the language used in tweets is mostly informal, and therefore the words occurring in a tweet may not easily match those terms in external corpora.

A simple, intuitive use of the tweet-relationship matrix R consists in expanding the tweet content by adding the words from the related tweets (tweets with the observed tweet relationships discussed in Sect. 3). In this approach, we add only words that are not already occurring in the original tweet. Our implementation of this content expansion is denoted as *eLDA* in this paper. A possible drawback of this method is that the added words might not be related to the tweet, therefore introducing noise.

4.3   *intLDA:* Incorporating the Tweet Relationship to Improve the Tweet-Topic Distributions

In LDA, each tweet i defines a multinomial distribution θ_i of topics. The global tweet-topic distribution θ can be learned based on the observed words present in each tweet through a Markov Chain Monte-Carlo algorithm such as Gibbs sampling [6].

Since working only on content makes LDA suffer from the sparsity problem, we extend the model to directly incorporate the observed relationships between tweets R in the process of learning θ. We use R to add an additional constraint to the θ distributions, so that if two tweets are related, then the θ of those two tweets will be simultaneously adjusted based on the sampled topic.

The difference between LDA and *intLDA* is in the process of sampling the tweet-topic distribution using Gibbs sampling. In each iteration of Gibbs sampling, LDA updates the document-topic counts of each tweet i independently of each other. In contrast, *intLDA* updates the document-topic counts of tweet i, as in LDA, but in addition it updates the document-topic counts for the sampled topic z of all tweets j that are related to i as defined by $R_{i,j}$. In other words, the estimation of the document-topic distribution θ_i for tweet i is affected by information from related tweets.

The posterior probability used to estimate the parameters in the Gibbs sampling is shown in Eq. 5.

$$P(z_{(d,t)}|z_{-(d,t)}, W, R, \alpha, \beta) = \frac{P(z_{(d,t)}, z_{-(d,t)}, W, R, \alpha, \beta)}{P(Z_{-(d,t)}, W, R, \alpha, \beta)} \tag{5}$$

where $z(d,t)$ denotes the z hidden topic of the nth word token in the dth tweet, W is the vocabulary, and R denotes the relationship between tweets. In Algorithm 1, the difference between LDA and *intLDA* is the addition of lines 14 to 16.

Algorithm 1. *intLDA* Gibbs Sampling

INPUT: tweets t, number of tweets D, number of topics K
OUTPUT: topic assignments z and counts cdt, cwt and ct

1: randomly initialize z and increment counters
2: **for** $i = 1 \to D$ **do**
3:    **for** $l = 1 \to N_i$ **do**
4:       $w \leftarrow t_{i,l}$
5:       $topic \leftarrow z_{i,l}$
6:       $cdt_{i,topic} - = 1; cwt_{w,topic} - = 1; ct_{topic} - = 1$
7:       **for** $k = 1 \to K$ **do**
8:          $p_k = (cdt_{i,k} + \alpha_k)\frac{cwt_{k,w} + \beta_w}{ct_k + \beta \times W}$
9:       $n\_topic \leftarrow$ sample from p
10:      $z_{i,l} \leftarrow n\_topic$
11:      $cdt_{i,n\_topic} + = 1;$
12:      $cwt_{w,n\_topic} + = 1;$
13:      $ct_{n\_topic} + = 1$
14:      **foreach** j such that $R_{ij} == 1$ **do**
15:          $cdt_{j,topic} - = 1$
16:          $cdt_{j,n\_topic} + = 1$
17: **return** z, cdt, cwt, ct

---

5   Experiments

In this section, we discuss the details of our experiments, including the experimental dataset, the baseline methods and the evaluation metrics, and the results.

5.1   Dataset

For the experiments, we use Twitter messages collected from 03 March 2014 to 07 March 2014 using the Twitter public stream API[2]. Our experiments deal with only English tweets. Our data set includes 729,334 tweets involving 509,713 users, 12,221 reply tweets and 101,272 retweets.

A preprocessing step was performed against the test dataset by removing all irrelevant characters (e.g., emoticons, punctuations) and stop words, and performing spelling correction and lemmatization using NLTK python packages. For the purposes of evaluation, around 20 % of the tweets were manually labeled as the training set (one label/topic for every tweet).

5.2   Baseline Methods

We evaluate *eLDA* and *intLDA* against the following alternatives.

- *LDA*. This is a straight use of LDA [2].
- *Plink-LDA*. This is a variant of LDA that uses relationships between documents as prior information for topic derivation [18]. This variant of LDA is thus closest to our approach. However, the implementation of the prior information in the topic sampling process seems to have no direct impact on the document topic distributions, as the sparse relationship between content and vocabulary still has a higher negative effect on the quality of the topics. For the purpose of this evaluation, we use our observed tweet relationships as the link information between tweets.
- *NMF*. This is a popular algorithm of Non Negative Matrix Factorization that factorizes a tweet-term matrix into tweet-topic and topic-term matrices [10].

5.3   Evaluation Metrics

We evaluated both the quality of tweet-topic distributions and the coherence of words in the topics.

As mentioned in Sect. 2, for each tweet we chose the topic with highest value in the topic distribution. We subsequently clustered the tweets by their chosen topic and compared the clusters against the clusters generated by our manually labeled training set. We used pairwise *F Measure* and Normalized Mutual Information (*NMI*) metrics to compare the clusters with the annotations.

---

[2] https://dev.twitter.com/streaming/overview.

The pairwise *F-Measure* [11] computes the harmonic mean of both precision p and recall r.

$$F = 2 \times \frac{p \times r}{p + r}. \tag{6}$$

where precision p is calculated as the fraction of pairs of tweets correctly put in the same cluster, and recall r is the fraction of actual pairs of tweets that were identified.

NMI [16] measures the mutual information shared between tweet-topic clusters and the training set $I(K; C)$, normalized by the entropy of the clusters $H(K)$ and training set $H(C)$. The value of *NMI* ranges between 0 and 1 (higher is better).

$$NMI(K, C) = \frac{I(K; C)}{[H(K) + H(C)]/2}. \tag{7}$$

To measure the coherence between words in a topic, we adopt the metric defined in Eq. 8, in which $Co(k, W)$ is the measurement of *topic coherence* for a topic k described by its topic-terms in W [12].

$$Co(k, W) = \sum_{m=2}^{M} \sum_{l=1}^{m-1} \log \frac{T(w_m, w_l) + 1}{T(w_l)} \tag{8}$$

where $w_m, w_l \in W$; $T(*)$ and $T(*, *)$ are document frequency and co-document frequency functions, representing the number of tweets which contain a given term or a pair of terms respectively; M is the size of the set W of topic-terms.

5.4   Discussion

We have conducted experiments on several possible setups for all the methods. We set the number of the topics starting from 20 ($k = 20, 40, 60, 80, 100$) to assess the performance of the methods for a different number of topics. For every value of k, we ran the algorithms over the dataset 30 times and noted the mean of each evaluation metric. In each experiment, we retrieved the 10 words with highest values in the topic probability distribution as the representative words for the topic.

Figure 2 shows that *intLDA* presents a significant improvement of *F-measure* in comparison to the other methods for every evaluation setup. The method of expanding the tweet content (*eLDA*) also provides an improvement over the straight *LDA* method, *Plink-LDA* and *NMF*. However, the performance of *eLDA* remains below that of *intLDA*. This suggests that incorporating the observed tweet relationships directly in the Gibbs sampling process is more robust to noise than introducing words from the related tweets.

The noise from expanded content on the *eLDA* method has a big impact on the entropy. As shown by Fig. 3, the *eLDA* method has the worst performance due to a higher entropy of information. In the *NMI* evaluation, our proposed

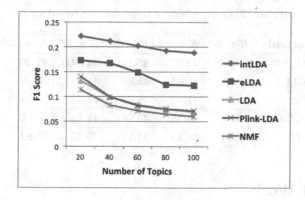

Fig. 2. Experiment results using F-Measure metric

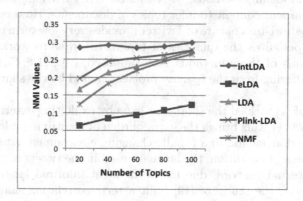

Fig. 3. Experiment results using *NMI* metric

method *intLDA* gives the best result over the other baseline methods. *Plink-LDA* is the next best method, showing that incorporating the relationships between tweets can produce higher mutual information than straight LDA.

Our evaluation of the topic coherence for each method (Table 2) confirms the results of the F-measure of cluster quality. A higher topic coherence value means that the topic is more readable [12]. Table 2 shows that *intLDA* always performs best on any number of topics. The expanded *eLDA* method shows only a small improvement over the original LDA.

The improvement of *intLDA* over the original LDA method for topic derivation in Twitter shows that incorporating social interactions is useful to improve topic quality. Our model tries to introduce additional information directly into the original LDA process, which previously worked solely on content. By having the ability to incorporate additional information on LDA, this method could potentially be extended for different tasks in Twitter, such as recommendation systems or collaborative filtering.

Table 2. Comparison of topic-coherence values

Methods	$K = 20$	$K = 40$	$K = 60$	$K = 80$	$K = 100$
intLDA	**59.12**	**48.97**	**45.69**	**42.30**	**41.27**
eLDA	58.51	47.93	43.96	41.79	40.00
LDA	58.39	47.52	43.75	41.52	38.39
Plink-LDA	55.42	46.34	43.78	41.13	38.68
NMF	54.04	44.48	43.72	40.43	37.82

6   Related Work

Popular topic modeling methods, such as PLSA [7], LDA [2] and NMF [10], exploit the document content to infer topics of documents. However, as already mentioned, the short-text nature of Twitter provides very low term co-occurrence which heavily penalizes the qualities of topics. In order to work on Twitter, certain extensions of these methods were proposed, e.g., [4,8,15,19]; however, they are still suffering from the sparsity problem caused by the short-text nature of Twitter.

The study of [1] tackled the short-text issue by exploiting external document collections. However, this brings the extra burden of identifying relevant corpora to augment the documents. In a rapidly changing environment such as Twitter, this is problematic. In addition, the language used in the tweets might not match that of the external corpora, due to the frequent informal language used on Twitter. Likewise, the study of [19] built a term-correlation matrix from the content of the documents, then jointly use document-term and term-correlation matrices to address the sparsity problem in short-text environments. However, as shown in Table 1, the term-to-term relationships as the term-correlation matrix only provides a small improvement with respect to density in comparison with the original tweet-to-term relationships.

The study of [15,17] exploited content based social features such as *hashtag* and *url* to improve the quality of the topics. The user's *following-follower* mechanism has also been investigated [3] for determining the popularity of authors to refine the topic learning process in Twitter. However, analyzing the relationships based on *following-follower* suffers from scalability issues in the Twitter's streaming environment, since user details information needs to be queried apart from the dataset itself.

Plink-LDA [18] is a variant of LDA that is close to our approach as it uses relationship information. This approach has been developed to analyze a collection of publications and their links via citations. It uses the link between documents as prior information. In contrast, we work on much shorter documents, and we integrate the link between tweets in the Gibbs sampling algorithm. As discussed in Sect. 5, our approach outperformed *Plink-LDA* in the Twitter data.

Within the domain of social media, [14] applied user context to topic modeling. This approach takes into consideration only conversation patterns, ignoring the tweet contents. The study of [9] suggested that the topics discussed through interactions on social networks had higher credibility than those specified by content-based extraction methods. These studies are aligned with our experiments with respect to the impact of interactions, in their case on topic qualities. However, our research discovered that deriving topics from only the socially connected tweets will lose a great number of important topics in the Twitter environment, as the self-contained tweets occupy the majority of the total tweets. Taking this research into account, *intLDA* effectively incorporates both social interactions and content similarities in the topic derivation process to achieve high quality results.

7   Conclusion

In this paper, we present a method that incorporates information about tweets relationship for topic derivation. *intLDA* is an extension of LDA that incorporates the relationship information directly in the Gibbs sampling process.

We have conducted several experiments of topic derivation on a Twitter dataset. Our experiments demonstrate that the defined relationships between tweets are helpful to improve the quality of the topic derivation result. Our evaluation results show that *intLDA* consistently outperforms *eLDA*, *Plink-LDA* and other methods that do not incorporate relationship information.

The relationships *intLDA* takes into account are based on the interactions of people, actions and content similarity between tweets. We are currently investigating more complex social features to observe their effects on topic derivation. Having achieved an improvement over *LDA*, *Plink-LDA* and *NMF*, we will also extend the study to incorporate the tweet-relationships for topic derivation in a real-time situation using an online and incremental version.

Acknowledgments. This work is supported by the Indonesian Directorate General of Higher Education (DGHE), Macquarie University, CSIRO and Australian Research Council Linkage Project (LP120200231).

References

1. Albakour, M., Macdonald, C., Ounis, I., et al.: On sparsity and drift for effective real-time filtering in microblogs. In: Proceedings of the 22nd ACM International Conference on Information and Knowledge Management, pp. 419–428. ACM (2013)
2. Blei, D., Ng, A., Jordan, M.: Latent Dirichlet allocation. J. Mach. Learn. Res. **3**, 993–1022 (2003)
3. Cha, Y., Bi, B., Hsieh, C.C., Cho, J.: Incorporating popularity in topic models for social network analysis. In: Proceedings of the 36th International ACM SIGIR Conference on Research and Development in Information Retrieval, pp. 223–232. ACM (2013)
4. Choo, J., Lee, C., Reddy, C.K., Park, H.: UTOPIAN: user-driven topic modeling based on interactive non-negative matrix factorization. IEEE Trans. Vis. Comput. Graph. **19**(12), 1992–2001 (2013)

5. Erk, K.: Vector space models of word meaning and phrase meaning: a survey. Lang. Linguist. Compass **6**(10), 635–653 (2012)
6. Griffiths, T.L., Steyvers, M.: Finding scientific topics. Proc. Nat. Acad. Sci. U.S.A. **101**(Suppl. 1), 5228–5235 (2004)
7. Hofmann, T.: Probabilistic latent semantic indexing. In: Proceedings of the 22nd Annual International ACM SIGIR Conference on Research and Development in Information Retrieval, pp. 50–57. ACM (1999)
8. Hu, Y., John, A., Wang, F., Kambhampati, S.: ET-LDA: joint topic modeling for aligning events and their twitter feedback. AAAI **12**, 59–65 (2012)
9. Kang, B., O'Donovan, J., Höllerer, T.: Modeling topic specific credibility on twitter. In: Proceedings of the 2012 ACM International Conference on Intelligent User Interfaces, pp. 179–188. ACM (2012)
10. Lee, D., Seung, H.: Algorithms for non-negative matrix factorization. Advances in Neural Information Processing Systems, pp. 556–562. MIT Press, Cambridge (2000)
11. Manning, C., Raghavan, P., Schütze, H.: Introduction to Information Retrieval, vol. 1. Cambridge University Press, Cambridge (2008)
12. Mimno, D., Wallach, H., Talley, E., Leenders, M., McCallum, A.: Optimizing semantic coherence in topic models. In: Proceedings of the Conference on Empirical Methods in Natural Language Processing (EMNLP), pp. 262–272. Association for Computational Linguistics (2011)
13. de Moor, A.: Conversations in context: a twitter case for social media systems design. In: Proceedings of the 6th International Conference on Semantic Systems, p. 29. ACM (2010)
14. Pochampally, R., Varma, V.: User context as a source of topic retrieval in twitter. In: Workshop on Enriching Information Retrieval (with ACM SIGIR), pp. 1–3 (2011)
15. Ramage, D., Dumais, S.T., Liebling, D.J.: Characterizing microblogs with topic models. ICWSM **10**, 1–1 (2010)
16. Strehl, A., Ghosh, J.: Cluster ensembles – a knowledge reuse framework for combining multiple partitions. J. Mach. Learn. Res. **3**, 583–617 (2003). http://dx.doi.org/10.1162/153244303321897735
17. Vosecky, J., Jiang, D., Leung, K.W.T., Xing, K., Ng, W.: Integrating social and auxiliary semantics for multifaceted topic modeling in twitter. ACM Trans. Internet Technol. (TOIT) **14**(4), 27 (2014)
18. Xia, H., Li, J., Tang, J., Moens, M.-F.: Plink-LDA: using link as prior information in topic modeling. In: Lee, S., Peng, Z., Zhou, X., Moon, Y.-S., Unland, R., Yoo, J. (eds.) DASFAA 2012, Part I. LNCS, vol. 7238, pp. 213–227. Springer, Heidelberg (2012)
19. Yan, X., Guo, J., Liu, S., Cheng, X., Wang, Y.: Learning topics in short texts by non-negative matrix factorization on term correlation matrix. In: Proceedings of the SIAM International Conference on Data Mining. SIAM (2013)
20. Yan, X., Guo, J., Lan, Y., Cheng, X.: A biterm topic model for short texts. In: Proceedings of the 22nd International Conference on World Wide Web, International World Wide Web Conferences Steering Committee, pp. 1445–1456 (2013)

Information Retrieval and
Question-Answering

Detecting Vital Documents Using Negative Relevance Feedback in Distributed Realtime Computation Framework

Shun Kawahara[1]($\boxtimes$), Kazuhiro Seki[2], and Kuniaki Uehara[1]

[1] Graduate Schools of System Informatics, Kobe University, Kobe, Japan
kawahara@ai.cs.kobe-u.ac.jp
[2] Faculty of Intelligence and Informatics, Konan University, Kobe, Japan

Abstract. Existing knowledge bases including Wikipedia are typically written and maintained by a group of voluntary editors. Meanwhile, numerous web documents are being published partly due to the popularization of online news and social media. Some of the web documents contain novel information, called "vital documents", that should be taken into account to update articles of the knowledge bases. However, it is virtually impossible for the editors to manually monitor all the relevant web documents. As a result, there is a considerable time lag between an edit to knowledge base and the publication dates of the web documents. This paper proposes a realtime detection framework of web documents containing novel information flowing in massive document streams. The framework consists of two-step filter using statistical language models. Further, the framework is implemented on the distributed and fault-tolerant realtime computation system, Apache Storm, in order to process the sheer amount of web documents. The validity of the proposed framework is demonstrated on a publicly available web document data set, the TREC KBA Stream Corpus.

Keywords: Negative feedback · Realtime processing · Text data streams · Wikipedia

1 Introduction

Large knowledge bases, such as Wikipedia and Freebase, are used by many people in their daily lives and also utilized to improve the performance in various information processing tasks, such as query expansion [9,21], entity linking [16], question answering [6] and entity retrieval [3]. For this reason, maintaining the quality of these knowledge bases is very important.

Knowledge bases typically contain a large number of articles. For example, the English version of Wikipedia has over 4.5 million articles and they are maintained by small workforces of humans, about 1,300 editors[1]. If those editors

---

[1] http://en.wikipedia.org/wiki/List_of_Wikipedias.

© Springer Science+Business Media Singapore 2016
K. Hasida and A. Purwarianti (Eds.): PACLING 2015, CCIS 593, pp. 193–208, 2016.
DOI: 10.1007/978-981-10-0515-2_14

took charge of the same number of articles for the total of 4.5 millions, an editor would be responsible for maintaining about 3,500 articles. In the meantime, the amount of web documents continues to grow due to the exploding popularity of social networking service (SNS), such as Twitter and Facebook, across the world. Currently, editors manually monitor relevant document streams and edit articles when they notice novel information. Consequently, there is a considerable time lag between the date of an edit to knowledge base and the publication date of vital documents. It is reported that the length of the time lag often become a year [11].

In this paper, we propose a realtime detection framework of such vital documents containing novel information flowing in massive document streams. Here, novel information is defined as those which requires an update of articles of knowledge bases. The Text REtrieval Conference (TREC) Knowledge Base Acceleration (KBA) track [10] targeted this particular problem, referred to as the "vital filtering" task. The participants of the track have developed a variety of system, but they are generally suffered from the three issues, that is, (1) no consideration of poor training data, (2) poor performance of detection of web documents containing novel information in relevant documents, and (3) no consideration as to how to process massive document streams in realtime. To deal with these issues, we take advantage of a pseudo relevance feedback model for non-relevant documents and use statistical language models representing documents containing novel information. Furthermore, our proposed framework is implemented on the distributed and fault-tolerant realtime computation system, Apache Storm[2], in order to process massive document streams in realtime.

The remainder of this paper is structured as follows: Sect. 2 reviews representative approaches developed for the TREC KBA vital filtering task. Section 3 briefly introduces Apache Storm and its components and describes our proposed framework. Section 4 evaluates our framework by reporting the results of empirical experiments, and Sect. 5 concludes this paper with a brief summary and possible future directions.

2   Related Work

Various approaches to detecting novel information in text streams have been developed for the TREC KBA vital filtering task. Liu et al. [14], Dietz and Dalton [8] proposed a feature expansion technique using topic information related to the target entity (see Sect. 3.1 for the definition). Abbes et al. [1] employed a classifier with a number of features, including the relative positions of keyword occurrences in a document related to the target entity and whether or not document titles mention the keywords. Kenter [12] used the similarity between documents and the target entity, such as cosine and Jaccard similarities. Bellogín et al. [4] and Wang et al. [19] also trained classifiers using the features mentioned above. While Bellogín et al. trained a unique classifier for each target entity, Wang et al. trained a general classifier for the whole topic set, achieving

---

[2] http://storm.apache.org/.

the best performance at TREC KBA 2013. The reason why the general classifier outperformed per-entity classifiers is that the number of training instances was relatively small and thus insufficient if split across entities. In the present work, we take advantage of pseudo feedback of non-relevant documents so as to remedy the problem of small training data and build a unique language model for each target entity. Most proposed approaches in the vital filtering task reported high recall and low precision [10], which means there are a plenty of negative feedback documents that can be used for our proposed framework.

Despite the various approaches proposed for the vital filtering task, there is much room to improve for the performance in detecting web documents containing novel information. In fact, all the approaches in KBA 2013 did not make a significant difference from a rather simple baseline [10]. It is presumably due to the fact that there were no features used for representing documents containing novel information. For instance, while term-based cosine similarity between a document and the target entity would be an effective feature for identifying documents related to the entity [2], it has nothing to do with novelty. In the present work, we build two statistical language models describing documents containing novel information. One is built from a knowledge base article corresponding to the target entity. Then, a document is judged to contain novel information when the similarity between the language model and the document is lower. Note that lower similarity means a small overlap between the two, which potentially indicates the existence of novel information. Another language model is built from a collection of documents containing novel information. This model is intended to capture the common vocabularies to be used with novel information. Based on the model, a document is judged to contain novel information when the similarity between the language model and the document is higher.

In addition, the previous work mentioned above do not consider the processing time. In order to recommend web/social media documents to the editors of knowledge bases, it is important to achieve not only high accuracy in detecting novel information but also to do realtime processing. To this end, our proposed framework is implemented on the distributed realtime computation system, Apache Storm.

3   Proposed Framework

Our proposed framework is developed on Storm, consisting of multiple filters using statistical language models. The next sub-sections first provide the term definitions necessary to describe our proposed framework and then introduce Apache Storm. After that, our proposed framework and other details are presented.

3.1   Term Definitions

This sub-section provides the definitions of key terms used throughout this paper, which follows those of TREC KBA.[3]

---

[3] http://trec-kba.org/trec-kba-2014.

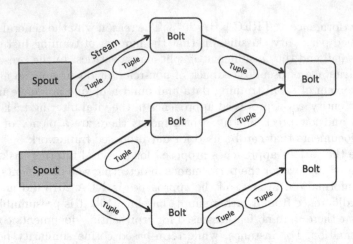

Fig. 1. Storm topology

Entity is a person, facility, organization and concept which is an article title of a knowledge base, such as "Barack Obama", "White House" and "Democratic Party". The aim of this study is to detect web documents containing novel information related to a given entity.

Vital documents are those containing novel information that at the time it entered the stream would motivate an update to the entity's article of knowledge base.

On the one hand, *useful* documents are those documents containing information related to a target entity but not contain novel information, e.g., background bio, primary or secondary source. Vital and useful documents are collectively called *relevant* documents.

3.2 Apache Storm

Apache Storm is a distributed realtime computation system, processing unbounded streams of data. McCreadie et al. [15] proposed online event detection approach from embarrassingly high volume social streams using Strom [18] describes the use of Storm at Twitter Inc. To use Storm, one needs to define "topologies" illustrated in Fig. 1. A topology is a graph of computation and each node in a topology has processing logic and edges between nodes indicate how data should be passed around between nodes.

There are two types of nodes, called "spouts" and "bolts". A spout is a source of streams (sequences of tuples) and a tuple is a unit of data processed in Storm. In case of our proposed framework, a spout would read document data from the provided corpus and emit them as a stream. A bolt receives any number of input streams, does some processing, and may emit new streams. For our framework, bolts would determine whether inbound documents from the streams are relevant. Each node in a Storm topology executes in parallel and one can specify how much parallelism he/she wants for each node.

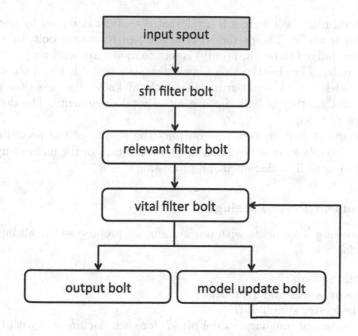

Fig. 2. Topology of our system developed on Storm.

3.3 Overview

Figure 2 depicts the topology of our proposed framework, where input spout reads documents from a data source and sends them to surface form name (sfn) filter bolt, followed by relevant filter bolt, vital filter bolt, and so on. These bolts process the input stream of documents in parallel for a given target entity. Our framework consists of two-step filter: relevant filter detects relevant documents in input documents, vital filter detects vital documents in relevant documents. The following paragraphs provide brief descriptions of the each type of nodes of the topology.

First, input spout reads individual documents from the input stream and sends them to sfn filter bolts. Note that each document is preprocessed as described in Sect. 3.4.

Sfn filter bolt checks if each input document contains any surface form names of a given target entity. Only the documents containing the surface form name(s) are sent to the succeeding processes. There may be more than one surface form name(s) for each entity. For instance, the surface form names of the entity "Barack Obama" are "Barack Obama", "Barack Hussein Obama", "Barack H Obama", and so on.

Relevant filter bolt judges whether an input document is relevant (i.e., vital or useful) or not. If judged to be relevant, the document is sent to vital filter bolt. For this purpose, a negative language model built from a set of non-relevant documents for the target entity is used. More details are found in Sect. 3.5.

Then, vital filter bolt judges if a relevant document detected by our framework is vital or useful. The predicted class are sent to output bolt. In addition, the document judged to be vital (only) is sent to model update bolt (see Sect. 3.7 for more details). The classification between vital or useful is based on other two language models; one is built from an article of knowledge base for the target entity, and another is built from a set of vital documents. The details are described in Sect. 3.6.

Lastly, output bolt collects and outputs the results of the preceding vital filter bolts. The following sub-sections give more details of the main components of the system as well as document preprocessing.

3.4   Document Preprocessing

Before processing documents with our system, we preprocess the all input documents as follows:

- Uncapitalize words.
- Remove stop words and symbols.
- Apply the Porter stemmer [17].
- Build a document language model $p(w|d)$ for each document d with Dirichlet smoothing [22]:

$$p(w|d) = \frac{c(w, d) + \mu p(w|\mathcal{C})}{|d| + \mu} \tag{1}$$

where Google-Ngram[4] (unigrams) is used to calculate the background language model $p(w|\mathcal{C})$, the value of μ is 2,000 described in [22].

3.5   Relevant Filter Bolt

Relevant filter bolt judges whether an input document is relevant (i.e., vital or useful) or not. For this purpose, we use a negative language model (NLM) built from non-relevant documents for the target entity in question adopting the concept of MultiNeg [20], which has been shown effective for difficult queries (topics) where the search results are poor.

MultiNeg is a model to improve ad-hoc retrieval by negative relevance feedback, which takes advantage of (pseudo) feedback of non-relevant documents. More specifically, according to the similarity between the language models built from non-relevant documents and an input document, the relevance score of the document is adjusted. The non-relevant documents here mean those irrelevant to search intention within the initial search result. For example, consider the case where a user would like to search for information regarding Apple Inc. and uses a query "apple". The search results would contain documents regarding apples (fruit), which are considered non-relevant documents in this case.

MultiNeg builds a NLM $\Theta = \{\theta_1, ..., \theta_f\}$ for each of such irrelevant documents $L = \{l_1, ..., l_f\}$ using the standard EM algorithm [7]. In MultiNeg, the relevance

---

[4] http://googleresearch.blogspot.jp/2006/08/all-our-n-gram-are-belong-to-you.html.

score of the document $S(q, d)$ is defined KL-divergence retrieval model [13], computed based on the negative KL-divergence between query model θ_q and document model θ_d, i.e.,

$$S(q, d) = -D(\theta_q \| \theta_d) = - \sum_{w \in V} p(w|\theta_q) \log \frac{p(w|\theta_q)}{p(w|\theta_d)} \tag{2}$$

Adjusted relevance score is defined as Eq. (3):

$$S(q, d) - S(NLM, d) \tag{3}$$

where $S(NLM, d)$ is penalty term based on NLM, defined as Eq. (4):

$$S(NLM, d) = \max(\bigcup_{i=1}^{f} \{S(\theta_i, \theta_d)\})$$
$$= -\min(\bigcup_{i=1}^{f} \{D(\theta_i \| \theta_d)\}) \tag{4}$$

This study uses Eq. (4) to filter out irrelevant documents. Specifically, our system judges document d as relevant when Eq. (5) is satisfied:

$$S(NLM, d) < t_r \tag{5}$$

where t_r is predefined threshold.

3.6   Vital Filter Bolt

Vital filter bolt judges if an input document is vital or useful using two language models, that is, Knowledge base Article Language Model (KALM) and Vital Language Model (VLM). KALM is a unigram language model, built from an article of knowledge base for the target entity. In addition, known vital documents (i.e., training data) for the target entity are used in building KALM because the information in those vital documents should be included in the corresponding article. VLM is also a unigram language model, built from a set of known vital documents. We first identify the terms characterizing vital documents based on chi-square statistics using a known vital documents set vs. a useful documents set. Table 1 shows the cross table, where V_{w+} (V_{w-}) denotes the number of documents when a term in question appeared (did not appear) in the vital document set. Similarity, U_{w+} (U_{w-}) are the number of documents when a term in question appeared (did not appear) in the useful document set. Chi-square statistics χ^2 is calculated for each word w for each entity as in Eq. (6).

$$\chi^2 = \sum_{i \in \{+,-\}} \frac{(V_{wi} - E_{wi}^V)^2}{E_{wi}^V} + \sum_{i \in \{+,-\}} \frac{(U_{wi} - E_{wi}^U)^2}{E_{wi}^U} \tag{6}$$
$$\text{where } E_{wi}^C = A_{wi} \cdot \frac{C}{A} \ (C \in \{V, U\})$$

Table 1. Cross table for computing chi-square statistics.

	Vital	Useful	Sum
Appear	V_{w+}	U_{w+}	A_{w+}
Not appear	V_{w-}	U_{w-}	A_{w-}
Sum	V	U	A

Among the terms with high scores, those satisfying Eq. (7) is excluded. The remaining terms are used as the vocabularies of VLM.

$$V_{w+} < E_{w+}^V \tag{7}$$

In filtering, the similarity between the language models and input documents are computed based on Eq. (2), from which the document is judged to be vital or not (i.e., useful). For KALM, the document is judged as vital if the similarity is lower than a predefined threshold t_{vk}. The rationale behind is that a document more different from an article of knowledge base would contain more, and possibly relevant, information not described in the article. For VLM, conversely, the document is judged as vital if the similarity is greater than a predefined threshold t_{vv}. The assumption here is that the vocabularies often found in vital documents, and the language model built on it, would capture some features characteristic to vital documents and a document similar to it would be also vital.

3.7   Model Update Bolt

Model update bolt receives a document which is judged as vital in the preceding vital filter bolt and updates KALM or VLM. Specifically, the number of occurrence of each term in the received document is added to the current statistics of KALM/VLM. Note that terms with low chi-square scores are not used to update VLM. The updated model is sent back to vital filter bolt and will be used afterwards. This update simulates the editing of knowledge base articles in the light of new information related to the target entities.

4   Evaluation

4.1   Experimental Settings

We follow the evaluation methodology adopted at the TREC 2014 KBA vital filtering task. The KBA track provided its participants with a large corpus, called the TREC KBA Stream Corpus 2014[5]. This corpus covers the time period from October 2011 to April 2013, containing 20,494,260 documents, including blogs, forum posts, and web pages. Each document in the corpus is associated

---

[5] http://s3.amazonaws.com/aws-publicdatasets/trec/kba/index.html.

with a time-stamp corresponding to its date of publication. The participants do documents filtering in time order[6]. Documents within the predefined time range is available as training data regardless of time-stamp. The number of target entities is 67. The official metric of the vital filtering task is the macro-averaged F_1-measure (harmonic mean between precision and recall).

$$F_1 = \frac{2 \cdot P_{ave} \cdot R_{ave}}{P_{ave} + R_{ave}} \tag{8}$$

$$P_{ave} = \frac{1}{|E|} \sum_{e \in E} P(e) \tag{9}$$

$$R_{ave} = \frac{1}{|E|} \sum_{e \in E} R(e) \tag{10}$$

where $P(e)$ and $R(e)$ are precision and recall of entity e, respectively, and E denotes the set of 67 target entities. Using F_1, the performance of the participating systems was evaluated.

We used canonical names as the surface form names of target entities. The canonical names were provided along with the Stream Corpus by the TREC KBA organizers. In addition, for those entities which have their Wikipedia articles, redirect[7] information extracted from the Wikipedia dump on 1/4/2012[8] were also utilized.

To estimate the NLM θ_i, our system used non-relevant documents in the training data in the Stream Corpus. We considered documents which contain surface form name(s) of a target entity but do not have a "vital" or "useful" label as non-relevant documents. Note that if the number of documents containing a surface form name is too large (>100k for our experiments), the name is unlikely informative and thus was not utilized. Also, if a target entity did not have non-relevant documents, relevant filter bolt was disabled for the entity. The threshold t_r was set to the smallest value among the thresholds based on which vital or useful documents in the training data would be judged to be relevant.

To build the KALM, we used vital documents in training data. Similarly to the extraction of redirect information described above, we also used the article in the Wikipedia dump on 1/4/2012 for entities which have the Wikipedia article. The same preprocessing described in Sect. 3.4 was applied to the extracted articles. The VLM was built using vital and useful documents in training data. The threshold t_{vk} and t_{vv} were set for each entity using the vital and useful documents in the training data such that F_1 measure is maximized based on their similarity scores with the language model.

---

[6] More precisely, it was also allowed to do hourly batch processing.
[7] http://en.wikipedia.org/wiki/Wikipedia:Redirect.
[8] http://s3.amazonaws.com/aws-publicdatasets/trec/kba/enwiki-20120104/index.html.

4.2 Results

Table 2 summarizes the five different settings of our system, where system_id "Exact Match" simply treated the documents which went through sfn filter bolt as vital. That is, the documents containing surface form name(s) of the target entities were judged as vital. Exact Match was treated as the baseline in the KBA vital filtering task [10]. The other system, "KALM" and "VLM", are results by our developed system. Specifically, "KALM" used KALM at vital filter bolt, whereas "VLM" used VLM. Note that "w/o updates" indicates that the system does not use the model update bolt. In the other words, KALM or VLM was not updated.

Table 3 shows the performance of vital documents detection and Table 4 shows that of relevant documents detection.

For the "vital documents detection" setting, both KALM and VLM improved the baseline, suggesting the effectiveness of our language model-based filters. VLM yielded the best result on average as shown in Table 3. However, statistical significance was found only between Exact Match and KALM at the 5 % significance level by pair-wise t-test. For the "relevant documents detection" setting, vital and useful documents are not distinguished and thus the performance of KALM and VLM are exactly the same. In other words, this experiment focuses on the effectiveness of relevant filter bolt only. The improvement from Exact Match were found statistically significant at the 1 % significance level, showing the effectiveness of the language model built from irrelevant documents.

Table 2. Summary of our system settings.

System_id	Description
Exact Match (baseline)	Documents which went through sfn filter were judged as vital
KALM	Using KALM in vital filter
KALM (w/o update)	Using KALM without update in vital filter
VLM	Using VLM in vital filter
VLM (w/o update)	Using VLM without update in vital filter

Table 3. Performance of our system (vital documents detection), where bold font marks the best performance.

System_id	Prec.	Recall	F_1
Exact Match	0.099	**0.953**	0.179
KALM	0.112	0.845	0.197
KALM (w/o update)	0.109	0.853	0.193
VLM	0.129	0.609	**0.213**
VLM (w/o update)	**0.143**	0.407	0.211

Table 4. Performance of our system (relevant documents detection), where bold font marks the best performance.

System_id	Prec.	Recall	F_1
Exact Match	0.191	**0.666**	0.297
KALM/VLM	**0.209**	0.655	**0.317**

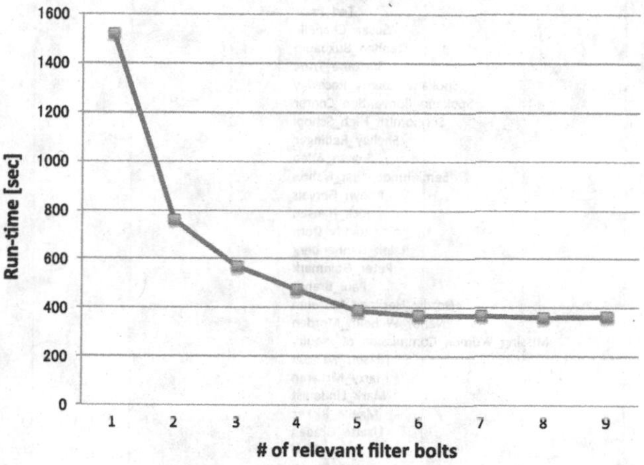

Fig. 3. Runtime under different parallelisms of relevant filter bolt.

Figure 3 show the runtime needed to process all the documents in the corpus under different parallelisms, i.e., the number of relevant filter bolts. When the number of bolts was increased (until around five), the runtime became shorter.

4.3 Discussion

As shown in the previous sub-section, there was no statistical significance for VLM, which is due to its larger variance of the performance than that of KALM as contrasted in Fig. 4 for KALM and Fig. 5 for VLM. KALM improved over the baseline for the majority of the entities, even though around a half of them are marginal. On the other hand, while VLM's improvement is more noticeable, it also showed strong negative effects for some entities, including "Lizette_Graden" and "Corisa_Bell". It may be caused by the largely different number of training data for each entity used in computing chi-square statistics. Moreover, we found that some training data of entities were imbalanced even when there were sufficient data.

Then, we examined the effect of the updates of the KALM and VLM. We observed that there were slight improvement in the performance in F_1 for both KALM and VLM with the model updates. This result suggests that model updates are effective if the original system (without updates) has high performance.

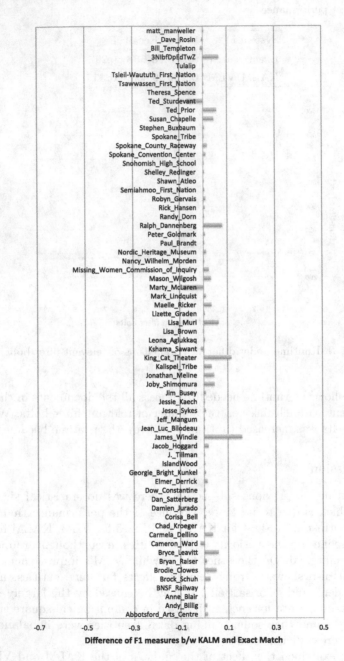

Fig. 4. Per-topic difference of F_1 measures for each entity between KALM and Exact Match.

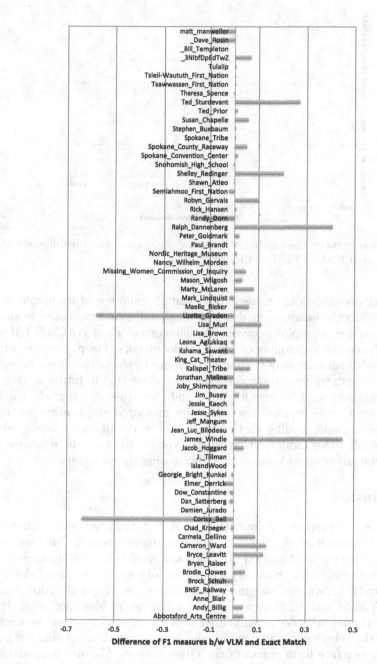

Fig. 5. Per-topic difference of F_1 measures for each entity between VLM and Exact Match.

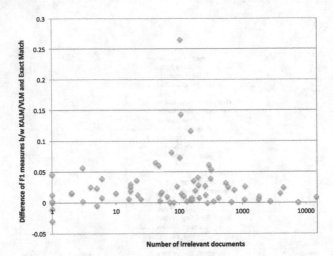

Fig. 6. Relation between the number of irrelevant documents and the difference of F_1 measures between KALM/VLM and Exact Match.

In further investigation, we also noted that the number of irrelevant documents in building the language models was largely different from entity to entity. Figure 6 shows a scatter plot between the difference of F_1 of KALM/VLM and Exact Match and the log number of irrelevant documents. The plot suggests that the number of documents may have some influence to the performance improvement. We will plan to investigate and leverage the relation in future work.

Regarding runtime, it became flat at around 6 min (360 s), where the number of relevant filter bolts reached five. We then measured the runtime of input spout for reading and sending all the documents in the Stream Corpus, which took about 6 min. This indicates that our proposed system is able to process the massive document streams in realtime by increasing the parallelism.

5   Conclusion

In this paper, we proposed a framework to detect vital web documents containing novel information flowing in massive document streams. Our framework employed a language model-based approach and used irrelevant documents for identifying relevant (vital or useful) documents and articles of knowledge base or, alternatively, known vital documents for further identifying vital documents, where the KALM and VLM were updated given newly identified vital documents. The framework was implemented as a distributed realtime processing system and the effectiveness was empirically demonstrated, improving the baseline using the surface form names of the target entities. We also demonstrated that our proposed system was able to process massive document streams in realtime by increasing the number of bolts.

There are several directions to improve our framework. One is to incorporate time-aware features, which have been considered effective to detect vital documents [2,5]. We are planning to combine time-aware features with natural language features using our models.

Acknowledgments. The authors would like to thank Sayaka Kitaguchi at Kobe University for processing the KBA corpus. This work is partially supported by JSPS KAKENHI Grant Numbers 25330363 and MEXT, Japan.

References

1. Abbes, R., Pinel-Sauvagnat, K., Hernandez, N., Boughanem, M.: IRIT at TREC knowledge base acceleration 2013: cumulative citation recommendation task. In: Proceedings of the Text REtrieval Conference (TREC) (2013)
2. Balog, K., Ramampiaro, H., Takhirov, N., Nørvåg, K.: Multi-step classification approaches to cumulative citation recommendation. In: Proceedings of the 10th Conference on Open Research Areas in Information Retrieval, pp. 121–128 (2013)
3. Balog, K., Serdyukov, P., Vries, A.P.d.: Overview of the TREC 2011 entity track. In: Proceedings of the Text REtrieval Conference (TREC) (2011)
4. Bellogín, A., Gebremeskel, G.G., He, J., Lin, J., Said, A., Samar, T., de Vries, A.P., Vuurens, J.B.: CWI and TU Delft at TREC 2013: Contextual suggestion, federated web search, KBA, and web tracks. In: Proceedings of the Text REtrieval Conference (TREC) (2013)
5. Bonnefoy, L., Bouvier, V., Bellot, P.: A weakly-supervised detection of entity central documents in a stream. In: Proceedings of the 36th International ACM SIGIR Conference on Research and Development in Information Retrieval, pp. 769–772. ACM Press (2013)
6. Dang, H.T., Kelly, D., Lin, J.J.: Overview of the TREC 2007 question answering track. In: Proceedings of the Text REtrieval Conference (TREC) (2007)
7. Dempster, A.P., Laird, N.M., Rubin, D.B.: Maximum likelihood from incomplete data via the EM algorithm. J. Roy. Stat. Soc. B **39**(1), 1–38 (1977)
8. Dietz, L., Dalton, J.: UMass at TREC 2013 knowledge base acceleration track: bi-directional entity linking and time-aware evaluation. In: Proceedings of the Text REtrieval Conference (TREC) (2013)
9. Elsas, J.L., Arguello, J., Callan, J., Carbonell, J.G.: Retrieval and feedback models for blog feed search. In: Proceedings of the 31st Annual International ACM SIGIR Conference on Research and Development in Information Retrieval, pp. 347–354 (2008)
10. Frank, J.R., Bauer, S.J., Kleiman-Weiner, M., Roberts, D.A., Tripuraneni, N., Zhang, C., Re, C., Voorhees, E., Soboroff, I.: Evaluating stream filtering for entity profile updates for TREC 2013 (KBA Track Overview). In: Proceedings of the Text REtrieval Conference (TREC) (2013)
11. Frank, J.R., Kleiman-Weiner, M., Roberts, D.A., Niu, F., Zhang, C., Ré, C., Soboroff, I.: Building an entity-centric stream filtering test collection for TREC 2012. In: Proceedings of the Text REtrieval Conference (TREC) (2012)
12. Kenter, T.: Filtering documents over time for evolving topics-the university of amsterdam at TREC 2013 KBA CCR. In: Proceedings of the Text REtrieval Conference (TREC) (2013)
13. Lafferty, J., Zhai, C.: Document language models, query models, and risk minimization for information retrieval. In: Proceedings of the 24th Annual International ACM SIGIR Conference on Research and Development in Information Retrieval, pp. 111–119 (2001)

14. Liu, X., Darko, J., Fang, H.: A related entity based approach for knowledge base acceleration. In: Proceedings of the Text REtrieval Conference (TREC) (2013)
15. McCreadie, R., Macdonald, C., Ounis, I., Osborne, M., Petrovic, S.: Scalable distributed event detection for twitter. In: 2013 IEEE International Conference on Big Data, pp. 543–549. IEEE (2013)
16. Mihalcea, R., Csomai, A.: Wikify!: linking documents to encyclopedic knowledge. In: Proceedings of the Sixteenth ACM Conference on Conference on Information and Knowledge Management, pp. 233–242 (2007)
17. Porter, M.F.: An algorithm for suffix stripping. Prog. Electron. Libr. Inf. Syst. **14**(3), 130–137 (1980)
18. Toshniwal, A., Taneja, S., Shukla, A., Ramasamy, K., Patel, J.M., Kulkarni, S., Jackson, J., Gade, K., Fu, M., Donham, J., et al.: Storm@ twitter. In: Proceedings of the 2014 ACM SIGMOD International Conference on Management of Data, pp. 147–156. ACM (2014)
19. Wang, J., Song, D., Lin, C.Y., Liao, L.: BIT and MSRA at TREC KBA CCR Track 2013. In: Proceedings of the Text REtrieval Conference (TREC) (2013)
20. Wang, X., Fang, H., Zhai, C.: A study of methods for negative relevance feedback. In: Proceedings of the 31st Annual International ACM SIGIR Conference on Research and Development in Information Retrieval, pp. 219–226 (2008)
21. Xu, Y., Jones, G.J., Wang, B.: Query dependent pseudo-relevance feedback based on wikipedia. In: Proceedings of the 32nd International ACM SIGIR Conference on Research and Development in Information Retrieval, pp. 59–66 (2009)
22. Zhai, C., Lafferty, J.: A study of smoothing methods for language models applied to Ad Hoc information retrieval. In: Proceedings of the 24th Annual International ACM SIGIR Conference on Research and Development in Information Retrieval, pp. 334–342 (2001)

Language Learning

Measuring Readability for Learners of English as a Foreign Language by Linguistic and Learner Features

Katsunori Kotani[1]([✉]) and Takehiko Yoshimi[2]

[1] Kansai Gaidai University, Osaka, Japan
kkotani@kansaigaidai.ac.jp
[2] Ryukoku University, Kyoto, Japan

Abstract. The Internet serves as a source of authentic reading material, enabling learners to practice English in real contexts when learning English as a foreign language. An adaptive computer-assisted language learning and teaching system can assist in obtaining authentic materials such as news articles from the Internet. However, to match material level to a learner's reading proficiency, the system must be equipped with a method to measure proficiency-based readability. Therefore, we developed a method for doing so. With our method, readability is measured through regression analysis using both learner and linguistic features as independent variables. Learner features account for learner reading proficiency, and linguistic features explain lexical, syntactic, and semantic difficulties of sentences. A cross validation test showed that readability measured with our method exhibited higher correlation ($r = 0.60$) than readability measured only with linguistic features ($r = 0.46$). A comparison of our method with the method without learner features showed a statistically significant difference. These results suggest the effectiveness of combined learner and linguistic features for measuring reading proficiency-based readability.

Keywords: Computer-assisted language learning and teaching · English as a foreign language · Readability · Linguistic and learner feature

1 Introduction

When teaching English as a foreign language (EFL), teachers need to choose reading materials that suit an EFL learner's reading proficiency. The choice of the materials plays an important role, especially when material is chosen from resources that are not prepared for pedagogical purposes, but from those used by English speakers in daily situations which can be inappropriate for a particular learner's capabilities. Appropriate materials will support effective EFL learning, and inappropriate materials can reduce the learning motivation [1, 2] and be detrimental to the learning process.

Finding appropriate materials is a time consuming task for teachers. When teachers gather teaching resources, they need to check the difficulty of the resources in order to choose reading materials that suit for learners' proficiency. The burden of this check-up can be reduced if teachers use readability measuring methods, and calculate readability scores for each candidate material.

© Springer Science+Business Media Singapore 2016
K. Hasida and A. Purwarianti (Eds.): PACLING 2015, CCIS 593, pp. 211–222, 2016.
DOI: 10.1007/978-981-10-0515-2_15

Here, readability is defined as the difficulty for EFL learners in understanding a reading material. The readability is supposed to depend on the linguistic features of a text such as the sentence length and word length.

The use of a readability measuring method has advantages not only for teachers but also EFL learners. If a readability measuring method is available for EFL learners, they can calculate the readability of resources found on the Internet, for instance. Thus, EFL learners can choose for themselves materials that fit their interests from whatever resources they can find, which enhances their learning motivation [1, 2].

Previous studies developed readability measurement methods for native English speakers [3, 4]. However, the previous methods should not be used in calculating the readability for EFL learners since EFL learners' reading proficiencies differ from those of native English speakers. Therefore, it is necessary to develop readability measurement methods specifically for EFL learners [5–7]. Since the range of EFL learners' reading proficiencies is wider than that of native English speakers, it is necessary to take into consideration each individual EFL learner's proficiency when calculating readability. The previous studies neglected the individual differences between EFL learners' reading proficiencies. Thus their methods account for a collective reading proficiency. Therefore, measured materials' readability might fit some EFL learners, but not to others.

As a solution for this problem, we propose to measure readability based on both linguistic and EFL learners' features. EFL learners' features demonstrate reading proficiency such as learning experience and reading comprehension test scores, and linguistic features are classified into lexical, syntactic, and semantic features of a material. Our readability measurement method was developed using these linguistic and learner features as independent variables and readability as a dependent variable in a regression analysis. In this study, we compared two types of readability: readability based on linguistic features, and readability based on both the linguistic and learner features. The experimental results showed that the latter readability expressed the readability for EFL learners more accurately, which suggests the requirement of learner features in measuring the readability.

2   Previous Studies

Ozasa et al. [5] proposed a readability measuring method for EFL learners that examined linguistic features on lexical and syntactic difficulties. Lexical difficulty was calculated in terms of word and phrase difficulty as determined by teachers and researchers, and syntactic difficulty was calculated by the sentence length. The performance of their method was unremarkable in that it could correctly measure readability with an accuracy of 41.2 % in terms of the contribution rate ($r^2 = 0.412$).

Petersen and Ostendorf [6] proposed another readability measurement method for EFL learners that examined linguistic features in more detail. Their method determined the readability level on a four-point scale based on N-gram language models with scores determined by examining the word and sentence length (Flesh-Kincaid readability). The performance of this method was also unremarkable in that it could correctly measure readability with an accuracy of 43.0 % in terms of the contribution rate ($r^2 = 0.430$).

Pilán et al. [7] proposed another method for learners of Swedish as a second or foreign language that measures sentence readability as a binary classification, or in other words, is suitable or unsuitable for learners. Their method employs machine learning, and determines the readability levels based on lexical, syntactic, and semantic features. The performance of this method is high in that it could correctly measure readability with an accuracy of 71 % in terms of the contribution rate ($r^2 = 0.710$).

Stenner [5] proposed a method that measures English native speakers' reading comprehension by examining syntactic and semantic features of a text. The syntactic features account for the difficulty of sentence form in terms of the sentence length, as used in the previous readability measuring methods [4]. However, the semantic features account for the semantic difficulty in terms of the frequency of words used in the corpus: the idea being that the more frequently a word is used, the more easily it is understood. The performance of this method is high, in that it could correctly measure readability with an accuracy of 86.5 % in terms of the contribution rate ($r^2 = 0.865$).

3 Data to Develop Readability Measurement Methods

3.1 Data Outline

As our readability measuring method was developed with regression analysis, it was necessary to collect training/test data consisting of dependent and independent variables. Dependent variables needed to show the readability for EFL learners. We used readability scores of a sentence, scored on a five-point Likert scale for ease of reading comprehension judged by EFL learners where 1: easy, 2: somewhat easy, 3: average, 4: somewhat difficult, and 5: difficult. Independent variables consisted of learner and linguistic features. As described in Sect. 4, the learner features showed reading proficiency, and linguistic features showed the lexical, syntactic, and semantic difficulties of a sentence.

3.2 Learners

Fifty-eight university EFL learners (43 males and 15 females; mean age 21.5 years, standard deviation (S.D.) 2.9) took part in data collection and were paid for participation. The EFL learners were asked to submit valid TOEIC (Test of English for International Communication) scores, taken that year or the year prior then were checked for basic computer literacy such as typing with a keyboard and controlling a mouse since a computer was to be used for data collection.

3.3 Materials

The materials used in this study were news articles since they are often used as practice reading materials for university EFL learners. Each news article included five multiple-choice comprehension questions to let learners work on the reading task as they would in an actual English language test. The questions were made in the [8] format: two true questions to choose a correct description about the article; two false questions to choose an incorrect description about the article; and one content question to choose a correct brief description of the article.

The news articles were chosen from the sections of the Voice of America (VOA) site (http://www.voanews.com): the special section for English learners and the editorial section for native English speakers. The English learners' section's news articles consisted of short, simple sentences that avoided using idiomatic expressions and used the 1,500 basic vocabulary of VOA. The editorial section's news articles were made without any restriction on vocabulary or sentence construction as long as they were appropriate as news articles for English speakers.

3.4 Task

Each learner was asked to read four news articles, a total of 80 sentences, sentence-by-sentence only once. After reading each sentence, they assigned a readability score for the sentence from the five-point Likert scale. After reading the entire article, the EFL learner answered five multiple-choice comprehension questions.

The EFL learners carried out the reading task using a data collecting tool. The tool displayed a sentence to read on a computer screen, and icons to move on to the next sentence and to select multiple-choice items for a readability score and comprehension questions. It did not allow EFL learners to return to a sentence for reading again after moving on to another sentence. It recorded the EFL learner's choices of the readability scores and answers for the comprehension questions.

The EFL learners were asked to complete the reading task as fast as possible during the allotted time (8 min for each news article), and to stop working when the task was completed or the experimenter and the data collecting tool alerted them of the end of the allotted time. They were prohibited from using dictionaries or any other reference books.

3.5   Readability Score

The training/test data consisted of 4,640 instances (58 learners × 80 sentences) of readability scores. The mean readability score was 2.8 (S.D. 1.2). Figure 1 shows how readability scores distribute according to the listening proficiency level. Learners were classified into three proficiency levels based on TOEIC reading comprehension scores: 18 advanced (score range: 335–480), 20 intermediate (score range: 230–330), and 20 beginner (score range: 100–225).

The largest group was the readability score 3 "average" in these three groups, and the smallest group was either the readability score 5 "difficult" or 1 "easy". That is, the reading materials were neither too difficult nor easy for the EFL learners.

As expected, the distribution of readability scores followed the proficiency levels. Advanced learners tended to judge the reading materials as easy, intermediate learners tended to judge them as moderate, beginner learners tended to judge them as difficult. As a reviewer pointed out to us, this distribution supports the reliability of the readability score data.

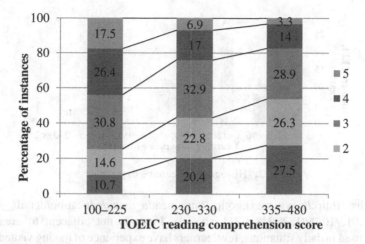

Fig. 1. Readability score distribution by the EFL learners' proficiency levels

4   Features for Measuring Readability

4.1   Learner Feature

Learner features need to explicate EFL learners' reading proficiency. We used learner features in terms of the English learning experiences, experiences of having visited English speaking areas, frequencies of reading English, and reading comprehension test scores (TOEIC reading comprehension scores).

Because EFL learners continue to study English, these learner features dynamically change. From viewpoint of practical use of our method, it is necessary to update the learner feature data, and to reconstruct a readability measuring method.

4.1.1   English Learning Experience
EFL learners' reading proficiency is supposed to increase according to the learning experience. Accordingly, we inquired how many months they had been studying English.

The learning experiences are summarized in Fig. 2. Most EFL learners had been learning English for more than 72 months. This is the baseline of learning experiences for university students in Japan, where English is taught for six years at least in junior- and senior-high schools.

4.1.2   Visiting Experience
Similarly to learning experience, experience of having visited English speaking areas is crucial for developing reading proficiency. As such, we asked EFL learners how many months they had spent in English speaking areas.

The visiting experiences are summarized in Fig. 3. Most EFL learners had visiting experience of less than 12 months. This visiting experience follows the Japanese government survey on visiting experience of high school students. Among more than three thousand high schools students, only 3.4 % had visiting experience for more than

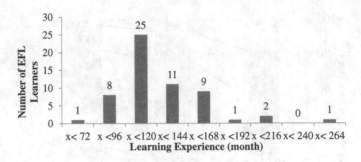

Fig. 2. Histogram of learning experience

12 months (http://www.mext.go.jp/component/a_menu/education/detail/__icsFiles/ afieldfile/2013/10/09/1323948_02_1.pdf). As Japan is not adjacent to areas where English is used in daily situations, few learners have experience of having visited English speaking areas.

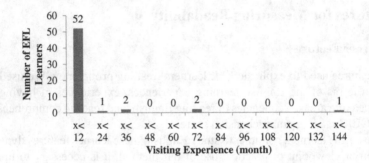

Fig. 3. Histogram of visiting experiences

4.1.3 Frequency of English Reading

If EFL learners read English texts outside classes, the reading proficiency grows. We asked EFL learners how often they read English texts per week in a five-point Likert scale: 1 infrequently, 2 somewhat infrequently, 3 moderate, 4 somewhat frequently, or 5 frequently.

The frequency of English reading is summarized in Fig. 4. Most EFL learners infrequently read English texts, mostly because English is not a principal language in both daily and academic situations in Japan.

4.1.4 Reading Comprehension Test Score (TOEIC Reading Comprehension Score)

Among the learner features, reading comprehension test scores directly reflect the EFL learners' reading proficiency. Among various English language tests, TOEIC is the most popular in Japan since companies utilize university students' TOEIC scores as selection

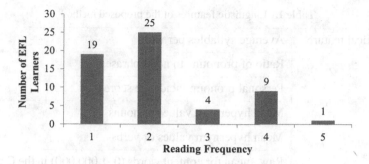

Fig. 4. Histogram of reading frequency

criteria to determine an applicant's English proficiency. As TOEIC scores consist of listening and reading comprehension parts (5–495 points for each part), we asked the EFL learners for their scores on the reading comprehension part.

The TOEIC reading comprehension scores are summarized in Fig. 5. A Kolmogorov-Smirnov test showed that the distribution of the TOEIC comprehension scores does not differ from a normal distribution pattern ($K = 0.51$, $P = 0.57$).

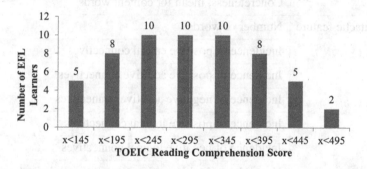

Fig. 5. Histogram of TOEIC reading comprehension scores

4.2 Linguistic Feature

Linguistic features need to explicate linguistic difficulties of a sentence. We used the linguistic features shown in Table 1 that were extractable from sentences through linguistic analyses by a computational linguistic analysis tool (Coh-Metrix [9]). The Coh-Metrix-based analyses can explain the linguistic difficulties of a sentence from the lexical, syntactic, and semantic perspectives. These linguistic features include well-known features such as the number of words (the sentence length) and average syllable per word (the word length).

Table 1. Linguistic features of the proposed method

Lexical feature	Average syllables per word
	Ratio of pronouns to noun phrases
	Personal pronoun incidence score
	Mean hypernym values of nouns
	Mean hypernym values of verbs
	Raw, mean for content words (0–1,000,000) in the Celex lexical database
	Logarithm, mean for content words (0–6) in the Celex lexical database
	Raw, minimum in sentence for content words (0–1,000,000) in the Celex lexical database
	Logarithm, minimum in sentence for content words (0–6) in the Celex lexical database
	Concreteness, mean for content words
Syntactic feature	Number of words
	Incidence of positive causal connectives
	Incidence of positive additive connectives
	Incidence of negative additive connectives
	Incidence of positive logical connectives
	Incidence of negative logical connectives
	Noun phrase incidence Score (per thousand words)
	Logical operator incidence score (and + if + or + conditional + negation)
	Mean number of modifiers per noun-phrase
	Mean number of higher level constituents per word
	Mean number of words before the main verb of main clause in sentences
Semantic feature	Incidence of causal verbs, links, and particles
	Ratio of causal particles to causal verbs
	Incidence of intentional actions, events, and particles
	Mean of location and motion ratio scores

5 Experiment

5.1 Method

The readability measurement method was constructed by support vector regression [10] with readability scores as dependent variables and all the learner and linguistic features shown in Sect. 4 as independent variables. Support vector regression was performed using an algorithm implemented in the mySVM software [11]. The first order polynomial was set as a type of kernel function, and the other settings were retained as the default ones.

Our readability measuring method was examined in a five-fold cross validation test by comparing sample methods (Method I-IV) developed using linguistic features with each type of the learner features. The baseline method (Method V) was developed using only the linguistic features. The features used in each method are marked in Table 2. Each method was examined by comparing the readability scores assigned by the EFL learners and readability scores measured with one of the methods.

Table 2. Readability measuring methods

	Our method	Method I	Method II	Method III	Method IV	Method V
Linguistic features	●	●	●	●	●	●
Learning experience	●	●				
Visiting experience	●		●			
Reading frequency	●			●		
TOEIC reading comprehension score	●				●	

5.2 Result

The correlation coefficients in Table 3 were statistically significantly different from zero (the significant level $\alpha = 0.05$). The difference in correlation coefficients with the baseline method (Method V) was examined using the Meng-Rosenthal-Rubin method [12]. The results showed that there was not a statistically significant difference between the baseline method and Method I (learning experience), but significant differences were found in the other methods (the significant level $\alpha' = 0.01$ after Bonferroni correction for five comparisons). The correlation coefficient of our method was marked as the highest. This suggests that the readability for EFL learners is affected by both learner and linguistic features.

Table 3. Correlation coefficients (an asterisk: p < 0.01)

	Our method	Method I	Method II	Method III	Method IV	Method V
Learner feature	all	learning experience	visiting experience	reading frequency	TOEIC reading comprehension score	none
Correlation coefficient	0.60*	0.47	0.49*	0.50*	0.57*	0.46

Measurement errors from the cross validation test results are plotted in Fig. 6. Measurement error was calculated as an absolute value of the difference between a readability score measured with a method and a readability score assigned by an EFL learner. Our method had more instances in the ranges of small measurement error (0.0–1.0) than the other methods, as seen in Fig. 6.

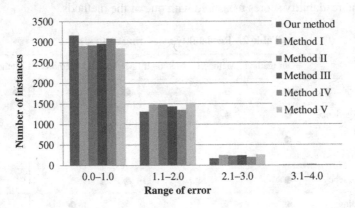

Fig. 6. Error distribution

5.3 Discussion

Our readability measuring method improved the performance of evaluating material by combining linguistic and learner features, although the improvement by combining the learner features was lower than expected. However, the results suggest the validity of the use of learner features, as follows.

Among the learner features, the TOEIC reading comprehension scores showed the highest contribution in measuring the readability for EFL learners as seen in Method IV. This fact suggests that the readability for EFL learners highly depends on the reading comprehension test scores. Hence, it is considered that the experimental result supports our readability measuring method using the TOEIC reading comprehension scores.

The visiting experience (Method II) and the reading frequency (Method III) also contributed to the readability for EFL learners. As the EFL learners' proficiency depends on the visiting experience and the reading frequency, these learner features are considered to function as indices showing the EFL learners' proficiency.

However, the learning experience (Method I) showed no significant contribution to the readability for EFL learners. We expected that the learning experience would function as an index for the EFL learners' proficiency, but the learning experience did not reflect the proficiency. This is apparent since the learning experience showed the fact that the EFL learners in this study merely had English learning experience in junior- and senior high schools and university.

6   Conclusion

We proposed a method for automatically measuring readability for EFL learners. Unlike the previous studies on readability, our method directly takes into account the EFL learners' reading proficiency as well as linguistic features of a text. Reading proficiency consists of the learning experience, visiting experience, reading frequency, and TOEIC reading comprehension scores.

In the experiment, the performance of our readability measuring method was confirmed by comparing the method without the learner features. The experimental results showed that among the learner features, learning experience was not statistically significant for measuring readability. However, the use of learner features surely improved the performance of a readability measuring method.

It is still unclear whether our method is practical for the effective choosing of reading materials for EFL learners. Hence, further examination of the validity of our method when used by teachers is required.

References

1. Hubbard, P.: Learner training for effective use of CALL. In Fotos, S., Browne, C. (eds.) New Perspectives in CALL for Second Language Classrooms, pp. 45–67. Lawrence Erlbaum, Mahwah (2004)
2. Petrides, J.R.: Attitudes and motivation and their impact on the performance of young english as a foreign language learners. J. Lang. Learn. 5(1), 1–20 (2006)
3. Flesch, R.F.: A new readability yardstick. J. Appl. Psychol. 32(3), 221–233 (1948)
4. Stenner, A.J.: Measuring reading comprehension with the lexile framework. Paper presented at the California Comparability Symposium (1996)
5. Ozasa, T., Weir, G.R.S., Fukui, M.: Measuring readability for Japanese learners of english. In: Proceedings of the 12th Conference of Pan-Pacific Association of Applied Linguistics, UNSPECIFIED (2007)
6. Petersen, S.E., Ostendorf, M.: A machine learning approach to reading level assessment. Comput. Speech Lang. 23, 89–106 (2009)
7. Pilán, I., Volodina, E., Johansson, R.: Rule-based and machine learning approaches for second language sentence-level readability. In: Proceeding of the ACL 2014 9th Workshop on Innovative Use of NLP for Building Educational Applications, pp. 174–184. Association for Computational Linguistics (2014)
8. Nation, P., Malarcher, C.: Reading for Speed and Fluency. Compass Publishing, Seoul (2007)
9. Graesser, A.C., McNamara, D.S., Louwerse, M.M., Cai, Z.: Coh-metrix: analysis of text on cohesion and language. Behav. Res. Methods Instrum. Comput. 36(2), 193–202 (2004)
10. Vapnik, V.: Statistical Learning Theory. Wiley-Interscience, New York (1998)

11. Rüping, S.: mySVM-Manual. University of Dortmund, Lehrstuhl Informatik VIII (2000). http://www-ai.cs.uni-ortmund.de/SOFTWARE/MYSVM/
12. Meng, X.L., Rosenthal, R., Rubin, D.B.: Comparing correlated correlation coefficients. Psychol. Bull. **111**(1), 172–175 (1992)

Machine Translation

Machine Translation Method Based on Non-compositional Semantics (Word-Level Sentence-Pattern-Based MT)

Jun Sakata[✉], Jin'ichi Murakami, Masato Tokuhisa, and Masaki Murata

Information and Knowledge Engineering, Tottori University, Tottori, Japan
{d112004,murakami,tokuhisa,murata}@eecs.tottori-u.ac.jp

Abstract. To overcome the conventional machine translation method, Ikehara et al. proposed a machine translation scheme based on non-compositional semantics. This machine translation scheme requires many sentence patterns which can preserve the semantics of the expression structure. To use this machine translation scheme for Japanese-English machine translation, a compound and complex sentence pattern dictionary, called "ToribankSPD", have been developed. This dictionary has three levels of sentence patterns: "word-level", "phrase-level", and "clause-level". In this paper, according to the machine translation scheme based on non-compositional semantics, we implemented the Japanese-English sentence-pattern-based machine translation method using the word-level sentence patterns of ToribankSPD. In our experiments, the pattern matching rate was low (about 10%). However, 72 out of 100 evaluated sentences used the sentence patterns that had an appropriate expression structure, and the translation accuracy of 55 sentences was high.

Keywords: Non-compositional semantics · Sentence-pattern-based machine translation · Word-level sentence pattern · Linear component · Non-linear component

1 Introduction

The conventional machine translation method based on compositional semantics has a problem in that it cannot generate the semantics of the sentence when it generates the target sentence. To resolve this problem, Ikehara et al. proposed a machine translation scheme based on non-compositional semantics [1]. This machine translation scheme requires many sentence patterns that can preserve the semantics of the expression structure. The sentence patterns have linear components and non-linear components. Linear components are defined as components that don't change the semantics of the sentence when being replaced with other components. And non-linear components are defined as components that change the semantics of the sentence when being replaced with other components. In translation, we conduct local translation of matched morphemes for the linear components and insert these results into the target sentence pattern.

© Springer Science+Business Media Singapore 2016
K. Hasida and A. Purwarianti (Eds.): PACLING 2015, CCIS 593, pp. 225–237, 2016.
DOI: 10.1007/978-981-10-0515-2_16

To use this scheme for Japanese-English machine translation, a compound and complex sentence pattern dictionary, called "ToribankSPD", have been developed [2]. The dictionary has 226,817 sentence pattern pairs from Japanese/English compound/complex sentences pairs. It also has three levels of sentence patterns: word-level (121,904 pattern pairs), phrase-level (79,438 pattern pairs), and clause-level (25,475 pattern pairs) [3]. Each level indicates the range of alignments that are replaced with variables in Japanese/English sentence pairs.

In this paper, according to the machine translation scheme based on non-compositional semantics, we implement a Japanese-English sentence-pattern-based machine translation method that involves ToribankSPD, a structural pattern matching (SPM) system [4], and a generation system. We evaluate the translation accuracy of our word-level sentence-pattern-based machine translation method and describe the efficiency of and problems with the method. It is said that machine translation methods with sentence patterns have high translation accuracy when the sentence patterns match to the input sentence. Most of the machine translation methods with sentence patterns have only several hundreds or thousands sentence patterns [5]. This paper is the first attempt as the machine translation methods with about hundred thousands sentence patterns to compound and complex sentences. As compound and complex sentences have complicated structure, Our sentence-pattern-based machine translation method is considered effective for these sentences.

2 ToribankSPD: Compound and Complex Sentence Pattern Dictionary

To resolve the problem of the conventional machine translation method, Ikehara et al. proposed a machine translation scheme based on non-compositional semantics [1]. This machine translation scheme uses sentence patterns that have linear components and non-linear components. This scheme is available to various languages, and is especially effective in the language pairs that have different language structure. To use this machine translation scheme for Japanese-English machine translation, a compound and complex sentence pattern dictionary, called "ToribankSPD", have been developed [2]. The original sentences of ToribankSPD were collected from various Japanese-English and English-Japanese dictionary. In total, 226,817 sentence patterns have been created.

Table 1 shows an example of our sentence patterns. Sentence patterns have letters, variables, functions, and markers. Japanese/English word/phrase/clause alignments are replaced with variables that are equivalent to the linear components. Word-level patterns have word variables. Phrase-level patterns have word and phrase variables, and clause-level patterns have all of three variables. The variables in Japanese sentence patterns have semantic codes. These codes are used for sentence pattern selection.

Non-linear components are described as letters and functions. The terms ".hitei" and ".kako" are modality and tense functions, respectively. ".hitei" matches negative expressions, and ".kako" matches the past tense. English functions have a role to assign a word form. "$N2$^poss" means $N2$ is the possessive case in English. "$V5$^past" means $V5$ is the past tense. In Japanese, a subject is often omitted, so $<N1\ は\ >$ means whether the subject is omitted in the pattern. In English patterns, $<I|N1>$ is "$N1$" if Japanese matches $N1$, or "I" if not.

The semantics of the expression structure is composed from non-linear components, word forms, parts of speech of linear components, and an order of components. The sentence patterns preserve the semantics of the expression structure of sentence.

Table 1. Example of sentence pattern pairs in ToribankSPD

Japanese Sentence	彼 の お母さん が ああ 若い と は 思わ なかっ た 。
English Sentence	I never expected his mother to be so young.
Word-Level Japanese Pattern	$<N1\ は\ >N2$(NI:23,NI:24) の $N3$(NI:80,NI:49) があ $AJ4$(NY:5) とは $V5$(NY:32,NY:31).hitei.kako。
Word-Level English Pattern	$<I|N1>$ never $V5$^past $N2$^poss $N3$ to be so $AJ4$.
Phrase-Level Japanese Pattern	$<\ N1\ は\ >\ NP2$(NI:49,NI:80) があ $AJ3$(NY:05) とは $V4$(NY:31,NY:32).hitei.kako。
Phrase-Level English Pattern	$<I|N1>$ never $V4$^past $NP2$ to be so $AJ3$.

3 Japanese-English Word-Level Sentence-Pattern-Based Machine Translation Method (Proposed Method)

In this section, we describe our word-level sentence-pattern-based machine translation method. Figure 1 shows an overview of the method. The translation steps are as follows.

Step 1) Sentence pattern matching is conducted.
Step 2) Pattern selection with semantic codes is conducted.
Step 3) Candidates of English sentences are generated using the word-level generation system.
Step 4) Only one English sentence is selected with use of the translation probability and word trigram.

3.1 Japanese Sentence Pattern Matching

We developed the structural pattern matching (SPM) system [4]. It implements the augmented transition network (ATN) algorithm [6] with breadth-first search and uses sentence patterns. The input sentence for the SPM is already morphological and has semantic codes added. It conducts pattern matching between the input sentence and sentence patterns. Moreover, it outputs the pattern matching results. Figure 2 shows an example of an input sentence.

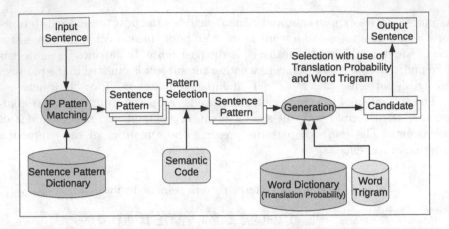

Fig. 1. Word-level sentence-pattern-based machine translation method

---

1. /彼 (1710,{NI:23,NI:48})
2. +の (7410)
3. /お母さん (1100,{NI:80,NI:49})
4. +が (7410)
5. /ああ (1110)
6. /若い (3106,{NY:5})
7. +と (7420)
8. +は (7530)
9. /思わ (2392, 思う, 思わ,{NY:32,NY:31})
10. +なかっ(7184, ない, なかっ)
11. +た (7216)
12. +。 (0110)
13. /nil

Fig. 2. Example of input sentence

In the first line in Fig. 2, "彼"[he] is a Japanese morpheme, "1710" is the tagging code, and "NI:23,NI:48" are indeclinable semantic codes [7]. In the sixth line, "NY:5" is a declinable semantic code. Each line shows a Japanese morpheme and semantic information.

Table 2 shows the SPM results. "Japanese Pattern" is a matched Japanese pattern for input sentence. "English Pattern" is a corresponding English pattern to that Japanese pattern. In "Matched Morpheme", for example, "$N2=$彼" shows that the morpheme "彼 [he]" matches the noun variable $N2$.

3.2 Sentence Pattern Selection with Semantic Code

If several sentence patterns match, we select sentence patterns with semantic codes. We use the semantic codes in "Nihongo-Goi-Taikei" [7]. These codes consist of indeclinable and declinable semantic codes, which have a hierarchical structure. The steps of sentence pattern selection are as follows.

Step 1) Semantic codes of the input sentence and matched sentence patterns are extracted.

Step 2) A range for sentence pattern selection is extracted from a matched morpheme for a variable. A parent code of a matched morpheme and all its children codes are determined as this range.

Step 3) If all semantic codes of variables in the Japanese sentence pattern are included within those ranges, these sentence pattern pairs are used for translation.

3.3   Word-Level Sentence-Pattern-Based Machine Translation

Word Dictionary. In the word-level generation system, word translation of a morpheme is done with a word bilingual dictionary. ToribankSPD has alignments of words, phrases, and clauses. We use this word alignments for creating a word dictionary.

In this dictionary, translation probabilities are given to each Japanese-English word pair. Table 3 lists examples of the word dictionary.

Translation probabilities in Table 3 are calculated using Equation (1).

$$P = \frac{C(e,j)}{C(j)} \times \frac{C(e,j)}{C(e)} \tag{1}$$

where $C(e,j)$ is the number of co-occurrences of each word pair in the alignments list, $C(j)$ is the number of occurrences of each Japanese word, and $C(e)$ is the number of occurrences of each English word. The first to fourth rows in Table 3 show English verbs "hit", "kick", "turn down", and "stamp out" coupled with the Japanese verb "蹴る", and the translation probabilities are "0.01", "0.29", "0.05", and "0.06", respectively.

Word-Level Generation System. An English sentence is translated with matched sentence pattern pairs with the word-level generation system. The word-level generation system performs word translation for the Japanese morphemes of the SPM results. Word translation is done using the word dictionary. Several results of word translation are inserted into the English pattern, and a single maximum likelihood sentence is selected with use of the translation probability and English word trigram. The translation steps of the word-level generation system are as follows.

Table 2. Results of SPM

Japanese Pattern	N2, の,N3, が, ああ,AJ4, とは V5,.hitei,.kako,。
English Pattern	<I|N1> never V5^past N2^poss N3 to be so AJ4.
Matched Morpheme	N2=彼 {NI:23,NI:24}, N3=お母さん {NI:80,NI:49},
	AJ4=若い {NY:5}, V5=思わ (思う){NY:32,NY:31}

Table 3. Example of word dictionary

Japanese word (POS)	English word (POS)	Translation probability
蹴る [kick] (V)	hit (V)	0.01
	kick (V)	0.29
	stamp out (V)	0.05
	turn down (V)	0.06
翻訳 [translation] (N)	translation (N)	0.53
	translate (V)	0.20

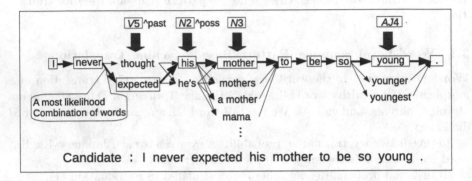

Fig. 3. Example of generation

Step 1) Word translations of Japanese morphemes are done.
Step 2) Word translation results are changed to the assigned form.
Step 3) Candidates of word translation are inserted into the English sentence pattern.
Step 4) The maximum likelihood combination of words is selected with use of the translation probability and English word trigram.

Example of English Sentence Generation. In the last generation step, the maximum likelihood combination of words is selected with use of the translation probability and English word trigram. Figure 3 shows an example of English sentence generation.

Selection of an Output Sentence from Candidates. If several sentence patterns are obtained in pattern matching and pattern selection, all matched sentence patterns are used for translation. As one translation candidate is obtained from one sentence pattern, in this case, several translation candidates are obtained. One translation candidate with the maximum translation probability and English word trigram (Sect. 3.3) is selected as an output sentence.

4 Experiments

4.1 Experimental Conditions

We carried out an open-test to investigate the effectiveness of the proposed method. We used 100,000 sentence patterns for translation experiments and created a word dictionary from word alignments extracted from these 100,000 sentence patterns. Word trigrams were trained from about 280,000 English sentences. In these sentences, 100,000 were original English sentences of these 100,000 English patterns and about 180,000 were English sentences from another Japanese-English parallel corpus [8]. We used 5,000 original Japanese sentences of the remaining sentence patterns as input sentences.

4.2 Baseline System

We used the phrase-based SMT (MOSES) [9] as the baseline system for comparison. We used 100,000 sentence pairs (same as sentence pairs of sentence patterns for pattern matching) for training of the translation model and about 280,000 English sentences (the same as in Sect. 4.1) for training of the language model. We conducted parameter tuning with MERT.

4.3 Evaluation Method

Translation accuracy was measured using automatic metrics and manual evaluation. We used the evaluation tools BLEU [10], TER [11], METEOR [12], and RIBES [13]. Manual evaluation was done from the point of view of adequacy [14], and Table 4 shows the scoring criteria.

4.4 Results

Out of the 5,000 input sentences, 502 sentences had at least one matched sentence pattern. Table 5 lists the automatic evaluation results of these 502 sentences. In all metrics, the proposed method outperformed the baseline.

We carried out manual evaluation for 100 randomly extracted sentences from the 502 sentences. Table 6 lists the manual evaluation results of these 100 sentences. The value of each evaluation criteria is the number of sentences. In Table 6, the number of Eval. 1 and Eval. 2 of proposed method are smaller than baseline, and the number of Eval. 4 and Eval. 5 are larger than baseline. And the average of proposed method is higher than baseline. These results show that the proposed method outperformed the baseline.

An example of the translation results is shown in Table 7. "Japanese Sentence Pattern" and "English Sentence Pattern" is the sentence pattern pair used for translation of output sentence. "Original Japanese Sentence" is the original sentence of this Japanese sentence pattern, and "Original English Sentence" is the original sentence of this English sentence pattern.

Table 4. Criteria of manual evaluation

Eval. 5	The meaning of the input sentence is correctly recognized.
Input	きみ は お父さん の 意見 に 従った ほう が いい 。
Output	You had better follow your father's opinion.
Reference	You should take your father's advice.
Eval. 4	Although a part is not appropriate grammatically, the meaning of the input sentence is correctly recognized.
Input	彼 は 彼女 を きびしい 目 で 見た 。
Output	He looked at her with harsh regard.
Reference	He regarded her sharply.
Eval. 3	The meaning of the input sentence is recognized somewhat.
Input	彼女 は とても 涼しい 目 を して いる 。
Output	She is very bright eyes.
Reference	She has very bright eyes.
Eval. 2	Only a part of the input sentence is recognized or output sentence is grammatically correct but the meaning is significantly different from the input sentence.
Input	彼 は 時計 を 出して 時間 を 見た 。
Output	He set the clock to look at the time own .
Reference	He took out his watch and glanced at the time.
Eval. 1	Nothing is recognized.
Input	彼 は なに が 起こって も 無神経だ 。
Output	He is might happen.
Reference	He is insensible of anything that happens around him.

Table 5. Automatic evaluation results

	BLEU	TER	METEOR	RIBES
Proposed	0.358	0.489	0.642	0.806
Baseline	0.307	0.549	0.583	0.780

Table 6. Manual evaluation results

	Eval. 1	Eval. 2	Eval. 3	Eval. 4	Eval. 5	Average
Proposed	4	26	15	11	44	3.65
Baseline	21	37	11	9	22	2.74

5 Discussion

The translation accuracy of the proposed method was high (3.65 : the average of human evaluation), but the pattern matching rate was low (about 10 %: 502/5,000). In this section, we discuss the reasons for these results and describe the efficiency of and problems with the proposed method.

Table 7. Example of translation results

Input	彼 が 帰国する 可能性 は ない 。
Reference	There is no question of his going home.
Output of proposed method	There is no possibility of his coming home.
Value of manual evaluation	5
Japanese Sentence Pattern	$N1$ が ($V2$^rentai|$ND2$ をする) $N3$ は ' 無い'#1(.genzai|.kako)。
English Sentence Pattern	There @be#1(^present|^past) no $N3$ of $N1$^poss $V2$^ing .
Matched morpheme	$N1$=彼, $V2$=帰国する, $V3$=可能性
Original Japanese Sentence	彼 が 当選する 可能性 は ない 。
Original English Sentence	There is no possibility of his winning the election.
Output of baseline	There is no possibility of his home country.
Value of manual evaluation	2

5.1 Efficiency of Proposed Method

We assumed that a expression structure can be preserved in a sentence pattern. We discuss whether a used sentence pattern for output is appropriate. In the 100 sentences used for manual evaluation, 72 sentences were appropriate and 28 sentences were not. Table 8 lists the causes of not using an appropriate sentence pattern in the 28 sentences.

In Table 8(c), (d) and (e) were caused by an error in each process. The error of annotations of semantic codes to morphemes causes the problem of (c). We can improve this problem by adding the words to the annotation list used by the annotation program. To improve the problem of (d), We need to correct these sentence pattern pairs manually. We omit the discussion about the problem of (e).

If we assume these processes were correctly performed, only 8 sentences did not use an appropriate sentence pattern. These results suggest that 72 out of the 80 sentences matched an appropriate pattern when all processes were correctly performed. Fifty-five out of these 72 sentences had high translation accuracy (Eval. 4 or 5). The other 17 sentences had problems in word translation, and the translation accuracy of those sentences was low. Therefore we confirmed that the proposed method obtained high translation accuracy by using appropriate sentence patterns.

Problem in Way of Making Sentence Patterns. Table 9 shows an example of cause (a) in Table 8. This example has two problems. One is concerning English functions. English functions have a role to determine word form of word translation results. This input sentence is an imperative sentence, but the verb variables in the used English pattern are not added a function which assign an original form of verb. This results in the wrong form in the output, such as "gets". This problem can be resolved by adding appropriate English

Table 8. Causes of not using appropriate sentence pattern

Cause	Number of sentences
(a) Problem in way of making sentence patterns	5
(b) Multi-word expression is decomposed and matched for variable	3
(c) Failure in pattern selection	14
(d) Error in sentence pattern	4
(e) Error in morphological analysis and SPM	2

Table 9. Example of problem in way of making sentence patterns

Input	子供 は 早く 寝て 早く 起き なさい 。
Output	Lie down its speed and gets up early .
Reference	Children should go to bed early and get up early.
Value of manual Eval.	1
Japanese Sentence Pattern	$< \quad N1$ は $>$ $ADV2$ $V3$ (て $\mid$ で) $ADV4$ ($V5$^meirei$\mid V5$.meireigo)。
English Sentence Pattern	$V3$ <your$\mid N1$^poss> $N2$ and $V5$ $ADV4$.
Matched morpheme	$N1$=子供, $ADV2$=早く, $V3$=寝 (寝る) $ADV4$=早く, $V5$=起き (起きる)
Original Japanese Sentence	十分 食べ て 十分 眠り なさい 。
Original English Sentence	Eat your fill and sleep well.

functions. The other problem concerns markers for a zero pronoun. In general Japanese imperative sentence, the object ordered by speaker at input is not included in that sentence. This input is a unique sentence that includes the object (("子供" [children]) of order as a subject 子供は" [children are]). The Japanese pattern in Table 9 matches the input by a marker for a zero pronoun ("$< N1$ は $>$" matches "子供は"). In this case, adding this marker to this sentence pattern is not necessary. This problem can be resolved by deleting unnecessary markers from each sentence pattern.

Problem of Multi-word Expression. Table 10 shows an example of cause (b) in Table 8. In the input, "情の細やかな" is a multi-word expression. The meaning of this expression is closest to "sensitive". However, a corresponding expression in the output is "tinier sensibilities". This result is caused by splitting this expression and matching each morpheme "情の細やかな" to each variable ($N2$ and $AJ3$). If we use word-level sentence patterns, we need a sentence pattern that describes ("情" and "細やかな") as letters to obtain an appropriate result. However, it is possible to obtain an appropriate result by using phrase-level sentence patterns.

Low Translation Accuracy of Word Translation. With the proposed method, word translation is done using the word dictionary, and a single maxi-

Table 10. Example of multi-word expression decomposed and matched for variables

Input	彼女 は 情 の 細やかな 人 だ 。
Output	She has tinier sensibilities.
Reference	She is a warm and considerate woman.
Value of manual Eval.	2
Japanese Sentence Pattern	$N1$ は $N2$ の $AJV3$^rentai(人 ｜ ひと ｜ ヒト) だ。
English Sentence Pattern	$N1$ @have $AJ3$ $N2$.
Matched morpheme	$N1$=彼女, $N2$=情, $AJV3$=細やかな (細やかだ)
Original Japanese Sentence	彼 は 心 の まっすぐな 人 だ 。
Original English Sentence	He has an upright mind.

Table 11. Example of problem in word selection

Input	彼 の 言う こと は 無意味だ 。
Output	He is fruitless.
Reference	There is no meaning in what he says.
Value of manual Eval.	2
Japanese Sentence Pattern	$N1$ の (言う ｜ いう ｜ 謂う ｜ 云う) ことは $AJV2$。
English Sentence Pattern	$N1$ @be $AJ2$.
Matched morpheme	$N1$=彼, $AJV2$=無意味だ
Original Japanese Sentence	君 の 言う こと は 本当 だ 。
Original English Sentence	You are truthful.

mum likelihood sentence is selected with use of the translation probability and English word trigram. In Sect. 5.1, 55 out of 72 sentences that had an appropriate sentence pattern had high translation accuracy. However, the remaining 17 sentences had low translation accuracy due to problems in word translation.

If a matched morpheme is not in the word dictionary, the morpheme is outputted as an unknown word. Nine out of the 17 sentences had this problem. This problem can be resolved by adding new words to the word dictionary.

The remaining 8 sentences exhibited a problem of not selecting an appropriate word from the translation probability and word trigram. Table 11 shows an example of the problem in word selection. "Fruitless" in the output is different from the meaning of "無意味だ" [nonsense]. There are appropriate candidates in the word dictionary, for example "meaningless", but "fruitless" is selected with use of the translation probability and word trigram.

5.2 Pattern Matching Rate

The pattern matching rate was about 10 %, which means that 100,000 word-level sentence patterns are not enough to cover compound and complex sentences for translation. Our sentence pattern dictionary has word-level, phrase-level, and clause-level sentence patterns. We have already carried out a pattern matching test with phrase-level patterns in the same situation as Sect. 4.1, and the pattern matching rate was about 40 %. In the future, we will evaluate the translation accuracy of our sentence-pattern-based machine translation method with those phrase-level sentence patterns.

6   Conclusion

The conventional machine translation method based on compositional semantics has a problem in that it cannot generate the semantics of the sentence when it generates the target sentence. To resolve this problem, Ikehara et al. proposed a machine translation scheme with sentence patterns based on non-compositional semantics. In this paper, according to this machine translation scheme, we implemented a Japanese-English sentence-pattern-based machine translation method using our word-level sentence patterns. We carried out translation experiments with compound and complex sentences as inputs. In the experiments, the pattern matching rate was low (about 10 %). However, 72 out of the evaluated 100 sentences used the sentence patterns that had an appropriate expression structure, and the translation accuracy of 55 sentences was high. For future work, we will evaluate the translation accuracy of the machine translation method, using our phrase-level sentence patterns.

Acknowledgments. The development of a compound and complex sentence pattern dictionary, called "ToribankSPD", was supported under the CREST program of the Japan Science and Technology Agency.

References

1. Ikehara, S., Tokuhisa, M., Murakami, J., Saraki, M., Miyazaki, M., Ikeda, N.: Pattern dictionary development based on non-compositional language model for Japanese compound and complex sentences. In: Matsumoto, Y., Sproat, R.W., Wong, K.-F., Zhang, M. (eds.) ICCPOL 2006. LNCS (LNAI), vol. 4285, pp. 509–519. Springer, Heidelberg (2006)
2. Ikehara, S., Tokuhisa, M., Murakami, J.: Non-compositional language model and pattern dictionary development for Japanese compound and complex sentences. In: Proceedings of the 22nd International Conference on Computational Linguistics, vol. 1, pp. 343–360, Manchester (2008)
3. Tori-Bank (2007). http://www.unicorn/toribank
4. Tokuhisa, M., Murakami, J., Ikehara, S.: Pattern search by structural matching from Japanese compound and complex sentence pattern dictionary (in Japanese). IPSJ SIG Technical report, 2006-NL-176, pp. 9–16 (2006)
5. Yin, D., Zhang, D.: Construct chunk-level templates for improving rule-based machine translation. J. Comput. Inf. Syst. **9**(14), 5505–5512 (2013)
6. Shapiro, S.C.: Generalized augmented transition network grammars for generation from semantic networks. Am. J. Comput. Linguist. Arch. **8**(1), 12–25 (1982)
7. Ikehara, S., Miyazaki, M., Shirai, S., Yokoo, A., Nakaiwa, H., Ogura, K., Ooyama, Y., Hayashi, Y.: Goi-Taikei: A Japanese Lexicon (in Japanese). Iwanami Shoten (1997)

8. Murakami, J., Hujinami, S.: Japanese-English parallel sentences collection from digital media (in Japanese). JCL Workshop 2012 (2012)
9. Koehn, P., Hoang, H., Birch, A., Callison-Burch, C., Federico, M., Bertoldi, N., Cowan, B., Shen, W., Moran, C., Zens, R., Dyer, C., Bojar, O., Constantin, A., Herbst, E.: Moses: open source toolkit for statistical machine translation. In: Proceedings of the 45th Annual Meeting of the Association for Computational Linguistics on Interactive Poster and Demonstration Sessions, pp. 177–180, Prague (2007)
10. Kishore, P., Roukos, S., Ward, T., Wei-Jing, Z.: BLEU: a method for automatic evaluation of machine translation. In: Proceedings of the 40th Annual Meeting of the Association for Computational Linguistics, pp. 311–318, Philadelphia, Pennsylvania (2002)
11. Snover, M., Dorr, B., Schwartz, R., Micciulla, L., Makhoul, J.: A study of translation edit rate with targeted human annotation. In: Proceedings of the 7th Conference of the Association for Machine Translation in the Americas, pp. 223–231, Cambridge (2006)
12. Banerjee, S., Lavie, A.: METEOR: an automatic metric for MT evaluation with improved correlation with human judgments. In: Proceedings of the 43th Annual Meeting of the Association of Computational Linguistics on Intrinsic and Extrinsic Evaluation Measures for MT and/or Summarization, pp. 65–72, Ann Arbor (2005)
13. Isozaki, H., Hirao, T., Duh, K., Sudoh, K., Tsukada, H.: Automatic evaluation of translation quality for distant language Pairs. In: Proceedings of the 2010 Conference on Empirical Methods in Natural Language Processing (EMNLP), pp. 944–952, Massachusetts (2010)
14. Koehn, P., Monz, C.: Manual and automatic evaluation of machine translation between European languages. In: Proceedings of the Workshop on Statistical Machine Translation, pp. 102–121, New York (2006)

The Application of Phrase Based Statistical Machine Translation Techniques to Myanmar Grapheme to Phoneme Conversion

Ye Kyaw Thu[1]([✉]), Win Pa Pa[2], Andrew Finch[1], Jinfu Ni[3], Eiichiro Sumita[1], and Chiori Hori[3]

[1] Multilingual Translation Laboratory, NICT, Kyoto, Japan
{yekyawthu,andrew.finch,eiichiro.sumita}@nict.go.jp
[2] Natural Language Processing Lab, UCSY, Yangon, Myanmar
winpapa@ucsy.edu.mm
[3] Spoken Language Communication Laboratory, NICT, Kyoto, Japan
{jinfu.ni,chiori.hori}@nict.go.jp

Abstract. Grapheme-to-Phoneme (G2P) conversion is a necessary step for speech synthesis and speech recognition. In this paper, we attempt to apply a Statistical Machine Translation (SMT) approach for Myanmar G2P conversion. The performance of G2P conversion with SMT is measured in terms of BLEU score, syllable phoneme accuracy and processing time. The experimental results show that G2P conversion with SMT is outperformed a Conditional Random Field (CRF) approach. Moreover, the training time was considerably faster than the CRF approach.

Keywords: G2P · SMT · CRF · Phoneme · Myanmar language

1 Introduction

G2P conversion is the task of predicting the pronunciation of words given only the spelling. A grapheme is the smallest semantically distinguishing unit in a written language analogous to the phonemes of spoken languages. The correspondence between graphemes and phonemes of the Myanmar language is not as simple as one to one. The relationship between syllables and pronunciations is context dependent, depending on adjacent syllables, and there are many exceptional cases. Some syllables can be pronounced in more than 4 ways depending on the context and Part of Speech (POS) of the syllable.

This is the reason Myanmar G2P conversion cannot be performed sufficiently well using Dictionary based approaches or rule-based approaches. Some Myanmar words' pronunciation can vary across different dialects of Myanmar. We will focus only on standard Myanmar pronunciation in this paper.

We took into account Myanmar subscript words or Pali words and foreign words in this work. The transcription of foreign words pronunciation is not standardized for Myanmar language, therefore some foreign words can be written in

© Springer Science+Business Media Singapore 2016
K. Hasida and A. Purwarianti (Eds.): PACLING 2015, CCIS 593, pp. 238–250, 2016.
DOI: 10.1007/978-981-10-0515-2_17

Myanmar in more than one way and there can be an out of vocabulary (OOV) problem.

We applied phrase based SMT for sentence level Myanmar language G2P conversion. Phoneme tagged training and test sentences are prepared manually. The performance of G2P conversion on SMT was compared with CRF approach.

The rest of this paper is organized as follows. Section 2 describes Related Work for G2P and Sect. 3 explains G2P Mapping. Preparing Training Data and Pronunciations of syllables is explained in Sects. 4 and 5. Section 6 is Experiment of G2P with SMT and CRF, Sect. 7 presents results of experiment, Sect. 8 is about discussion and Sect. 9 concludes the paper.

2 Related Work

There is only one published paper for Myanmar language G2P conversion so far. It was a dictionary-based approach and worked on only Myanmar syllables and did not consider Pali or subscript consonants [1]. The main drawback is out of vocabulary word (OOV) since it was a dictionary-based approach. G2P conversion for English and non-English languages have been proposed using rule-based, data-driven and statistical methods [8–11]. [8] compared different G2P methods and found that data-driven methods outperform rule-based methods. A novel modified Expectation-Maximization (EM)-driven G2Psequence alignment algorithm that supports joint-sequence language models, and several decoding solutions using weighted finite-state transducers (WFST) is presented in [10].

G2P conversion using SMT is proposed by [2, 3]. In [2], it shows that applying SMT gives better results than a joint sequence model-based G2P converter for French. The automatic generation of a pronunciation dictionary is proposed in [3] and it used the Moses phrase-based statistical machine translation toolkit [12] as G2P conversion.

3 Grapheme to Phoneme Mapping

The Myanmar Language Commission (MLC) Pronunciation Dictionary can be used as a basis for pronunciation mapping [4]. We found it necessary to extend the dictionary with foreign pronunciations. In the proposed mapping table there are 23 phonetic symbols for 33 consonants (some consonants share the same pronunciation, for example "ဒ", "ဓ", "ဍ" and "ဎ" in Table 1), 87 vowels combinations and 20 special symbols for foreign word pronunciations.

Characters are grouped according to their pronunciation; the groups are un-aspirated, aspirated, voiced and nasal and are shown in Table 1. Many Myanmar syllables containing un-aspirated and aspirated consonants are pronounced as voiced consonants depending on the neighboring context.

Some foreign pronunciations have to be expressed by special vowel combinations because Myanmar pronunciations do not include some pronunciations. See Table 1. MLC dictionary was extended by defining 26 more symbols to include

Table 1. Groups of Myanmar consonants

Grouped consonants				
Unaspirated	**Aspirated**	**Voiced**		**Nasal**
က /k/	ခ /kh/	ဂ /g/	ဃ /g/	င /ng/
စ /s/	ဆ /hs/	ဇ /z/	ဈ /z/	ဉ/ည /nj/
ဋ /t/	ဌ /ht/	ဍ /d/	ဎ /d/	ဏ /n/
တ /t/	ထ /ht/	ဒ /d/	ဓ /d/	န /n/
ပ /p/	ဖ /hp/	ဗ /b/	ဘ /b/	မ /m/
ယ /j/	ရ /j/ or /r/	လ /l/	ဝ /w/	သ /th/
	ဟ /h/	ဠ /l/	အ /a/	

phoneme mappings for foreign words for example, the Myanmar phonetic representation of the foreign name "Alex" "အဲလက်(စ်)" is e:le'S (here, S is for (စ်)) and "Swift" "ဆွစ်(ဖ်)(ထ်)" is hswi'HPHT (here, HP is for (ဖ်) and HT is for (ထ်)).

4 Preparing Training Data

We built two types of data for training. The first one was a phonetic dictionary based on the MLC phonetic dictionary that contains pronunciations of 26,588 unique words. Myanmar language data from the multilingual Basic Travel Expression Corpus (BTEC) [6], which is a collection of travel-related expressions, was the second type of data used for training.

4.1 Building the Phonetic Dictionary

The phonetic dictionary was built for training the G2P conversion model by modifying entries for existing words, and by adding new words to the MLC phonetic dictionary. The following steps were applied for syllable-to-phoneme alignment to the dictionary in order:

1. Words from MLC dictionary were broken into syllables using a heuristic approach, which is 100.
2. Syllables were aligned to their phonemes using a combination of rules and human annotation. Initially, single syllable words were used to align by exact match on the phoneme sequences. This was sufficient to unambiguously align about 80.
3. Map MLC phonemes to the proposed phoneme set using a manually prepared conversion table.

The size of the upgraded dictionary was 28,393 unique words (2,489 unique syllables, 1,906 unique phonemes).

4.2   Sentence Selection with a Greedy Algorithm

The size of BTEC1 subset of the BTEC corpus used in these experiments was 160 K sentenced and manually phoneme-tagging all these sentences would be a time consuming task. Therefore a phonetically balanced sample was taken that contained all syllables by applying the greedy algorithm proposed in [7]. We briefly describe this algorithm below.

To select such a sentence set S from a large text corpus, it is necessary to define the metric of unit coverage of the sentence set. Let unit type, X, have elements $\{\mu_1^x, \mu_2^x, \ldots, \mu_{nx}^x\}$, where n_x is the number of elements. X can be a syllable, a diphone, or other defined unit. Assume $p(\mu_i^x)$ the occurrence frequency of μ_i^x in the text corpus. By definition, $\sum_{i=1}^{n_x} p(\mu_i^x) = 1$. The unit coverage of S to X, denoted by C_S^X, is defined as $C_S^X = \sum_{i=1}^{n_x} p(\mu_i^x) \times \sigma(\mu_i^x)$, where $\sigma(\mu_i^x) = 1$, if $\mu_i^x \in S$. Otherwise, $\sigma(\mu_i^x) = 0$. When given a text corpus and the size of S in the number of sentences, say n, the goal is to select in sentences from the text corpus to maximize C_S^X. In this paper, four types of units are considered, namely, syllable, di-phone spanning two syllables, tri-phone.

The main steps of the algorithm are briefly described as follows.

Step 1: Calculate the occurrence frequency of units in the text corpus and set none to S.

Step 2: Scan the whole text corpus to select one sentence and add the sentence to the current sentence set S. The selected sentence is that which maximizes the unit coverage of S according to the following priority:

 (1) Maximizing $C_S^{syllable}$ (or simply denoted by C_S^{syl}).
 (2) Maximising $C_S^{diphone\ spanning\ two\ syllables}$, if (1) is satisfied.
 (3) Maximizing $C_S^{diphone}$, if (1)–(2) are satisfied.
 (4) Maximizing $C_S^{triphone}$, if (1)–(3) are satisfied.

In this way, the algorithm can find the best sentence set that simultaneously maximizes the coverage of syllables, di-phone spanning two syllables, di-phones, and tri-phones in the priority mentioned above.

Step 3: Halt, if a predefined set size is reached. Otherwise, repeat Step 2.

We extracted 5,276 sentences from BTEC1 and used them for training using SMT and CRF models. The 5276 sentences were tagged with their phonemes manually. The selected sentences set contain foreign names and which should allow for the coverage of non-Myanmar words.

The pronunciation is formed from syllables and syllable boundaries have to be defined since Myanmar language is written continuously. Words from MLC Dictionary and selected sentences were first broken into syllables using a heuristic approach [13]. Then each syllable was labeled with its phoneme based on MLC Dictionary. Labeling phonemes on selected 5,276 sentences was manually done by three Myanmar native speakers. Some phoneme tagged sentences are shown in Fig. 1 and it can be seen that pronunciations of some same syllables are different.

ကျေး ဇူး တင် ပါ တယ် ။
kyei: zu: tin ba de pm
(Thank you.)

မင်း စဉ်း စဉ်း စား စား လုပ် တတ် တယ် ။
min: sin: zin: sa: za: lou' ta' te pm
(You usually do carefully.)

မိ ချောင်း သား ရေ သား က ဘာ လဲ ။
mi. gyaun: tha- jei dha: ga. ba le pm
(what is crocodile skin?)

Fig. 1. Phoneme tagged sentences

5   Pronunciations of Syllables

Pronunciations of Myanmar syllables can be different from the original pronunciation of orthographic structure. The following two sub-sections explain the original pronunciation of syllables and how they can change according to their context.

5.1   Contextually Independent Pronunciation

This section explains how the pronunciation of Myanmar syllables is normally derived from orthographic structure. Myanmar syllables are generally composed of consonants and (zero or more) vowel combinations starting with a consonant. Here, vowel combinations can be single vowel, sequences of vowels starting with a consonant that modifies the pronunciation of the first vowel. The pronunciations of consonants when they are combined with vowels are shown in Table 2.

Table 2. Examples of vowel combinations and their pronunciations

အိ i	အိ i.	အိး i:	အစ် i'	အင် in	အင် in.	အင်း in:
အေ ei	အေ့ ei.	အေး ei:	အိတ် ei'	အိန် ein	အိန့် ein.	အိန်း ein:
အယ် e	အယ့် e.	အဲ e:	အိုက် ai'	အိုင် ain	အိုင့် ain.	အိုင်း ain:
အာ a	အာ့ a.	အား a:	အတ် a'	အန် an	အန့် an.	အန်း an:
အော် o	အော့ o.	အော o:	အောက် au'	အောင် aun	အောင့် aun.	အောင်း aun:
အု u	အု u.	အူး u:	အွတ် u'	အွန် un	အွန့် un.	အွန်း un:
အို ou	အို့ ou.	အိုး ou:	အုပ် ou'	အွန် oun	အွန့် oun.	အွန်း oun:

In general, the pronunciation of syllables can be obtained directly from the pronunciation of these components. All of the pronunciations of consonants are shown in Table 1 and some example pronunciations of vowel combinations are

Table 3. Standard pronunciation of syllables

Syllable	Consonant+Vowel	Standard Pronunciation
သ	သ	tha.
တင်:	တ+င်:	t+in:
စ	စ+၁	s+a
ပိုင်:	ပ+ိုင်:	p+ain:
ချေ	ခ+ေ၁	ch+ei
ပု	ပ+ု	p+u
လေ	လ+ေ	l+e:
မင်	မ+င်	m+in
ကျောင်	ကျ+ောင်	ky+aun

shown in Table 2. The pronunciation of full syllable is a concatenation of the pronunciations of each component. The pronunciations do not modify each other. This type of pronunciation will be referred as the "standard pronunciation". Table 3 shows examples of standard pronunciations of some syllables according to their composition of consonant and vowels.

5.2 Contextually Dependent Pronunciations

Some Myanmar syllables do not conform to these standard rules of pronunciation. The pronunciation of the syllables can depend on the context of syllables.

Table 4. Examples pronunciations of some words

No.	Words	Standard	Correct
1	သတင်းစာ (newspaper)	tha. tin: sa	dha- din: za
2	ပိုင်းဝေ (denominator)	pain: chei	pain: gyei
3	ပုလဲ (pearl)	pu. le:	pa- le:
4	ပညာ (knowledge)	pa. nja	pjin nja
5	မင်ကျောင် (tatoo)	min kyaun	mhin gyaun

Differences between standard pronunciations and correct pronunciations of some words are shown in Table 4 as examples. It can be also seen in Table 2 that pronunciations of some same syllables are different depend on the context.

In [5], 10 patterns are proposed to capture the dependencies. Most of the patterns changed unaspirated or aspirated syllables to their voiced form. The first word in Table 4 is one pattern of deviation to standard pattern. The pattern is of that word's pronunciation is "A syllable's pronunciation can be changed if the syllable before it was changed". This phenomenon can cause a cascade of changes that can affect several syllables. The next pattern is changing the pronunciation of successive aspirated or aspirated syllable to voiced sound if the vowel combination of first syllable is (/in/, /an/, /e/, /aun/, /ein/, /un/). The second word in Table 4 is an example of that pattern. The pronunciation of some vowel combinations is occasionally non-standard. An example of that pattern is the third word in Table 4. Vowel sounds of some syllables are omitted and sometime nasal vowel is added to the pronunciation. The fourth and fifth words in Table 4 follow that pattern. Another pattern relates to compound words. If a noun and verb combine to form a noun phrase, the final syllable (unaspirated or aspirated) is changed to the voiced form.

We found every pattern has exceptions and the amount of exceptions is not small. In one pattern, the number of exceptions is 2,659 in 6,446 occurrences of that pattern and number exception of another pattern is 344 of 4,817 of occurrences. There are 224 exceptions in out of 388 occurrences in the pattern of omission of vowel sound. From this fact, it is obvious that only rule based or dictionary based approaches cannot predict correctly for Myanmar G2P conversion.

6 Experiments

6.1 Data Settings

We use three training data settings: extended version of MLC Dictionary (28,393 unique words) that we prepared (see Sect. 4.1), selected 5,276 sentences (see Sect. 4.2) with a greedy algorithm and combination of two of them. Training data were mapped to our phoneme symbols to create the training data for building CRF models and phrase based translation models.

We prepared 4 open test sets that were randomly selected from BTEC corpus; 3 sentence level test sets (Test set 1, Test set 2, Test set 3) and 1 word level test set (Test set 4). Each sentence level test set has 500 sentences. In detail, the unique number of Test sets are: Test set 1 contains 831 syllables and 837 phonemes, Test set 2 contains 836 syllables and 844 phonemes, and Test set 3 contains 824 syllables and 822 phonemes. Word level test set 4 contains 414 words, 461 syllables and 480 phonemes.

6.2 Conditional Random Field (CRF) Models

We used the CRFsuite tool [15] for training and testing CRF models. The feature set consisted of unigrams and bigrams of syllables, and unigrams, bigrams and trigrams of pronunciation change labels for each feature, and is shown below:

s[t-2], s[t-1], s[t], s[t+1], s[t+2]
s[t-1]—s[t], s[t]—s[t+1]
l[t-2], l[t-1], l[t], l[t+1], l[t+2]
l[t-2]—l[t-1], l[t-1]—l[t], l[t]—l[t+1], l[t+1]—l[t+2]
l[t-2]—l[t-1]—l[t], l[t-1]—l[t]—l[t+1], l[t]—l[t+1]—l[t+2]

Where s[t] is the syllable at position t (t being the position of the syllable being labeled), and l[t] is the label at position t; and s[t-1]s[t] is a bigram of syllables, and so on. In addition the model includes transition features for up to bigrams of phonemes.

6.3 Phrase Based Translation Models

We use the phrase based SMT system in Moses for training machine translation model [12]. The Myanmar source segmented by syllable segmentation method is aligned to the syllable level phoneme using GIZA++ [16]. The alignment is symmetrized by grow-diag-final-and heuristics [17]. The lexicalized reordering model is trained with the msd-bidirectional-fe option [18]. We use SRILM to training 5-gram language model with interpolated modified Kneser-Ney discounting on phoneme training data [19,20]. In decoding, we adopt the default settings of the Moses decoder. Since the size of manually phoneme tagged data is small, tuning was not done for all SMT experiments in this paper.

6.4 Evaluation Criteria

We used two criteria for evaluation; Bilingual Evaluation Understudy (BLEU) [14] for SMT and phoneme accuracy for comparison between CRF and SMT approaches.

7 Results

The results of the SMT experiment with dictionary model, selected sentences model and combination of dictionary and selected sentences model are shown in Table 5. From the results, generally, translation model trained with sentence level give better G2P translation than word level for Test Set 1, 2 and 3. The highest BLEU score 86.29 achieved from the Dictionary+Sentence SMT model.

Table 5. Test set BLEU score of Myanmar G2P

Test data	Dictionary	Sentence	Dict+sentence
Test set 1	37.15	**74.63**	74.59
Test set 2	34.70	73.73	**74.18**
Test set 3	38.55	75.33	**75.57**
Test set 4	80.34	79.17	**86.29**

The comparison in terms of phoneme accuracy between CRF and SMT approaches is shown in Table 6. It can be seen clearly that G2P conversion using SMT approaches outperformed that of CRF.

We also measured training time difference between CRF and SMT approaches. Here, we used three different servers with similar specification. Training time for dictionary model, sentence model and dictionary + sentence

Table 6. Phoneme accuracy of CRF and SMT approaches

	CRF			SMT		
Test-data	Dictionary	Sentence	Dict+sent	Dictionary	Sentence	Dict+sent
Test set 1	50.48	73.56	74.21	65.34	**89.66**	89.59
Test set 2	49.60	73.82	74.36	63.64	89.24	**89.45**
Test set 3	51.31	74.55	75.17	65.69	89.94	**90.12**
Test set 4	75.93	72.71	77.71	92.79	91.85	**94.29**

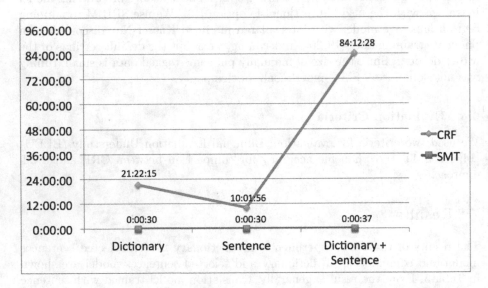

Fig. 2. Training time comparison between CRF and SMT approaches

model can be seen in Fig. 2. From this results, SMT approach considerably faster than CRF and able to train in less than one minute.

8   Discussion

There are 1816 unique syllables and 1829 unique phonemes in BTEC and the coverage of syllables and phonemes of selected 5276 sentences from BTEC is shown in Table 7.

There is usually more than one pronunciation for some syllables and all pronunciations of each syllable are included in dictionary. From the results presented in Sect. 7, it can be concluded that models training with a dictionary is not enough for sentence level G2P for Myanmar language. Since, pronunciations of syllables can be contextually dependent such as some particles and conjunctions. Figure 3 shows an example sentence where SMT can predict the right pronunciation of the respective syllable.

Table 7. Syllable and phone coverage for the selected 5,276 sentences

	Syllables	Di-phone	Tri-phone
Unit	1,833	5,121	35,295
Coverage	99.77 %	90.95 %	88.78 %

Myanmar Sentence: ဒါအတော်ပဲ။

Syllable Breaked: ဒါ အ တော် ပဲ ။

Dictionary Model Output: da a- (do)(pe:) pm

Sentence Model Output: da a- to be: pm

Dictionary+Sentence Model Output: da a- to be: pm

Fig. 3. An example of three SMT model outputs

In predicting new compound words (OOV), all CRF models (dictionary, selected sentences model, dictionary+selected sentences model) predicted as its standard pronunciation but the sentence model and dictionary+sentence SMT model can predict the correct phonemes. An example OOV word, အ ခက် ခဲ ဆုံး (the most difficult)

> *standurd pronunciation:* a- khe' khe: **hsoun:**
> *correct pronunciation:* a- khe' khe: **zoun:**

where "ခက် ခဲ" is the stem word in the dictionary it combines with an affix "အ" and suffix "ဆုံး" to form an adjective. Some OOV words that are predicted erroneously by all CRF models and cannot be predicted by the SMT models are shown below with their correct pronunciations.

> တစ် လုံး လောက် (one piece please) ta- loun: lau'
> တစ် နေ ရာ ရာ (somewhere) ta- nei ja ja
> တို့ အောင် (to be shorter) tou aun
> ကမ် ဘော ဒီး ယား (Cambodia) kan bo: di: ja:
> န ယူး စ် ဝိခ် (Newsweek) na- ju:S wi.KH

But a foreign name ရုရှား (Russia) pronounce as ra- sha: that appeared only once in the training corpus is predicted correctly by the sentence SMT model but not by the CRFs and other SMT models.

An example imperative sentence that ends with stem verb without suffix and its outputs from different models are shown below:

အောက် ကို ကြည့် ။

Look below.

au' kou kyi.

CRF (dictionary model): au' kou **za- ga**

CRF (sentence/dictionary+sentence model): au' kou **ba**

SMT (dictionary model): au' kou ကြည့်

SMT (sentence/dictionary+sentence model): au' kou **kyi.**

The pronunciation of ကြည့် was predicted correctly by the SMT sentence and dictionary+sentence models. In the sentence level test sets 1, 2 and 3, the pronunciation of some syllables that have two phonemes, for example

$$ကျွန်ုပ်(I)=> kya- nou'$$

is predicted correctly by all SMT models but not by the CRF models.

The conjunctions and some (unaspirated/aspirated to voiced) changed pronunciations are correctly predicted by the sentence CRF models and sentence SMT models.

The outputs of the CRF models and SMT models for an input Myanmar sentence along with its meaning and correct pronunciation are shown in below.

ဒုက္ခ ခ ပဲ ပြော တဲ့ စ ကား က မ တူ ဘူး ။

So bad, we are speaking in different languages.

dou' kha. be: pjo: de. za- ga: ga. ma- tu bu:

CRF (dictionary model):

dou' kha. pe: pjo: te. za- ga: ka- ma- tu bu:

CRF (sentence/dictionary+sentence model):

dou' kha. be: pjo: de. za- ga: ga. ma- tu bu:

SMT (dictionary model):

dou' kha. pe: pjo: te. za- ga: ka- ma- du bu:

SMT (sentence/dictionary+sentence model):

dou' kha. be: pjo: de. za- ga: ga. ma- tu bu:

In the above example, all models except dictionary models can predict the correct pronunciations.

In all the CRF models, the dictionary+sentence model has achieved the highest accuracy but among the SMT models, the sentence model achieved similar accuracy to the dictionary+sentence model. This indicates that the sentence SMT model can work well without a dictionary since the training sentences are selected to cover all syllables and phonemes from the original BTEC corpus. One major advantage of using SMT rather than a CRF model is speed. The SMT model proved to be considerably faster in both decoding and training, making the approach far more practicable.

9   Conclusion

In this paper, we presented G2P conversion results applying phrase based SMT. The highest BLEU score 86.29 was achieved from training only with a dictionary plus selected 5,276 sentences. All the results using SMT outperformed CRF approaches in terms of phoneme accuracy. Furthermore, our experiments have shown that the SMT approach also has a great advantage at the sentence level. In future work we hope to extend our SMT experiments with extended phoneme tagged data and also with other syllable based languages such as Thai, Khmer.

Acknowledgment. We thank Ms. Aye Mya Hlaing (UCSY, Yangon, Myanmar) and Ms. Hay Mar Soe Naing (UCSY, Yangon, Myanmar) for their help in phoneme tagging and checking for MLC dictionary and selected 5,276 sentences.

References

1. Soe, E.P.P.: Grapheme-to-Phoneme Conversion for Myanmar Language. In: 11th International Conference on Computer Applications (ICCA), pp. 195–200, Myanmar (2013)
2. Laurent, A., Deleglise, P., Meignier, S.: Grapheme to phoneme conversion using an SMT system. In: INTERSPEECH, 10th Annual Conference of the International Speech Communication Association, pp. 708–711, Brighton, United Kingdom, 6–10 September 2009
3. Karanasou, P., Lamel, L.: Automatic generation of a pronunciation dictionary with rich variation coverage using SMT methods. In: Gelbukh, A. (ed.) CICLing 2011, Part II. LNCS, vol. 6609, pp. 506–517. Springer, Heidelberg (2011)
4. Dictionary, M.-E.: Department of the Myanmar Language Commission. Ministry of Education, Yangon, Myanmar (1993)
5. Thadda, M.: Myanmar Language Commission. Ministry of Education, Myanmar (2005)
6. Kikui, G., Yamamoto, S., Takezawa, T., Sumita, E.: Comparative study on corpora for speech translation. IEEE Trans. Audio Speech Lang. **14**(5), 1674–1682 (2006)
7. Ni, J., Hirai, T., Kawai, H.: Constructing a phonetic-rich speech corpus while controlling time- dependent voice quality variability for English speech synthesis. In: Proceedings of ICASSP, vol. 1, pp. I-881–I-884 (2006)
8. Damper, R.I., Marchand, Y., Adamson, M.J., Gustafson, K.: A comparison of letter-to-sound conversion techniques for English text-to-speech synthesis. Proc. Inst. Acoust. **20**(6), 245–254 (1999)
9. Black, A.W., Lenzo, K., Pagel, V.: Issues in building general letter to sound rules. In: 3rd ESCA on Speech Synthesis (1998)
10. Novak, J.R., Minematsu, N., Hirose, K.: WFST-based grapheme-to-phoneme conversion: open source tools for alignment, model-building and decoding. In: Proceedings of the 10th International Workshop on Finite State Methods and Natural Language Processing, Donostia-San Sebastían, pp. 45–49 (2012)

11. Chen, S.F.: Conditional and joint models for grapheme-to-phoneme conversion. In: Eurospeech (2003)
12. Koehn, P., et al.: Moses: open source toolkit for statistical machine translation. In: Proceedings of the ACL, pp. 177–180 (2007)
13. Thu, Y.K., Finch, A., Sagisaka, Y., Sumita, E.: A study of Myanmar word segmentation schemes for statistical machine translation. In: Proceedings of ICCA, Myanmar, pp. 167–179 (2013)
14. Papineni, K., Roukos, S., Ward, T., Zhu, W.J.: BLEU: a method for automatic evaluation of machine translation. In: Proceedings of ACL2002, pp. 311–318, Philadelphia, USA (2002)
15. Okazaki, N.: CRFsuite: a fast implementation of Conditional Random Fields (CRFs) (2007). http://www.chokkan.org/software/crfsuite/
16. Och, F., Ney, H.: Improved statistical alignment models. In: Proceedings of 38th Annual Meeting on Association for Computational Linguistics, pp. 440–447 (2000)
17. Koehn, P., Och, F.J., Marcu, D.: Statistical phrase- based translation. In: Proceedings of HTL-NAACL, pp. 48–54 (2003)
18. Tillmann, C.: A unigram orientation model for statistical machine translation. In: Proceedings of HTL-NAACL, pp. 101–104 (2004)
19. Stolcke, A.: SRILM-an extensible language modeling toolkit. In: Proceedings of ICSLP, pp. 901–904 (2002)
20. Chen, S.F., Goodman, J.: An empirical study of smoothing techniques for language modeling. In: Proceedings of the 34th Annual Meeting on Association for Computational Linguistics, pp. 310–318 (1996)

Collecting Bilingual Technical Terms from Japanese-Chinese Patent Families by SVM

Lijuan Dong[1], Zi Long[1], Takehito Utsuro[1(✉)], Tomoharu Mitsuhashi[2], and Mikio Yamamoto[1]

[1] Graduate School of Systems and Information Engineering, University of Tsukuba, Tsukuba 305-8573, Japan
utsuro@iit.tsukuba.ac.jp
[2] Japan Patent Information Organization, 4-1-7, Toyo, Koto-ku, Tokyo 135-0016, Japan

Abstract. This paper proposes how to collect bilingual technical terms from Japanese-Chinese patent families. In the proposed method, the phrase translation table of a statistical machine translation model is used within the procedure of estimating Japanese-Chinese translation of technical terms. In this procedure, first, we extract Japanese technical terms from the Japanese side of parallel patent sentences. Then, we collect all the sentences that contain the extracted Japanese term. Next, we generate Chinese translation of the Japanese technical term, where we refer to the phrase translation table of a statistical machine translation model. Finally, we apply the Support Vector Machines (SVMs) to the task of identifying bilingual technical terms. As the overall performance, we achieve over 90 % precision with the condition of more than or equal to 60 % recall.

Keywords: Translation acquisition · Statistical machine translation · Phrase translation table · SVM

1 Introduction

Manual compilation of bilingual lexicon requires huge manual labor. Research efforts on automatically compiling bilingual lexicons have been in the academic fields of knowledge acquisition from natural language text. Especially, the following types of techniques have been invented: translation term pair acquisition based on statistical co-occurrence measure from parallel sentences [8], translation term pair acquisition from comparable corpora [1,9], compositional translation generation based on an existing bilingual lexicon for human use [11]; translation term pair acquisition by collecting partially bilingual texts through the search engine [3,6], and translation term pair acquisition from multilingual resources included in Wikipedia [2].

This paper proposes to collect Japanese-Chinese technical terms from the phrase translation table. The phrase table is trained by a phrase-based statistical machine translation (SMT) model with parallel sentences automatically

© Springer Science+Business Media Singapore 2016
K. Hasida and A. Purwarianti (Eds.): PACLING 2015, CCIS 593, pp. 251–262, 2016.
DOI: 10.1007/978-981-10-0515-2_18

extracted from patent families. The proposed approach is advantageous in that Japanese-Chinese patent families, from which we collect Japanese-Chinese technical terms, continue to be published every year.

In this procedure, first, we extract Japanese technical terms from the Japanese side of parallel patent sentences. Then, we collect all the sentences that contain the extracted Japanese term. Next, we generate Chinese translation of the Japanese technical term, where we refer to the phrase translation table of a statistical machine translation model. Finally, we apply the Support Vector Machines (SVMs) to the task of identifying bilingual technical terms. As the overall performance, we achieve over 90 % precision with the condition of more than or equal to 60 % recall.

2   Japanese-Chinese Parallel Patent Documents

Japanese-Chinese parallel patent documents are collected from the Japanese patent documents and the Chinese patent documents. The Japanese patent documents are those published by the Japanese Patent Office (JPO) in 2004–2012. The Chinese patent documents are those published by State Intellectual Property Office of the People's Republic of China (SIPO) in 2005–2010. From them, 312,492 patent families are extracted. Then, Japanese and Chinese sentences are aligned by the method of Utiyama and Isahara [13]. In this alignment procedure, we used a Japanese-Chinese translation lexicon consisting of about 170,000 Chinese head words. From those sentence alignment result, we use 3.6M parallel patent sentences which have the highest scores of sentence alignment.

3   Phrase Translation Table of an SMT Model

We apply Moses [5] to the whole 3.6M parallel patent sentences as a toolkit of a phrase-based SMT model. Before applying Moses, we apply the Japanese morphological analyzer MeCab[1] with the morpheme lexicon IPAdic[2] to Japanese sentences and segment them into a sequence of morphemes. We also apply the Chinese morphological analyzer Stanford Word Segment [12] trained with Chinese Penn Treebank to Chinese sentences and segment them into a sequence of morphemes. When we apply Moses, the upper bound of the numbers of the morphemes of both Japanese and Chinese phrases is set as 15. The trained phrase translation table is in the direction of Japanese to Chinese translation and consists of 108M translation pairs with 76M Japanese phrases. Each entry in the phrase translation table has a Japanese to Chinese phrase translation probability $P(p_C \mid p_J)$ of translating a Japanese phrase p_J into a Chinese phrase p_C. The phrase translation table includes multiple Chinese translation candidates for each Japanese phrase. Those multiple translation candidates are ranked in descending order of Japanese to Chinese phrase translation probabilities.

---

[1] http://mecab.sourceforge.net/.

[2] http://sourceforge.jp/projects/ipadic/.

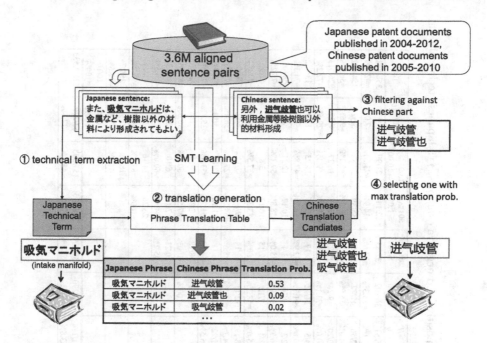

Fig. 1. Estimating the translation of a technical term based on a phrase translation table and a parallel sentence pair

4   Estimating the Translation of a Technical Term Based on a Phrase Translation Table and a Parallel Sentence Pair

As we show in Fig. 1, Chinese translation of a Japanese technical term is estimated based on a phrase translation table and a parallel sentence pair. When we have a parallel sentence pair $\langle S_J, S_C \rangle$ and a Japanese technical term t_J, we first refer to the phrase translation table and identify a bilingual technical term pair. Then, we collect candidates of Chinese translation of the Japanese technical term t_J and match them against the Chinese sentence S_C of the parallel sentence pair $\langle S_J, S_C \rangle$. Finally, we select $\hat{t}_C$ with the largest translation probability $P(t_C \mid t_J)$ among those found in S_C, and then we identify the bilingual technical term pair $\langle t_J, \hat{t}_C \rangle$ as the result.

5   Applying SVM to Translation Estimation

5.1   Japanese Technical Terms for Evaluation

This section presents how we select Japanese technical terms for evaluation. First, 1.2M noun phrases are extracted from the 3.6M parallel patent sentences. Next, according to the frequency within the whole parallel patent sentences,

Table 1. Positive examples' rates (number of positive examples/number of positive and negative examples, jf: Japanese technical term frequency, jcf: Japanese-Chinese co-occurrence frequency)

	$jf=1$	$2\leq jf\leq5$	$6\leq jf\leq10$	$11\leq jf\leq15$	$16\leq jf\leq20$	$21\leq jf\leq30$	$31\leq jf\leq50$	$51\leq jf\leq100$	$101\leq jf\leq200$	$201\leq jf\leq500$	$501\leq jf\leq1,000$	$1,001\leq jf\leq10,000$	$10,001\leq jf$	Total
$jcf=1$	36/58 =62.1%	27/35 =77.1%	20/26 =76.9%	27/43 =62.8%	31/55 =56.4%	21/37 =56.8%	25/45 =55.6%	26/51 =51.0%	36/102 =35.3%	32/85 =37.6%	52/149 =34.9%	21/99 =21.2%	4/57 =7.0%	358/842 =42.5%
$2\leq jcf\leq5$		56/57 =98.2%	32/36 =88.9%	17/23 =73.9%	25/37 =67.6%	18/27 =66.7%	28/35 =80.0%	27/50 =54.0%	41/72 =56.9%	33/62 =53.2%	35/89 =39.3%	37/82 =45.1%	5/52 =9.6%	354/622 =56.9%
$6\leq jcf\leq10$			36/37 =97.3%	25/25 =100%	21/24 =87.5%	22/24 =91.7%	21/23 =91.3%	10/20 =50.0%	19/26 =73.1%	17/27 =62.9%	31/53 =58.5%	16/27 =59.3%	8/27 =29.6%	226/313 =72.2%
$11\leq jcf\leq15$				29/30 =96.7%	16/17 =94.1%	11/11 =100%	11/11 =100%	4/5 =80.0%	11/12 =91.7%	9/17 =52.9%	10/15 =66.7%	11/23 =47.8%	1/11 =9.1%	113/152 =74.3%
$16\leq jcf\leq20$					20/20 =100%	17/17 =100%	4/4 =100%	2/3 =66.7%	9/10 =90.0%	3/4 =75.0%	10/17 =58.8%	12/21 =57.1%	2/9 =22.2%	79/105 =75.2%
$21\leq jcf\leq30$						19/19 =100%	10/11 =90.9%	3/4 =75.0%	7/12 =58.3%	12/15 =80%	10/12 =83.3%	3/8 =37.5%	6/10 =60.0%	67/91 =73.6%
$31\leq jcf\leq50$							20/21 =95.2%	18/19 =94.7%	12/13 =92.3%	11/14 =78.6%	9/14 =64.3%	3/11 =27.3%	4/11 =36.4%	78/104 =75.0%
$51\leq jcf\leq100$								21/22 =95.5%	22/22 =100%	6/11 =54.5%	11/12 =91.7%	7/13 =53.8%	5/14 =35.7%	72/94 =76.6%
$101\leq jcf\leq200$									21/21 =100%	18/18 =100%	7/8 =87.5%	9/15 =60.0%	7/14 =50.0%	62/76 =81.6%
$201\leq jcf\leq500$										20/21 =95.2%	17/18 =94.4%	6/10 =60.0%	3/4 =75.0%	46/53 =86.8%
$501\leq jcf\leq1,000$											26/26 =100%	14/16 =87.5%	1/2 =50.0%	41/44 =93.2%
$1,001\leq jcf\leq10,000$												18/18 =100%	7/9 =77.8%	25/27 =92.6%
$10,001\leq jcf$													10/10 =100%	10/10 =100%
Total	36/58 =62.1%	83/92 =90.2%	88/99 =88.9%	98/121 =81.0%	113/153 =73.9%	108/135 =80.0%	119/150 =79.3%	111/174 =63.8%	178/290 =61.4%	159/275 =57.8%	218/413 =52.8%	157/343 =45.8%	63/230 =27.4%	1,521/2,533 =60.4%

Table 2. Numbers of positive and negative reference examples

Positive	Negative	Total
1,531	1,002	2,533

Table 3. Positive examples (jf: Japanese technical terms frequency, jcf: Japanese-Chinese co-occurrence frequency)

	low frequency range ($1 \leqq jf \leqq 15$)	middle frequency range ($16 \leqq jf \leqq 100$)	high frequency range ($101 \leqq jf$)
low frequency range ($1 \leqq jcf \leqq 15$)	<レーザ/発振/素子, 激光/振荡/元件> (laser oscillation element) (jf=1, jcf=1)	<光/触媒/体/分散/液, 光催化/体/分散液> (photocatalytic body-dispersed liquid) (jf=23, jcf=3)	<シリサイド/層, 硅化物层> (silicide layer) (jf=300, jcf=4)
middle frequency range ($16 \leqq jcf \leqq 100$)		<摩擦/クラッチ, 摩擦/离合器> (friction clutch) (jf=59, jcf=56)	<無/段/変速/機, 无级/变速机> (continuously variable transmission) (jf=709, jcf=43)
high frequency range ($101 \leqq jcf$)			<炭素/繊維, 碳纤维> (carbon fibers) (jf=1,157, jcf=1,057)

the set of all the Japanese noun phrases are divided into 13 frequency ranges shown in Table 1. From each frequency range, we manually judge whether each of randomly selected 90 Japanese noun phrases is appropriate as a technical term to be used in the evaluation of Chinese translation estimation. 578 Japanese technical terms are selected for evaluation.

5.2 A Reference Set of Bilingual Technical Terms

Based on the procedure of translation estimation of Sect. 4, we collect Chinese translation candidates for each of the 578 Japanese technical terms selected in the previous section. In total, 2,533 candidates of Japanese-Chinese technical term translation pairs are obtained. We manually judge whether each of the 2,533 candidates is a correct technical term translation pair or not. As in Table 2, 1,531 correct translation pairs are obtained as positive examples, while the remaining 1,002 erroneous ones are judged as negative examples. In the evaluation of this paper, the set of those positive/negative examples is used as the reference set of Japanese-Chinese technical term translation pairs.

For each pair of the 13 frequency ranges of Japanese technical term frequency (jf) and Japanese-Chinese co-occurrence frequency (jcf), Table 1 also shows the numbers of positive/negative examples. For each pair of low/middle/high frequency ranges of Japanese technical term frequency (jf) and Japanese-

Chinese co-occurrence frequency (jcf), Table 3 further lists positive examples
of Japanese-Chinese technical term translation pairs.

5.3   Applying SVM

This section describes how we apply SVMs to the task of identifying bilingual
technical terms. The reference set of 2,533 bilingual technical terms are first
divided into 10 subsets[3].

We use TinySVM[4] as a tool for learning SVMs. We use the polynomial
(2nd order) kernel as the kernel function. 8 out of the whole 10 subsets are
used in the training of SVMs. In the tuning of SVMs classifier, the distance
from the separating hyperplane to each test instance is regarded as a confidence
measure and the lower bound of the confidence is tuned with one of the remaining two subsets. Tuning instances which satisfy the confidence measure over a
certain lower bound is only considered as positive samples. The lower bound is
tuned for maximizing precision while keeping recall more than or equal to 60 %,
or it is tuned for maximizing F-measure. The trained classifier is tested against
another one of the remaining two subsets. Test instances which satisfy the confidence measure over the lower bound is only returned as positive samples. This
procedure of training/tuning/testing is repeated 10 times, and the 10 results of
test performance are averaged.

5.4   Features of SVM

Features we used in this paper are shown in Table 4. We divide those features
into the following two types: i.e., f_1 and f_2, which are monolingual features, and
$f_2, \cdots, f_9$, which are bilingual features, representing various characteristics of
the input bilingual technical term pairs.

The monolingual features are f_1, the frequency of the Japanese term and f_2,
the frequency of the Chinese term. We represent their feature values as IDs of
the 13 frequency ranges.

The bilingual features are f_3, the translation probability, f_4, the rank of the
Chinese translation candidates, f_5, the co-occurrence frequency of the bilingual
technical term pairs, f_6, the difference of the frequency of the Japanese technical
term and the co-occurrence frequency of bilingual technical term pairs, f_7, the
number of Chinese translation candidates, f_8, the rate of parallel sentences where
phrase alignment is consistent with word alignments, and f_9, the translation
probability when generating the Chinese translation candidate compositionally
from constituents of the Japanese technical term.

Among those features, we employ features based on term frequencies simply
because a bilingual technical term pair usually constitutes a correct translation

---

[3] We collect Japanese-Chinese bilingual technical term pairs which are generated from
an identical Japanese term into one subset. We do not separate them into more than
one subsets.

[4] http://chasen.org/~taku/software/TinySVM.

Table 4. Features of SVM

Class	Feature	Definition
Monolingual features	f_1: frequency of Japanese term	the ID (1~13) of the frequency range of the Japanese technical term
	f_2: frequency of Chinese term	the ID (1~13) of the frequency range of the Chinese technical term
Bilingual features	f_3: translation probability	the translation probability $P(t_C \mid t_J)$
	f_4: rank of Chinese translation candidates (descending order)	the rank of t_C with respect to the descending order of the conditional translation probability $P(t_C \mid t_J)$
	f_5: co-occurrence frequency of bilingual technical term pairs	the ID (1~13) of the co-occurrence frequency range of the Japanese-Chinese technical term pairs
	f_6: difference of the frequency of Japanese technical term and the co-occurrence frequency of bilingual technical term pairs	returns 1 if the difference of the frequency of the Japanese technical term and the co-occurrence frequency of bilingual technical terms is less than or equal to the upper bound (we use 105 as this upper bound in this paper), while returns 0 otherwise.
	f_7: number of Chinese translation candidates	the number of Chinese translation candidates for the Japanese technical term t_J
	f_8: rate of parallel sentences where phrase alignment is consistent with word alignments	$f_8 = \dfrac{\text{the number of parallel sentences where the phrase alignment is consistent with word alignments}}{\text{co-occurrence frequency of the Japanese-Chinese technical term pair}}$
	f_9: translation probability of compositional translation generation	translation probability when generating the Chinese translation candidate compositionally from constituents of the Japanese technical term

of each other if their frequencies are close. Also, if a pair of bilingual terms has a high translation probability and/or one of them is ranked highly as the translation candidate of the other in the SMT phrase translation table, they are usually correct translation of each other. Thus, we employ f_3 and f_4. The number of translation candidates is also useful. This is because, if the number of translation candidates of a term is small, the term is usually a technical term. Furthermore, the rate of parallel sentences where the phrase alignment is consistent with word alignments is also employed because this rate is usually large if a bilingual term pair is a correct translation of each other.

Table 5. Results of evaluation (%)

		Precision	Recall	F-measure
Baseline		60.4	100	75.3
SVM	Maximum precision	91.8	59.7	72.3
	Maximum F-measure	76.2	88.6	81.9

5.5 Evaluation Results

Evaluation results for a baseline as well as for SVMs are shown in Table 5. We simply judge all of the input Japanese-Chinese technical term pairs as correct translation as the baseline. When maximizing precision, we achieve almost 92 % precision while keeping recall almost 60 %. When maximizing F-measure, we achieve almost 82 % F-measure with around 76 % precision and 88 % recall.

For each pair of the 13 frequency ranges of Japanese technical term frequency (jf) and Japanese-Chinese co-occurrence frequency (jcf), Table 6 shows the evaluation results. We achieve around 90 % or higher precision in most pairs of the 13 frequency ranges of Japanese technical term frequency and Japanese-Chinese co-occurrence frequency. As shown in the table, when the rates of positive examples are lower for certain frequency range pairs, we have lower recalls for the frequency range pairs.

Next, Table 7 shows examples of correct and erroneous SVMs' judgments. As shown in Table 7(a), a Japanese-Chinese technical term pair ⟨ "水性/樹脂/組成/物", "水性/树脂/组合物" ⟩ are correctly judged by SVM, mainly because its translation probability in the phrase translation table (f_3) as well as its translation probability of compositional translation generation (f_9) are high, and both the rank of the Chinese translation candidate (f_4) and the number of Chinese translation candidate (f_7) are 1. Also, another Japanese-Chinese technical term pair ⟨ "気/液/分離/器", "气液/反应器" ⟩ is correctly judged by SVM to be a translation error, mainly because its values of f_3 and f_9 are 0 or quite small, while those of f_4 and f_7 are fairly large.

Erroneous judgements by SVM shown in Table 7(b), on the other hand, are mainly due to errors in Chinese morphological analysis. The first bilingual technical term pair ⟨ "生物/処理/反応/槽", "生物/处理/反应/槽中" ⟩ is a translation error since the two Chinese morphemes 中 and 槽 are concatenated as the result of erroneous Chinese morphological analysis. Although it is expected that this bilingual technical term pair is to be rejected by SVM, it is judged by SVM as correct translation, mainly because its values of f_3 and f_9 are not quite small, while the rank of f_4 is relatively high and the value of f_7 is relatively small.

Table 6. Results of evaluation (precision/recall/F-measure (%), jf: Japanese technical term frequency, jcf: Japanese-Chinese co-occurrence frequency)

	$jf=1$	$2 \leq jf \leq 5$	$6 \leq jf \leq 10$	$11 \leq jf \leq 15$	$16 \leq jf \leq 20$	$21 \leq jf \leq 30$	$31 \leq jf \leq 50$	$51 \leq jf \leq 100$	$101 \leq jf \leq 200$	$201 \leq jf \leq 500$	$501 \leq jf \leq 1,000$	$1,001 \leq jf \leq 10,000$	$10,001 \leq jf$	Total
$jcf=1$	82.9/80.6 /81.7	88.2/55.6 /68.2	100/30.0 /46.2	100/25.9 /41.2	100/38.7 /55.8	75.0/14.3 /24.0	83.3/20.0 /32.3	50.0/3.8 /7.1	83.3/13.8 /23.8	100/6.3 /11.8	100/1.9 /3.8	0/0/0	0/0/0	87.5/24.0 /37.7
$2 \leq jcf \leq 5$		98.1/94.6 /96.4	100/78.1 /87.7	86.7/76.5 /81.3	85.7/48.0 /61.5	77.8/77.8 /77.8	85.0/60.7 /70.8	66.7/40.0 /50.0	81.3/31.7 /45.6	83.3/15.2 /25.6	66.7/5.7 /10.5	100/2.7 /5.3	0/0/0	87/47.5 /61.4
$6 \leq jcf \leq 10$			97.2/97.2 /97.2	100/100 /100	95.2/95.2 /95.2	95.7/100 /97.8	100/85.7 /92.3	100/50.0 /66.7	84.6/57.9 /68.8	75.0/35.3 /48.0	75.0/19.4 /30.8	100/31.3 /47.6	50.0/12.5 /20.0	93.3/67.7 /78.5
$11 \leq jcf \leq 15$				100/100 /100	94.1/100 /97.0	100/100 /100	100/90.9 /95.2	100/50.0 /66.7	100/81.8 /90.0	60/66.7 /63.2	75.0/60.0 /66.7	40.0/18.2 /25.0	0/0/0	90.2/81.4 /85.6
$16 \leq jcf \leq 20$					100/100 /100	100/94.1 /97.0	100/75.0 /85.7	50.0/50.0 /50.0	87.5/77.8 /82.4	0/0/0	85.7/60.0 /70.6	77.8/58.3 /66.7	0/0/0	90.9/75.9 /82.8
$21 \leq jcf \leq 30$						100/100 /100	90.0/90.0 /90.0	75.0/100 /85.7	62.5/71.4 /66.7	100/88.9 /94.1	100/80.0 /88.9	100/100 /100	100/83.3 /90.9	92.3/89.6 /90.9
$31 \leq jcf \leq 50$							95.0/95.0 /95.0	94.4/94.4 /94.4	100/83.3 /90.9	77.8/58.3 /66.7	77.8/77.8 /77.8	75.0/100 /85.7	100/25.0 /40.0	90.0/80.7 /85.1
$51 \leq jcf \leq 100$								95.5/100 /97.7	100/90.9 /95.2	62.5/83.3 /71.4	100/100 /100	75.0/42.9 /54.5	100/80.0 /88.9	92.8/88.9 /90.8
$101 \leq jcf \leq 200$									100/95.2 /97.6	100/88.9 /94.1	100/85.7 /92.3	85.7/66.7 /75.0	85.7/85.7 /85.7	98.2/87.1 /92.3
$201 \leq jcf \leq 500$										100/100 /100	100/100 /100	100/83.3 /90.9	100/66.7 /80.0	100/93.5 /96.6
$501 \leq jcf \leq 1,000$											100/96.2 /98.1	100/92.9 /96.3	100/100 /100	100/95.1 /97.5
$1,001 \leq jcf \leq 10,000$												100/94.4 /97.1	100/71.4 /83.3	100/88.0 /93.6
$10,001 \leq jcf$													100/100 /100	100/100 /100
Total	84.6/78.6 /81.5	95.4/79.5 /86.7	96.8/74.1 /83.9	98.5/77.6 /86.8	93.6/72.5 /81.8	95.1/79.4 /86.5	95.3/72.6 /82.4	83.1/59.3 /69.2	86.4/57.1 /68.8	89.0/42.2 /57.3	95.4/43.5 /59.7	91.3/44.1 /59.4	87.5/55.6 /68.0	91.8/59.7 /72.3

Table 7. Example results of applying SVM

(a) Correct Judgement by SVM

Japanese technical term for evaluation	Chinese translation candidate	feature f_1	feature f_2	feature f_3	feature f_4	feature f_7	feature f_9	reference judgement	judgement by SVM
水性/樹脂/組成/物 (aqueous resin composition)	水性/樹脂/组合物 (aqueous resin composition)	$11 \leq jf \leq 15$	$11 \leq jcf \leq 15$	0.95	1	1	0.73	correct translation	correct translation
気/液/分離/器 (gas-liquid separator)	气液/反应器 (gas-liquid reactor)	$1{,}000 \leq jf \leq 10{,}000$	$jcf = 1$	0.0008	9	13	0	translation error	translation error

(b) Erroneous Judgement by SVM

Japanese technical term for evaluation	Chinese translation candidate	feature f_1	feature f_2	feature f_3	feature f_4	feature f_7	feature f_9	reference judgement	judgement by SVM
生物/処理/反応/槽 (biological treatment reactor tank)	生物/处理/反应/槽中 (in + biological treatment reactor tank)	$21 \leq jf \leq 30$	$2 \leq jcf \leq 5$	0.06	3	5	0.05	translation error	correct translation
非/晶/質/シリコン (amorphous silicon)	非晶质/硅 (amorphous silicon)	$501 \leq jf \leq 1{,}000$	$jcf = 1$	0.005	7	13	0	correct translation	translation error

The second bilingual technical term pair ⟨ ``非/晶/質/シリコン", "非晶质/硅" ⟩, on the other hand, is a correct translation according to the reference judgement. However, this technical term pair is judged by SVM to be a translation error mainly because the value of the translation probability of compositional translation generation (f_9) is 0. This is caused by the results of Japanese and Chinese morphological analysis that are not consistent with each other. In the result of Japanese morphological analysis, 非/晶/質 is a sequence of consecutive three morphemes, while, in the result of Chinese morphological analysis, three morphemes corresponding to the Japanese ones 非/晶/質 are concatenated into one morpheme as 非晶质. This inconsistency causes the feature (f_9) of the translation probability of compositional translation generation to be 0, since the Chinese morpheme 非晶质 can not be decomposed into its constituents in the procedure of compositional translation generation.

6　Related Work

This section discusses related work. Itagaki et al. [4] studied automatic validation of translation pairs available in the phrase translation table trained by an SMT model. Yasuda and Sumita [14] also studied to extract bilingual terms from comparable patents. Kanji character similarity between Japanese and Chinese languages is used in Yasuda and Sumita [14]. Our approach is different from those of Itagaki et al. [4] and Yasuda and Sumita [14] mainly because we use various features extracted from parallel patent sentences as well as the phrase translation table of a SMT model. Lu and Tsou [7] studied to extract English-Chinese bilingual terms from patent families. In Lu and Tsou [7], they extract bilingual terms from parallel sentences by SVM. Our approach is different from that of Lu and Tsou [7] in that our features studied are much finer-grained and cover wider range of information. Morishita et al. [10] studied to acquire Japanese-English technical term translation lexicon from the phrase translation tables. Our approach is more advantageous than that of Morishita et al. [10]

because we concentrate on utilizing information that are available from patent families, but not rely on information source other than patent families. Also, features we employed in this paper cover much wider range of information that are available from patent families.

7 Conclusion

This paper proposed how to collect bilingual technical terms from Japanese-Chinese patent families. In the proposed method, the phrase translation table of a statistical machine translation model was used within the procedure of estimating Japanese-Chinese translation of technical terms. We then applied SVMs to the task of identifying bilingual technical terms. We achieved the performance of over 90 % precision with the condition of more than or equal to 60 % recall.

References

1. Bouamor, D., Semmar, N., Zweigenbaum, P.: Context vector disambiguation for bilingual lexicon extraction from comparable corpora. In: Proceedings of 51st ACL, pp. 759–764 (2013)
2. Erdmann, M., Nakayama, K., Hara, T., Nishio, S.: Improving the extraction of bilingual terminology from Wikipedia. ACM Trans. Multimedia Comput. Commun. Appl. 5(4), 31:1–31:17 (2009)
3. Huang, F., Zhang, Y., Vogel, S.: Mining key phrase translations from Web corpora. In: Proceedings of HLT/EMNLP, pp. 483–490 (2005)
4. Itagaki, M., Aikawa, T., He, X.: Automatic validation of terminology translation consistency with statistical method. In: Proceedings of MT Summit XI, pp. 269–274 (2007)
5. Koehn, P., Hoang, H., Birch, A., Callison-Burch, C., Federico, M., Bertoldi, N., Cowan, B., Shen, W., Moran, C., Zens, R., Dyer, C., Bojar, O., Constantin, A., Herbst, E.: Moses: open source toolkit for statistical machine translation. In: Proceedings of 45th ACL, Companion Volume, pp. 177–180 (2007)
6. Lin, D., Zhao, S., Van Durme, B., Paşca, M.: Mining parenthetical translations from the web by word alignment. In: Proceedings of 46th ACL: HLT, pp. 994–1002 (2008)
7. Lu, B., Tsou, B.K.: Towards bilingual term extraction in comparable patents. In: Proceedings of 23rd PACLIC, pp. 755–762 (2009)
8. Matsumoto, Y., Utsuro, T.: Lexical knowledge acquisition. In: Dale, R., Moisl, H., Somers, H. (eds.) Handbook of Natural Language Processing, chap. 24, pp. 563–610. Marcel Dekker Inc., New York (2000)
9. Morin, E., Hazem, A.: Looking at unbalanced specialized comparable corpora for bilingual lexicon extraction. In: Proceedings of 52nd ACL, pp. 1284–1293 (2014)
10. Morishita, Y., Utsuro, T., Yamamoto, M.: Integrating a phrase-based SMT model and a bilingual lexicon for human in semi-automatic acquisition of technical term translation lexicon. In: Proceedings of 8th AMTA, pp. 153–162 (2008)
11. Tonoike, M., Kida, M., Takagi, T., Sasaki, Y., Utsuro, T., Sato, S.: A comparative study on compositional translation estimation using a domain/topic-specific corpus collected from the web. In: Proceedings of 2nd International Workshop on Web as Corpus, pp. 11–18 (2006)

12. Tseng, H., Chang, P., Andrew, G., Jurafsky, D., Manning, C.: A conditional random field word segmenter for Sighan bakeoff 2005. In: Proceedings of 4th SIGHAN Workshop on Chinese Language Processing, pp. 168–171 (2005)
13. Utiyama, M., Isahara, H.: A Japanese-English patent parallel corpus. In: Proceedings of MT Summit XI, pp. 475–482 (2007)
14. Yasuda, K., Sumita, E.: Building a bilingual dictionary from a Japanese-Chinese patent corpus. In: Gelbukh, A. (ed.) CICLing 2013, Part II. LNCS, vol. 7817, pp. 276–284. Springer, Heidelberg (2013)

Author Index

Printed in the United States
by Bookmasters

Printed in the United States
By Bookmasters